JILL PRESCOTT'S

Ecole de Cuisine

JILL PRESCOTT'S

Ecole de Cuisine

Professional Cooking for the Home Chef

Jill Prescott

PHOTOGRAPHY BY KELLY SHIELDS

Ten Speed Press
BERKELEY TORONTO

To my children, the great joys of my life,

Shawn, Elisabeth, Scott,

and Christopher

A Kirsty Melville Book

Ten Speed Press
PO Box 7123
Berkeley, California 94707
www.tenspeed.com

Distributed in Australia by Simon and Schuster Australia, in Canada by Ten Speed Press Canada, in New Zealand by Southern Publishers Group, in South Africa by Real Books, in Southeast Asia by Berkeley Books, and in the United Kingdom and Europe by Airlift Book Company.

Library of Congress Cataloging-in-Publication Data
Prescott, Jill.
    Jill Prescott's ecole de cuisine : professional cooking for the home chef / Jill Prescott.
        p. cm
    ISBN 1-58008-290-4
    1. Cookery, French. I. Title: Ecole de cuisine. II. Title.
TX719.P755   2001
641.5944—dc21   00-066299

Jacket and text design by Catherine Jacobes
Food styling by Robin Krause

Some of the recipes in this book include raw eggs, meat, or fish. When these foods are consumed raw, there is always the risk that bacteria, which is killed by proper cooking, may be present. For this reason, when serving these foods raw, always buy certified salmonella-free eggs and the freshest meat and fish available from a reliable grocer, storing them in the refrigerator until they are served. Because of the health risks associated with the consumption of bacteria that can be present in raw eggs, meat, and fish, these foods should not be consumed by infants, small children, pregnant women, the elderly, or any people who may be immuno-compromised.

First printing, 2001
Printed in the United States of America

1 2 3 4 5 6 7 8 9 10 — 05 04 03 02 01

Contents

Acknowledgments

IT IS WITH THE DEEPEST SENSE OF GRATITUDE that I thank the many people who have helped and encouraged me along the way:

Marianne Montag, my guardian angel; Mark Weber, dear friend and professional giant; Paul Berg, and Tom Dinolfo for years of dedication; Marc Bianchini, for the Italian perspective; Richard Grausman, for opening the door; Bob McKinley, Brian and Laura Putnam, Beth Mannebach, Joe Fisco, Deb Christmann, John Schiiaparelli, Mark Collings, students who have worked tirelessly on both the TV show and the cookbook; Charlie White, my director and cheerleader; Julia Child, for her guidance and support; Lisa Prescott, for the show's opening design; Scott Danielson, for introducing Dacor Appliances; Tom Maclean, for his caring; Mara Trotter, for testing recipes; Dennis Getto, for his friendship and good humor; Joshua Foss, for exploring Provence; Ed Dudkowski, for teaching me how to teach to a camera; Lola Roeh, for her trust; Kirsty Melville, my publisher, for giving my book life; Holly Taines White, for superb and meticulous editing; Catherine Jacobes, for a perfect book design; James Stern, for excellent advice; Marcel and Shannon Biro, for their great spirit; the Ecole de Cuisine staff, for their hard work; my television crew, for their superb skills; my students, who have traveled to my school from all corners of the country; and the viewers who support and watch my series.

The following companies have also been instrumental: WKNO Memphis Public Television, Dacor Distinctive Appliances, Karl E. Klein S.C., Midwest Express Airlines, Richardson Furniture Emporium, August Lotz, Schwarz Fish, KitchenAid, Cuisinart, Kohler Company, George Watts and Son, Pickard China, Bistrot Margot, Lake Park Bistro, Osteria del Mondo, Golden Guernsey Dairy, Mauviel Copper, Le Creuset, John Boos and Company, Thoumieux, Nielsen-Massey Vanilla, Bragard Uniforms, Rockey Farms, Oenophelia, Illuminations, Romancing Provence, General Espresso, Pillivuyt, Rochester Inn, Pinehurst Inn, Victorian Village, and Wild Flour Bakery.

And I offer a special, heartfelt thanks to the artisans of the world, who continue to enrich our culture and my life.

Introduction

MY FIRST MOMENTS IN FRANCE will forever live in my memory as a mélange of sights and aromas that captured my soul and changed my life.

Though I was tired, cold, and even a little bit lost on the late night I arrived in Paris, I was enthralled, for just down the winding road outside my hotel room, I could see the Eiffel Tower all lit up against the dark sky.

The next morning I awoke to a ruckus of laughter and chatter. As I opened the bedroom's huge old shutters, I discovered that I was overlooking Rue Cler, one of the most famous market streets in Paris.

I made my way down the creaky old winding staircase and found myself before a fish vendor. For nearly an hour, I stood captivated by this tiny spot, no larger than an average American bedroom. This space contained more varieties of fish than I knew existed, and it smelled, amazingly, like fresh sea air. Next to the fish vendor was a cheese shop with over a hundred varieties of cheese ripening on beds of straw, many of them wrapped in chestnut leaves. Just thirty feet away from the cheese vendor were more discoveries: Bread bakeries scented with smoke from the wood-fired ovens; a pastry shop with exquisite pieces of edible art; butcher shops with numerous varieties of chicken; and a breathtaking shop full of fruits and vegetables that all looked too perfect to be real.

Encouraged by my mentor, Richard Grausman, I was in Paris to take classes at LaVarenne cooking school. When I began classes and saw the pots and pans, the simplicity of the equipment and the ovens, and the quality of ingredients, I was awestruck. Everything, absolutely everything, was different. It was then that I first observed the stark contrast between real French cuisine and the fabricated version marketed to the American public.

I had met Mr. Grausman, then U.S. teaching representative to Le Cordon Bleu, in the mid-seventies while taking demonstration classes from him. I later served as his assistant when he taught in my area. He was a great influence on me and opened the door to good cooking. After my four children were in school, he suggested that I seek professional culinary training in Paris. At that time, there simply wasn't a school in the United States. offering three-month intensive participation classes that I could immerse myself in. So I followed a lifelong dream and trekked off to Paris to learn to cook. At age thirty-eight, it changed my life.

Returning from Paris, I discovered that I had a passion for sharing my newfound knowledge with others who were interested in cooking. Thus, Ecole de Cuisine was born. Designed for the home chef, my cooking school is a place where anyone, at any age, can take professional cooking classes on a wide variety of topics. Many couples take my courses as a means of sharing a craft, as do men and women with high-stress jobs looking for a relaxing diversion. We spend the day cooking and end the class with an exceptional meal prepared by the students.

I teach one way—the right way. French cooking is mistakenly regarded as difficult, but if you follow the rules, it is very easy to learn. The rules are not arbitrary: they are based on classic methods that yield perfect results. The French theory of cooking is, "If it works, don't fix it." Once you have learned how to make a perfect emulsified sauce, you go on to learn another skill. There is no need to learn fifteen ways to make a hollandaise sauce once you have mastered the perfect one. Because I am a cooking teacher, I design my recipes to the limit, meaning I fit in as many techniques as possible. In practice, this means that some recipes may be finished with butter or cream to demonstrate a crucial technique—this is a cooking school, not a diet center.

If there is one idea I try to drill into my students' minds, it is *mise en place,* a French term that translates to "put in place," or, as I put it, "get your mess in place." The point is to prepare your kitchen and your ingredients ahead of time for maximum efficiency. Stocks can be made ahead and frozen, as can fresh tomato sauce. If you have prepped items on hand that are used in many different recipes, you'll always be ready to cook. I teach students how to set up their kitchens so that good cooking is as easy as driving a car. Once you have learned proper cooking techniques, you can make an outstanding meal in a short time.

I am very particular about who teaches at Ecole de Cuisine. I teach most of the classes myself, but have a stellar collection of chefs, committed as I am to providing the students with a professional culinary experience, that help with my extensive programs. In the early years, I invited the culinary elite to give demonstration classes, including

Richard Grausman, Julia Child, Jacques Pépin, Patricia Wells, Giuliano Bugialli, Lynne Rosetto Kasper, Anne Willan, and Guy LeGay. But during the past six years, my focus has been on participation and hands-on courses. It is through total immersion that a student masters cooking techniques. I have therefore designed courses that target specific topics, and the students learn by doing each step themselves.

It has become my mission to not only teach solid cooking techniques, but also to advise my students as to which ingredients, cooking equipment, and appliances are valid and of true high quality. Marketing campaigns claim that you need to buy a specific canned stock, or use a certain pot or pan, or own one particular knife to be a good cook. Good cooking does require quality food products and some specific high-quality equipment, but most of what is available on the market is over-rated and of poor quality. Therefore, I teach the importance of buying from and supporting artisan food, appliance, and cookware purveyors—not getting sucked in by the marketers' hype.

Yes, there are foods to fear in the common American diet, but the list does not include butter, cream, and eggs. I am amazed at the swill that lines the shelves of grocery stores and fills the vending machines in our children's schools. Should soda really be considered a daily beverage? Are brightly colored globs of gelatin made from chemical colors, scents, and flavors really good for us (or more important, our children)? Is canned soup containing massive amounts of salt, slimy noodles, and tiny cubes of meat finished with monosodium glutamate really something you want to swallow? It is shocking to see the horrific prices on a ridiculous boxed product claiming to be "Garlic Mashed Potatoes." What the consumer gets is a tiny amount of dehydrated potato with nasty onion flakes and preservatives. The boxed, bagged, and canned meals are not food. These are expensive products produced for profit. So, in my school, we use only top-quality ingredients. In the long run, I believe they cost less and foster good health.

Along the same lines, the cookware shop at the school carries only the highest quality, most useful items for a home kitchen. And I even go against the grain of typical marketing efforts and rarely advertise. It is the good reputation of my school that continues to attract students from all over the country. The simple facts are that I love teaching, and I love to ignite that same passion for cooking in others.

The recipes in this book are, for the most part, French and Italian, with the exception of the American pies. Recipes have been gathered from my extensive travels through the various regions of France and Italy. Whether I travel alone or with friends, chefs are always enthusiastic to share their creations. I have learned a great deal from a restaurant in Paris called Thoumieux, where the food is simple perfection. The owner, Jean Basserlet, and his staff continually open new doors for me to explore. I am lucky enough to have been influenced by many such phenomenal people throughout the years.

First as a student, then as an instructor, then as a national public television cooking show host, and now as a cookbook author, I have been blessed with the opportunity to work with some of the finest artisans in the world. I have returned to France more than twenty times since that first fateful trip to learn from these proud artists, appreciate their craft, adopt their lifestyle, and, ultimately, to bring back to the States the lessons which I have embraced as my own. I've discovered along the way that a person can become a good cook with a lot less study and equipment than we have been led to believe. Separating the reality from the myth has become a culinary art in itself.

I have designed a cooking school that I hope reflects my respect for all the chefs, restaurants, schools, and artisans that have influenced my life. My goal is that Ecole de Cuisine will have the same kind of impact on my students as learning to cook in Paris had on me so long ago. It is with the greatest pride that I carry on the culinary traditions of France. As with all my students, I am honored to share my discoveries and my passion with you.

Jill's Cooking Basics

THROUGH MY YEARS OF TEACHING AT ECOLE DE CUISINE, I've been asked the same questions time and again about ingredients, cooking techniques, cookware and appliances, and basic recipes. Not surprisingly, my students and most home chefs do not clearly understand basic professional cooking techniques. In an attempt to fill in these blanks, I've addressed some of the most common issues. Obviously, not every question can be answered, but I think these tips will get you started and will prove most beneficial as you expand your culinary horizons.

Ingredient Tips

Let me share my thoughts on various ingredients with you—what to buy, how to handle them, and what kind of quality to look for. Use these reference points, shop at good markets, and your cooking will improve overnight. This list is clearly not all-inclusive; it's just meant to cover those items my students often have questions about.

ANCHOVIES

Students often turn up their noses at the mere mention of anchovies. But there is a vast difference between oil-packed anchovies and the superior salt-packed product. Once you have tried salt-packed anchovies in the Puttanesca pasta recipe (page 143), you will feel very differently about anchovies.

Many Italian specialty stores carry whole tins of salt-packed anchovies, but unless you split it with five or six friends, you may have a hard time using 2 pounds of anchovies. Luckily, many delis have begun selling them by the ounce, and they last for months in the refrigerator. First, gently rinse the small fish to remove the surface salt, and pat them dry. Open up the fish along the belly to expose the backbone. The fish will have been gutted, but you must remove the backbone: using the tip of a small paring knife, loosen the bone at the head and gently lift the spine out. Each fish yields 2 fillets. If you must use canned anchovy fillets packed in oil, be sure to rinse off the oil, which is the lowest quality olive oil approved for human consumption. Pat the fillets dry with paper towels before using. Anchovies packed into glass jars and covered with oil are superior to the canned product, but are not as good as salt-packed anchovies.

BUTTER

I believe that butter is healthful, so it is a staple at the school. In my opinion, margarine is not a food product and cannot be substituted for butter in good cooking. I don't know much about margarine, nor do I care to. I do know that it is nothing more than oil emulsified into water through a chemical process. In the past, unfounded media reports instilled a tremendous fear of butter in Americans. However, more and more studies are showing that the "M" product may be causing more damage than natural butter. Recently, nutritionists actually stated that butter was better than margarine, which I knew all the time.

I use only unsalted butter, which contains more fat than salted butter does. And that is the reason we use butter—for the fat and the taste. Salt actually replaces some of the fat in butter. It is not added to help you season your food, but to preserve butter, giving it the shelf life of uranium. Most often, I use whole butter with a fat content of at least 80 percent, although this is not stated on the package. You'll find there are some brands of unsalted butter containing more fat than others (butter is made up of fat, water, and milk solids). Always buy the butter with the highest fat content, which will not necessarily be the bargain brand.

CHOCOLATE

I use one chocolate for everything at the school—a high-quality bittersweet. Bittersweet chocolate contains a high percentage of cocoa solids with very little sugar added.

Milk chocolate is the sweetest chocolate available. It's so sweet that I think it's really only useful for decoration. Semi-sweet chocolate is slightly darker, but is still too sweet for my recipes. I almost never use unsweetened chocolate, which contains no sugar at all. Be sure to buy bittersweet and not unsweetened—they are *not* the same. Using unsweetened chocolate in a recipe calling for bittersweet will yield a very mouth-puckering result.

For many years, my favorite chocolate has been the French brand, Valrhona. I have become accustomed to its superb flavor. Some California chocolate makers, such as Scharffen Berger, are also producing very good bittersweet bars.

CREAM

Cream comes under many different headings in this country. You will see it labeled as whipping cream, heavy cream, light cream, gourmet cream, and sweet cream. What do all these names mean to you? In reality, whatever the manufacturer wants them to. All you need to look for when purchasing cream is at least 40 percent milk fat. Anything less than that, even 38 percent, I consider not fit to cook with. The label should clearly state 40 percent milk fat and list cream as the first ingredient. It is quite easy to identify the inferior creams—rather than listing just cream in the ingredient list, they also contain caragheenan, guar gum, and/or a number of other preservatives and stabilizers that I'm not even interested in knowing about. Carrageenan is a thickener made from seaweed. Guar gum is the ground seed from an Indian plant that has eight times the thickening power of cornstarch. You don't want this stuff in your cream.

Have you ever whipped cream and put it on top of a pie, only to find that a watery substance leaks out of the cream onto the top of the pie? Don't worry, you didn't whip it incorrectly, there's just not enough fat in the cream to hold it together. Because the inferior cream sold to unsuspecting American consumers is held together with plant products, it breaks down. A similar thing may happen when you reduce inferior cream for a sauce—without enough fat, it often separates. Fat is a good word at Ecole de Cuisine, when it comes to cooking. Preservatives and chemicals are not. So what happens to the premium heavy creams? I find that they go to bakeries and restaurants where chefs understand the difference and demand high-quality ingredients. But if you frequent good markets and read labels carefully, you should be able to find the better cream.

EGGS

Large eggs are the standard at the school and, these days, in just about every cookbook published. They should be used in all of my recipes. If you use small or jumbo eggs in cake recipes that require precise amounts, the results may be disastrous. For the past few years, I have found that egg yolks seem to be getting paler and paler, which reflects the inferior diet of the chicken. If you buy eggs from upscale markets, organic farms, or direct from the farmer, you'll find the best ones—those with dark golden, flavorful yolks.

The presence of salmonella in eggs is certainly cause for concern, but it is only found in 1 out of every 20,000 eggs. In addition, salmonella only grows in optimum conditions: basically when infected eggs, or food containing infected eggs, are left in a warm place for too long. Properly storing and using eggs will prevent bacteria growth. Eggs should always be kept in the refrigerator in their container (where they'll typically keep for 3 to 5 weeks). They need to be brought to room temperature just before use in baking.

FENNEL

This mild-flavored vegetable, with a celery-like crunch and texture and a mild yet distinct anise flavor, appears in better markets and is often used in Italian and Provençal recipes. The bulb can be braised and added to stew, sautéed in a little olive oil and then stuffed into the pocket of a fish, or cooked and puréed for a base rather than using a sauce. I especially like it raw. The fern-like tops of the fennel bulb are superb in salads or in butter sauces for fish or shellfish.

FLOUR

When I returned from my professional training in France, one of the most bother-some problems was trying to find the kind of flour I had worked with there. On a frustrated call to one of my instructors, I complained that I couldn't make certain recipes work, and said that our flour is bad here in the United States. He assured me that this wasn't the case, that we have the best wheat in the world in North America, but nobody knows how to mill it properly. I was amazed that something as seemingly simple as the way flour is milled could make such a difference in the success or failure of a recipe. In many aspects of food production, we have come a long way in the last few years, and I can now find many interesting flours at organic health food stores and specialty markets.

As specified in each recipe, you should use unbleached all-purpose flour, unbleached bread flour, pastry flour, or cake flour for the recipes in this book. Since there are so many flours available, I recommend stocking just these basic ones. Bleached flour and self-raising flour are unnecessary, and I try to avoid them. Bleach simply makes your flour white, and the bromates added to self-raising flour are chemicals that give extra rise to your cake. If you know how to properly fold egg whites into batter, there is no need to have chemicals do it for you.

HERBS

With the exception of bay leaves and oregano, I use only fresh herbs at the school. Ecole de Cuisine has its own herb garden, where we grow all of our herbs except bay leaves. My dry bay leaf of choice is imported from Turkey and has a very earthy and mellow flavor compared to the more pungent flavor of fresh bay leaf. Oregano is often too assertive in its fresh form but takes on a toasty, mellow flavor when dried. For all other herbs, there is simply no comparison between fresh and dried. Fresh herbs can elevate any dish to its greatest heights.

Tender herbs—tarragon, basil, chervil, cilantro, curly and flat-leaf parsley—are normally added at the end of the recipe, because their flavor tends to cook away. Woody herbs—sage, rosemary, marjoram, and thyme—are put into braises, stews, stocks, or other recipes early in the cooking time. All of the above-mentioned herbs are commonly used at the school. In addition, some of my recipes call for fresh lavender blossoms, although lavender is a flower, not an herb. I use it because of its intense and distinct flavor. Since fresh lavender is only available in summer and early fall, purchasing dried lavender from a reputable vendor (see Sources, page 252) is acceptable. Just be sure not to get the perfumed potpourri variety.

Some quick herb-preparation tips: To chop chives, line them up in a bunch and cut into 1/8-inch pieces. Or, just snip them to size with sharp kitchen scissors. Only cut once to retain color and shape—repeated cuts will bruise the chives. The most efficient way to chop basil is to make it into a chiffonade: Stack the leaves on top of one another and roll them together as if rolling a cigar. Slice even, thin strips from the log, and then separate and fluff the strips with your fingers.

MILK

I use whole milk at the school and in all my recipes. Although you can use 2 percent or skim milk, the resulting dish will not taste the same. Milk fat gives a dish structure and flavor.

NUTS

I try to buy nuts in season in fall and winter so they are in perfect form and at good prices. If they are not to be used immediately, nuts should be stored in plastic freezer bags in the freezer. They tend to get rancid when left at room temperatures, which happens in about a month in hot climates. If nuts taste bitter, they are probably rancid. That's a good hint to not use them.

OLIVE OIL

Only extra virgin, cold pressed olive oil should be used—not "pure" olive oil. For extra virgin oils, the first cold pressing is the only technique used to extract the oil. But pressure alone does not extract all the oil from the fruit, so manufacturers press the same fruit again, using heat and chemicals to extract every last bit of oil. The resulting grade is designated as "pure," but is not suitable for fine cooking. It is amusing that the "pure" classification uses chemicals to extract the remaining juice. So, as it goes in the confusing world of food labeling, pure is not really pure.

Some restaurant chefs use the cheaper pure oil for sautéing because it has a higher smoke point than extra virgin. I never do. Instead, I recommend mixing extra virgin oil with a lighter vegetable oil, like safflower, sunflower, or grapeseed, for sautéing. If an assertive olive oil taste needs to be toned down for a dressing or other use, I recommend using a similar combination. The color of olive oil does not indicate quality; many factors, including the variety of olive, the degree of ripeness, and even the weather at harvest, determine the color of the oil. Store olive oil away from sunlight and the intense heat of the stove. Don't store oils in the refrigerator—condensation can form, which causes spoilage.

SALT

I use both finely ground and coarse French sea salt at the school. Sea salt is mined directly from salt marshes and has a very bright, fresh, and intense flavor. Regular table salt contains a preservative to prevent the kernels from sticking together in humid weather. Finely ground French sea salt contains this free-flowing agent as well, but in much smaller quantity. Coarse French sea salt contains no free-flowing agent at all because it will never compact and stick together.

The difference between French sea salt and common table salt available in America is quite distinct. Table salt is mined from the earth. Throughout the centuries, trace minerals have settled and compacted with the salts in the earth, giving it a bitter aftertaste. That, along with excessive amounts of the free-flowing agent, yields salt with an "off" flavor.

I use fine sea salt in sauces, soups, baking, and for salting meats. Coarse sea salt is used in cooking water for pasta or vegetables, or in any dish where it will dissolve in liquid.

Fleur de Sel: From France, this is the most expensive salt you will ever buy, but it is not to be used in cooking—only to season finished dishes. The taste is exquisite and it has the uncanny ability to draw out complex flavors from food. (See pages 251 and 252 for fleur de sel sources.)

Kosher Salt: Kosher salt is the same as common table salt, but it has been flattened through rollers by the manufacturer. It was designed to extract blood from animals for Jewish cooking—the flattened kernels give it more surface space for absorption. Kosher salt has a milder flavor than both table and sea salts, so the only time I use it at the school is for sprinkling on top of breads. Commercial salts for breads are not available to the public, but the judicious use of kosher salt on top of bread works well for the home chef.

SPICES

I am extremely passionate about the use of top-quality spices. Every student who comes to my school is given the phone number and address of my spice supplier (also one of my favorite shops in the country)—The Spice House (see Sources, page 252).

I recommend buying your spices from a shop that grinds their own every week. The taste difference between freshly ground and grocery store spices is dramatic. Spices can make or break a recipe.

SUGAR

I only use granulated cane sugar. Some sugar is made from beets, but I prefer the sugar cane variety. In cooking applications where you need sugar to dissolve quickly, superfine sugar is the best choice. It's easy to make—place 1 cup granulated sugar into the bowl of a food processor and process for 30 seconds to 1 minute. It should be stored in a tightly covered container.

TOMATOES

I use Italian Roma tomatoes, also called "plum" tomatoes. These oblong tomatoes are meatier than regular tomatoes and are used for making sauces. They also hold their shape during long cooking, so are used for dishes like Pasta with Kale and Spicy Italian Sausage (page 147) and Penne alla Puttanesca (page 143). Most fresh tomatoes are when eaten by themselves or in salads. They contain a great deal of liquid, so they do not produce thick sauces. During my early years as a devoted homemaker, a friend and I canned about a hundred quarts of tomatoes. But they were big juicy slicing tomatoes that cooked into red threads floating in pink-colored water. When you can find an abundance of Roma tomatoes, make my Fresh Tomato Sauce (page 139) and freeze 2-cup amounts. This is one of the best *mise en place* procedures (page x) you can do for quick meals. As a side note, buy tomato paste in tubes rather than opening the cans that often go to waste.

VANILLA BEANS

Vanilla beans are another staple in our kitchen. For recipes such as Basic Vanilla Custard Sauce (Crème Anglaise, page 222), ice cream, and infusions like Crème Brûlée (page 243) and Crème Caramel (page 241), I use beans exclusively, never extract. You want a pronounced vanilla flavor in these recipes, which only beans can produce. Vanilla extract is milder and is used in cake and cookie recipes. The vanilla plant is the only fruit-bearing orchid. I usually use the flavorful beans from Madagascar. Vanilla beans are also grown in Tahiti: the flavor is flowery and interesting, but I rarely use these pods.

Vanilla beans are usually infused in a hot liquid at the beginning of the cooking process. The pod is slit open lengthwise with the tip of a knife, then the seeds are scraped out and placed into the liquid (often milk or cream) along with the pod, which also contains a great deal of flavor. After the milk has been brought to a boil, it is taken off the heat, and vanilla bean is left to infuse its flavor into the milk for at least 30 minutes. The pod is then removed from the liquid and discarded. Extract can be substituted, but it must be added at the end of cooking, as the flavor will dissipate during the cooking process. I have read many times that the pod can be rinsed and put into sugar to make vanilla sugar. First of all, I would not want to put a milk-soaked pod—even one that has been rinsed—in sugar. And second, I have never in my culinary career used vanilla sugar. But if you do have a recipe calling for vanilla sugar, use a fresh vanilla bean, not one that has been drowned in milk.

WINE

When a recipe calls for red or white wine, you should use a freshly opened bottle. Only put wine in your food that you would also put in your glass. I keep opened white wine for one day and red wine for two days—after that they begin to turn to vinegar. You can also purchase a device to extract air from the bottles to give the wine a longer shelf life—this adds, perhaps, up to a week to its keeping time. Cooking wine is a vile pseudo-food product sold on grocery store shelves. It contains copious amounts of salt to discourage minors from buying it to drink. Heaven forbid that teenagers learn to appreciate wine with a meal, as a complement to food rather than an intoxicant. Instead, we steer our youth toward sugary soda, red and blue dyed "fruit" drinks, and chemical cocktails. Now that makes sense, doesn't it?

ZEST

An amazing concentration of flavor is found in the outermost peel, called the zest, of citrus fruits. Capturing and using this powerful punch brings a wonderful taste to both savory and sweet recipes. The best way to remove zest from fresh lemons and oranges is with a zester, which is designed to cut off strips of peel without any of the bitter underlying white pith. When removing the zest, be careful not to press too hard on the zester, or you may pick up some of the pith. If you need grated zest, you can procure strips with a zester and then finely chop them, or you can just use the finest holes of a grater.

I always wash fruit before zesting to remove any wax and residual chemicals that may have been used to extend the fruit's shelf life. Fill the sink with warm water, add a few drops of non-perfumed dish soap, drop in the fruit, and swish it around. Then rinse in cold water and dry with a towel.

Cookware and Appliance Notes

Home chefs often use the same tools used by professional chefs, though usually the home versions are smaller in scale. The best equipment costs a bit more, but will be part of your *batterie de cuisine* for your lifetime and that of your children. My students are surprised by the lack of gadgets in my kitchen. You don't need lots of gadgets: you need a few good-quality tools, and you must know how to use them. In my early cooking days, I bought just about all the trendy items available—all of them touted as great additions to my kitchen—but I've found that most of them are just expensive clutter. Since studying in France, I have become a crusader for top-quality cookware and appliance manufacturers.

POTS AND PANS: WHAT TO LOOK FOR WHEN BUYING

First step—buy a 2-quart saucepan. Take it home, pour one cup of cream into it. Place it over high heat and boil until the cream is reduced to a thick sauce. If you have a gas stove, adjust the flame so that it is on the highest flame possible without the flames lapping up the sides of the pan. If you have an electric stovetop, just do this over medium-high to high heat on a small burner. If the cream burns on the sides or bottom of the pan, take it back. It is an inferior pan.

Good construction equals good cookware. It is critical that the same thickness of heat-conducting metal (be it copper or aluminum) forms the walls of the pan, not just the base. If the copper or aluminum is only on the bottom, food will burn onto the sides. The only time that stainless steel sides and a copper or aluminum base is acceptable is in a stockpot. Stockpots are used for one purpose—making stock. Usually you pretty much only have water in them, which will never burn or stick.

Nonstick cookware has its place in every kitchen for omelets, sticky cheese potatoes, and so on, but there's no need to spend tons of money. Better to spend twenty dollars for a nonstick pan that you will eventually throw out than a hundred for a pan just to match your set.

When you purchase cookware, you are looking for a material that conducts heat without imparting taste to your food. Let's take a look at the various materials available.

Glass: Glass is 0 percent efficient in conducting heat. I am not sure why people would want it at all—it chips, it cracks, and it just doesn't spread heat.

Stainless Steel: Stainless steel is somewhere in the 9 percent category for heat conductivity, meaning that it doesn't conduct heat well. In fact, it tends to burn everything. The redeeming quality of stainless steel, however, is that it is a nonreactive metal—it will not impart an off flavor or taste to your food.

Aluminum: Aluminum is in the 50 to 60 percent category of efficient heat conductivity. This is very good, but the problem with aluminum is that it imparts a flavor to your food, particularly in long cooking processes, such as stews, braises, and long simmers. The flavor of the resulting food is much like that of a crumpled piece of aluminum foil.

Enameled Cast iron: Enameled cast iron conducts heat very well, slightly better than aluminum, ranging in the 55 to 65 percent efficiency category. Coating cast iron with enamel prevents the cast iron from passing taste to foods, especially sauces. My favorite Dutch ovens are made out of enameled cast iron. I use them for braising, stewing, and soups—they do a better job than aluminum.

Copper: Copper is the best conductor of heat, with an efficiency percentage of 90 to 95 percent. It is also a reactive metal, even toxic when used with certain foods, and therefore any pot or pan must be lined. (Copper bowls and sugar pans don't need to be lined because eggs react with the copper in a positive way and sugar is not a reactive food. Such bowls and pans should never be used with any foods other than eggs and sugar.) In France, the lining is usually tin, which conducts heat well but will eventually have to be replaced (depending on use). In the past ten years, stainless steel–lined copper has become readily available; this provides an interior surface that will not wear off or react with food. There are nice-looking models available with brass handles, but they're usually made with a thin-gauge copper. I use the heaviest gauge of copper with cast-iron handles and stainless steel lining. Look for copper pans at least 2.5 millimeters thick.

CONVENTIONAL AND CONVECTION OVENS

Convection ovens have recently begun making a big splash in the appliance world. I have started getting a lot of questions about them, so I think it's important that I explain the differences. Conventional ovens cook food primarily from the heat that radiates from the bottom element (conventional ovens have two elements—top and bottom). Casseroles, braises, and stews all cook perfectly well in conventional ovens.

Convection ovens are much more complicated. In convection ovens, the most important heat source is an additional third element in the back of the oven. A fan draws air out of the oven chamber and forces it through a filter and across the convection heating element. The heated air is then evenly directed back into the oven chamber. So what you're getting is constantly circulating hot air. The temperature stays perfectly accurate at all levels—top, center, and bottom—so your food cooks evenly. True convection ovens are unrivaled in producing perfectly baked breads, layers of just-right cookies, crisp pie crusts, and juicy roasted meats.

Beware though—not all ovens sold as convection are truly convection. Some simply have a fan that blows air around, but they lack the extra third heating element. There are many such inferior, though still expensive, ovens available. And your run-of-the-mill counter top models are definitely not convection. Dacor Distinctive Appliances located in Pasadena, California, produces an exceptional oven with the same pure convection benefits of the ovens I used in France.

STOVETOPS

I always cook on gas stovetops with 15,000 BTUs (British Thermal Unit—basically a measure of the heat output) of heat, which are high-quality appliances designed for homes, not chefs. Please don't get suckered in by the so-called simmer burners—they barely have a flame and do nothing more than create ambience in your kitchen. A 15,000 BTU burner will produce the perfect simmer because the control is very accurate. Though I recommend against electric stovetops, if you must use one, I suggest keeping one burner on a high heat and another on a low heat so that you can switch temperatures quickly by moving the pot back and forth rather than waiting for a burner to cool or heat.

MISCELLANEOUS TOOLS

Besides the best pots, pans, and appliances, it is important to pay attention to the quality of your everyday kitchen items. Plus, with all the stores full of gadgets, you need to know what you should really outfit your kitchen with.

Apple Corer: An easy method for quick removal of the core, it's just one of those things you need to have around. Indispensable for making the Caramelized Apple Tart (Tarte Tatin, page 236).

Bakeware: When baking, aluminum pans are ideal. (Batters will not pick up the aluminum taste as do liquids.) Choose heavy-gauge aluminum, because it will distribute the heat evenly for even baking. See the list below for a good range of sizes.

Chinois: Translating as "China cap," a chinois is a very fine-mesh conical strainer used for making fine sauces and stocks.

Colander: A large stainless steel colander is essential for rapidly draining water from cooked pasta, blanched vegetables, and rinsed fruit.

Cookware: I cover materials in some detail on pages 10 and 11. See the list below for what sizes you should have.

Cooling Racks: Large heavy duty wire cooling racks facilitate the cooling of baked goods by allowing air to circulate all around the food.

Copper Bowls: Nothing works better to whip egg whites than a copper bowl. Egg whites react with the copper to provide the highest volume and stability. When using copper, the cream of tartar often called for when whisking egg whites is not necessary.

BAKEWARE	COOKWARE
8-inch round cake pans	2-quart saucepan
9-inch round cake pans	4 1/2-quart saucepan with an offset "helper" handle opposite the main handle
9-inch springform cake pans (for cheesecake)	3-quart sauté pan
9 by 9-inch square baking pan	6-quart sauté pan
8 by 8-inch square baking pan	12-inch frying pan
3 by 9 by 12-inch baking pan (good for doughs that rise, such as Cinnamon Buns, page 75)	7- or 8-quart casserole (Dutch oven)
6 by 11-inch 4-sided jelly-roll pan	12-, 16-, or 20-quart stockpot
10 by 15-inch 4-sided jelly-roll pan	
2-sided baking sheets (for cookies)	

Crepe Pan: Black steel pans from France are the best choice for making crepes, because they give the traditional lacey look rather than the flat light color produced by nonstick pans and electric crepe makers. The most useful sizes are 5 and 7 inches. Before using, you must cure your crepe pan to make it nonstick. With a paper towel, rub the inside generously with plain vegetable oil and a teaspoon of salt. Place the pan over low heat and allow it to cure for about 15 minutes. The darker and nastier the pan gets, the more nonstick it becomes. You must take special care in washing your crepe pan—it really should only be wiped clean with a paper towel.

CUTLERY
3 1/2-inch paring
5-inch boning
8-inch serrated bread
9- or 10-inch meat slicer
8-inch chef's

Cutlery: Choose knives that are forged from a single block of steel for strength, balance, safety, and comfort. Good quality is important for sharpening and long-life. Use a good, long sharpening steel to keep your knives healthy. Knives that have been mistreated may need to be re-ground at either a reputable hardware store or some cookware shops. Then, you should be able to keep them in good condition with the steel.

Cutting Boards: I like to use high-quality wooden boards at least 1 1/2 inches thick. Periodically, you should treat wooden cutting boards with a nontoxic mineral oil to seal against impurities. Polyethylene cutting boards, at least 1 inch thick, are another good option. They are sturdy, warp-resistant, waterproof, and hygienic. A quick scrub with a little bleach will restore them to their pristine hygienic condition.

Dutch Oven: A Dutch oven should be heavy, preferably cast iron with enamel on the interior. These pots retain heat well with even temperature and no hot-spots, and can be used on all cook surfaces. Seven or eight quarts is the perfect all-purpose size.

Food Mill: One of the most useful tools in the kitchen, food mills make quick work of puréeing, creating silky smooth textures. For sauces, soups, and potato dishes, they are preferable over food processors, which do not strain out skins and seeds. Be sure to buy one with both a fine- and coarse-hole disk.

Food Processor: A good-quality, heavy-duty food processor is essential for puréeing, making pesto, chopping nuts, and a multitude of other kitchen tasks.

Grater: Most useful for cheese (obviously), a good grater is also needed when a recipe calls for freshly grated nutmeg. Almost always made with stainless steel, you should choose a grater with four sides and therefore four different grate sizes.

Ladles: Needed for stocks, soups, sauces, and batters, 1-, 2-, 4-, and 8-ounce ladles are good sizes to have on hand.

Liquid Measuring Cup: Heat-tempered, spouted glass cups let the cook quickly measure and dispense liquid ingredients. The measurements should be written on the outside so they can be read at eye level. You'll want the 1-, 2- and 4-cup sizes. For stock and dessert making, it's nice to have the larger 2-quart cup.

Mandoline: A peerless and very precise cutting instrument that is used to slice, julienne, and make waffle cuts on potatoes or other vegetables. Nothing compares to a mandoline for making paper-thin slices of potato. Though expensive, usually around $160, they are an excellent investment, often performing better than food processors for those exact cutting jobs.

Measuring Cups and Spoons: The ones I use are made from professional-quality stainless steel and engineered for precision and accuracy to ensure consistency in food preparation. They won't rust or get bent out of shape.

Mixing Bowls: At the school, we use flat-bottomed French bowls made from high-quality stainless steel. Nesting, heavy-gauge stainless steel bowls that are more upright than wide are the best choice.

Parchment Paper: With its multitude of kitchen uses, you'll wonder how you ever got along without parchment paper. In baking, it makes for easy cleanup and is often used for its nonstick properties. It's also perfect for wrapping around fish to create a mini–steam oven with moist, flavorful results. Do purchase a good quality paper—you won't regret it.

Pastry Bags and Tips: Use high-quality nylon pastry bags for all your piping needs, from potatoes to puff pastry to buttercream. They are reusable, but you need to wash them by hand and allow them to air dry. There are all kinds of tip sizes and shapes available, just make sure you have a 1/2-inch plain tip, and 1/4-inch, 1/2-inch, and 1-inch French star tips.

Pastry Brushes: A wood-handled natural bristle brush is the best choice, but avoid the ones with metal-bound bristles, which will rust. Brushes that are 1 1/2 to 2 inches wide will work for most applications.

Porcelain: For family-size casseroles and potato dishes, 2- and 3-quart porcelain bakers will do well. My favorite brand is Pillyvuit, from France. I have just about every piece of this wonderful porcelain, including ramekins, bakeware, terrines, serving platters, and place settings. Porcelain is the best option when you want to bake in and serve out of the same dish.

Ramekins: Ramekins should be made of a good-quality porcelain. For Classic French Chocolate Mousse (page 245) and Crème Caramel (page 241), use 4-ounce capacity ramekins, 3 1/2 inches in diameter. For Crème Brûlée (page 243), choose shallow dishes, 5 to 6 inches in diameter. This size also works well for Spinach Gnocchi (page 140) and Coquilles St. Jacques (page 158). If you're doing a cheese or dessert soufflé, you'll need a 4-cup capacity ramekin with a diameter of 8 inches.

Roasting Pan: Use an aluminum pan made of the highest grade available, which will conduct heat extremely well. Choose one with deep sides and good handles. The best on the market are made in France. As I do, you might find both a large and small one useful at home.

Rolling Pin: I can't say enough about the 20-inch-long French rolling pin. As opposed to conventional rolling pins, these are non-tapered, cylinder-shaped pins. Preferably made of boxwood, which will not transfer flavors from one product to another, this rolling pin is perfect for rolling crusts and cookie dough.

Salad Spinner: Salad dressing will not adhere to wet leaves. A salad spinner is absolutely the best way to dry salad greens. Depending on what model you buy, the inner basket can double as a colander, while the outer container can be used as a salad bowl.

Scale: Choose a model that is battery operated for exact measurements. It should also be capable of metric measurements (grams) as well as ounces.

Silpat, Exopat, or Fiberlux: These are all brand names for the same thing—a silicone rubber baking mat that is placed on baking sheets to make them nonstick. These mats can withstand very high heats and are reusable. They should be hand washed with warm soapy water and air-dried.

Skimmer: One of those tools that is in continual use at the school, a fine-mesh skimmer is perfect for retrieval of loose particles in stocks, skimming impurities off sauces and soups, or simply retrieving food from liquid. I use a flat fine-mesh Italian skimmer.

Spatulas, Metal: Also called turners, one of my favorite tools is one with a long handle, a long flexible blade, and open strips. I use this for deglazing pans and many other purposes.

Spatulas, Rubber: Rubber spatulas should be heat resistant to at least 600°. You'll want narrow, medium, and wide versions.

Spatulas, Wood: These spatulas look like flattened spoons. A favorite and most useful tools, a wooden spatula is especially good for the "trail" method of testing cream reductions. Look for boxwood spatulas (this wood does not transfer flavors).

Stand Mixer: Stand mixers are great workhorses in the kitchen. A 5-quart model serves the most uses, from mixing batters to kneading doughs to whipping egg whites. Many models have attachments for grating cheese and chocolate. I use a KitchenAid stand mixer at the school.

Stock Pot: To make a good soup, the stock must cook for hours in a deep, somewhat heavy pot. A pot with stainless steel sides and a layer of copper or aluminum on the bottom allows for even heat dispersal. The interior should always be stainless steel, though, since aluminum imparts a tinny flavor. For home use, a 12-, 16-, or 20-quart pot will be sufficient.

Strainer: A very fine-mesh strainer is an absolute must for sauces and clarifying butter. I like an Italian one that is approximately 7 inches in diameter.

Swiss Peeler: Shaped similarly to a wire-cutter cheese slicer, Swiss peelers have extremely sharp high-carbon blades that make quick work out of tedious peeling tasks, especially peeling tomatoes. Its shape offers incredible control, allowing jobs to be done in half the time.

Tart Pans: Tart pans should be made out of tin and have removable bottoms. This is becoming a pattern, but I do encourage you to buy French tart pans. The frauds made in other countries are made from alloy metals and therefore burn rather than brown the contents. I recommend that you have an 8-inch, a 9-inch, and six to eight individual 5-inch pans. You might also want to purchase 4-inch tins, 1 1/2 inches deep, for the Warm Bittersweet Chocolate Tarts (page 234). For the Caramelized Apple Tart (Tarte Tatin, page 236), you'll need an "official" Tarte Tatin mold—a tin-lined copper pan that is 11 1/4 inches in diameter at the rim and 2 1/4 inches deep.

Thermometer, Candy: Used for temperature monitoring while making candy and caramel and heating oils, find one with a large easy-to-read dial.

Thermometer, Meat: You'll want an instant-read thermometer also with a large easy-to-read dial. This is far superior to the old-fashioned thermometers designed to be left in a roast the entire time it's in the oven. Be sure to scan the instructions and be aware that an instant-read thermometer should not be immersed in water or left in a hot oven.

Tongs: Fourteen-inch tongs are the best for most kitchen uses. With a 3-inch scalloped head, this set of tongs is ample for turning a pork loin roast or plucking a custard cup from its bain-marie. The scalloped edges provide a fast hold and lessen the chance of piercing the item you're lifting.

Tweezers: Not often thought of as a kitchen tool, tweezers are useful for pulling bones out of fish.

Whisks: Solidly constructed stainless steel whisks are an absolute must. You want the working end of the whisk to have a resin connection to the handle, preventing rust and germ collection. A few different types are necessary—one with thin wires for sauces, one with medium wires for pastry creams, and a balloon one for beating egg whites. My favorite whisks are manufactured right here in the U.S. by a company called, appropriately, Best Whisks. I take them to France to give as gifts to my chef friends.

Zester: A zester is used for easy removal of the outermost layer of orange or lemon peel where the essential fruit oils (and flavor) are stored. A zester will create decorative strips that can be used whole or chopped.

Cooking Techniques

BLANCHING

For blanching, the liquid is brought to a full rolling boil and food is added for a short period of time. The food is then drained and rinsed in cold water to stop the cooking (this is sometimes called "shocking"). Blanching serves a multitude of purposes: vegetables are blanched to preserve their color and/or prepare them for further cooking at a later time. You would blanch vegetables before freezing them to make sure they still look fresh after thawing. Or you might blanch broccoli, for example, to soften it a bit before sautéing, so that the tough fibers will not scorch. Blanching is also done to remove skins from nuts, as well as from fruits such as tomatoes and peaches. If bacon or salt pork is to be used in a casserole or salad, they are blanched first to remove their excessive smoke flavor or saltiness, otherwise the strong flavor might overpower everything else in the dish.

BOILING

I always ask my beginning students if they know how to boil water for vegetables. It seems like a silly question, but do you begin them in hot or cold water? The general rule of thumb is that if the vegetable grows above the earth, like green beans, it is dropped into boiling, salted water. The heat is then adjusted to achieve a simmer and the vegetables cooked to al dente—firm, not crunchy, but not soft. Root vegetables that grow under the earth, like potatoes, are started in cold water, which is brought to a boil over high heat. Salt is only added after the water has reached a boil—salt sitting in cold water on the bottom of a pan may cause pitting. When food is dropped into a full rolling boil, the temperature of the water is immediately lowered. Once the water returns to a boil, the heat must be adjusted to maintain a moderate boil. Cooking at a full rolling boil will tear apart the outside of a potato while the inside remains uncooked.

There are four levels of boiling identified by observing the surface of the liquid. The following descriptions are helpful:

Shimmer: When the water begins to tremble, but no bubbles are breaking through. Shimmering is used when poaching fish.

Simmer: Tiny, evenly spaced, continual bubbles will cover the entire surface. A brisk simmer is the stage just before the water breaks out into a boil. Simmering is used for slow-cooking stews, braises, stocks, and soups.

Moderate boil: The water surface will break into medium bubbles. A moderate boil is used for cooking vegetables and pasta.

Rolling boil: Water bubbles will burst in the middle of the liquid and roll to the surface. A rolling boil is used for wilting leafy vegetables and some reductions.

BRAISING

Braising is most commonly used for cooking meat, but is also a cooking technique for vegetables. In a braise, one piece or pieces of meat are seared and browned, then cooked slowly, covered by two-thirds with a liquid, either on the stovetop or, preferably, inside the oven where the heat is more even. The flavor of a braise is enhanced by the browning of the meat, however, meat may be braised without the searing. A mirepoix—equal parts carrot, celery, and onion—is often added to the liquid when a braise goes into the oven.

Braising is a great cooking method for tough, large cuts of meat that will become very tender with slow cooking. Non-marbled meats are the most desirable, but any fat can be removed from the surface before serving.

Procedure for Braising

1. Bring the meat to room temperature.

2. Dry the meat thoroughly with paper towels. (Excess juice on the meat will create steam, which prevents browning.)

3. Season the meat with salt and pepper.

4. Follow the searing instructions through step 5 (pages 26–27).

5. Place the mirepoix in a large casserole, then place the meat on top of the vegetables. Add enough liquid, preferably homemade stock, to come two-thirds of the way up the sides of the meat.

6. Simmer the braise on the stovetop over medium-low heat or place into a 350° oven for about 2 hours. Whether on the stovetop or in the oven, the pan should be covered with a tight-fitting lid. I prefer to braise in the oven so the heat is more even. It is very important to never allow the braise to boil, which will make the meat very tough and stringy. Extra liquid, either stock, water, or wine, may be added if the liquid has reduced too much before the meat is done.

7. Once the meat is tender, remove it from the pan. If the sauce is too liquidy, place the pan on the stovetop and reduce the sauce to the desired consistency. If necessary, return the meat to the sauce to warm it through before serving.

DONENESS TEST FOR MEAT AND SEAFOOD

The steps detailed on the following page work perfectly when testing meat, such as steaks and chops, for doneness. This will also work for seafood, but remember that seafood is much more tender and will break apart if pushed too firmly. (Without breaking the fish up too much, you also need to check the level of opacity when testing fish for doneness— fish is done as it turns opaque and the juices become milky white. Undercooked fish is translucent with clear and watery juices. Overcooked fish is dry and falls apart easily.)

I've seen another doneness test that always makes me laugh. The instructions say that a skewer should be plunged into a piece of meat, then removed and placed flat against one's face in the crevice between the bottom lip and chin. Supposedly, warm indicates rare. I wonder how many people have scorch marks on their faces from practicing this "technique." Also, constant poking allows the juices to pour from the meat, leaving a dehydrated piece of leather. So if you see anyone with scorch marks across their chins, be certain to teach them my method. The skilled chef will know when a piece of meat is cooked to preference without having to cut into or skewer it.

FLAMBÉING

Flaming or, as the French say, flambéing, is quite spectacular to watch on TV or in a fine restaurant, but there is no earth-shattering need to flambé a dish. Most home kitchens do not have the same level of ventilation as restaurants, so I am rather hesitant to instruct my students to flambé at home. Although it is impressive to watch, it is not always practical. Also, chefs have 30,000 BTU burners. Even the better home ranges have only about 15,000 BTUs maximum. The more BTUs, the higher your flame, the easier it is to flambé.

Doneness Test for Meat and Seafood

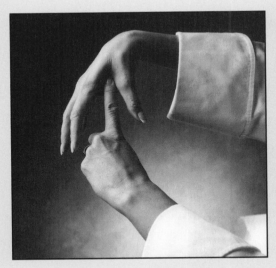

STEP 1—RARE

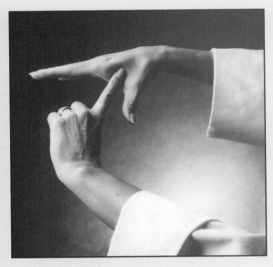

STEP 2—MEDIUM

STEP 3—WELL DONE

STEP 1 — Shake one hand and allow it to hang down limply from your wrist. With the forefinger of the opposite hand, firmly press the fleshy part between the thumb and forefinger of your limp hand. This is what rare meat feels like to the touch.

STEP 2 — Next, extend your hand with fingers pointing straight out. Again with the forefinger of your opposite hand, press between the thumb and forefinger. You'll feel more resistance and firmness. This is how medium-cooked meat feels to the touch.

STEP 3 — Now make a fist and feel the same spot. It will be very firm with little resistance. This is what well-done meat feels like. (I often think such meat is only fit for the dogs.)

Flambéing does, however, create an intense caramelization and resulting great flavor on the exterior of a steak. Cognac is generally the preferred flavor for flambéing, but other liqueurs will work. If you want to flame and have plenty of room, first warm some Cognac (however much is called for in the recipe) in a long-handled 1-cup soup ladle over a high heat burner until the Cognac is lukewarm. (Cognac is highly flammable. Never pour it directly from the bottle into the pan—the flame can easily travel up the stream of liquid into the bottle and cause the bottle to explode.) Then place the ladle slightly to the side of and above the flame of a gas burner, and tip one side slightly toward the flame. (If you are using an electric stove, warm the Cognac over a burner, then light it with a long match.) The alcohol will catch fire and can then be poured directly into the sauté pan. To be really safe, you can cool the pan slightly before you add the Cognac, then increase the heat to high and continue cooking over high heat.

POACHING

Poaching is a method of cooking food in hot, but not bubbling, water. It requires enough liquid to allow the food to be comfortably surrounded. Generally, poaching liquid consists of water and/or stock or wine, and vegetables and fresh herbs. The liquid from a simple poached chicken may be used as the base for a Velouté Sauce (page 51) or as a stock. The temperature of poaching liquid should range from 195 to 205°, which is always below boiling. You are looking for a shimmer, or at most a simmer, with only slight movement on top. It is important to maintain an even temperature, therefore the liquid should be checked occasionally. When poaching, undercook fish and shellfish slightly, because it will taste oily and strong and become tough if overcooked.

If poaching liquid is allowed to boil, the violent movement of the liquid will destroy the outside of the food before the center is cooked. Boiling liquid will tear poultry skin and toughen the flesh. So watch and adjust the heat to keep the liquid at the optimum temperature!

REDUCING, AND SAUCE CONSISTENCY

If you place a sauce or liquid over high heat, it will cook down to a reduced consistency. The goal is either to thicken the sauce or intensify the flavor—often both processes occur. You want the sauce to reduce as quickly as possible to concentrate the flavor.

You might also reduce a wine or liqueur to capture its essence before adding other ingredients, as with Béarnaise Sauce (page 56).

Reducing cream sauces: Cream sauces should be reduced over medium to high heat. If using a gas stove, the flame should never lap up the sides of the pan, but should come just to the edges of the base. Stir occasionally to prevent sticking as the sauce thickens. Sauces reduced in thin-bottomed, poorly made pans will burn on the sides and often on the bottom. (See pages 10 and 11.)

Sauce consistency: I find that students have a great of trouble deciding exactly when a sauce has reached the correct consistency, and everybody is afraid to turn up the heat! You need sufficient heat, at least medium-high, for the sauce to reduce to the right consistency. The best tip I can give you—use a wooden spoon. When you pull a wooden spoon out of a sauce, the sauce will coat the spoon. Draw your finger through the sauce on the back of the spoon. If your finger leaves a trail, the sauce is at the right consistency. If the sauce runs back together as your finger passes through, it must continue reducing—just give it a few more minutes over high heat and then test again.

ROASTING

Technically, roasting is cooking food, usually whole pieces of meat and poultry, at medium to high heat in an oven. The goal is to cook the food with dry, hot air. Most roasts are cooked in shallow pans (not surprisingly, they are commonly referred to as roasting pans). This kind of pan allows the hot air to circulate around the meat so that it cooks evenly. Roasting racks help in this endeavor, as they elevate the meat and provide air circulation around the entire roast. The pan must be large enough to hold the meat comfortably, but not so large as to let the meat drippings burn. Normally, roasts are placed fat side up in the pan so that the fat runs down over the roast as it cooks. I even roast my turkey upside down until the last hour, at which time I turn it over using old potholders. The breast meat is always juicy!

High-Heat Roasting: This is my preferred method of roasting. It's pretty simple—you begin the roasting process at a high temperature, around 425°, then, after a short time, usually 5 to 10 minutes, decrease the temperature to around 400°. This will produce a browned, crispy, and well-done exterior, while ensuring a juicy interior. Rack of lamb, Cornish game hens, and other small roasts respond particularly well to this technique.

Low-Heat Roasting: Low-heat roasting, at 325 to 350°, provides a uniformly cooked piece of meat throughout both the exterior and interior. A piece of meat that is slow-roasted will shrink less during the cooking process than one that is high-heat roasted. Large pieces of meat, such as rib roasts, are well suited for this method.

Roasting Vegetables: To roast vegetables, such as potatoes, you should first blanch them. This will partially cook and soften the vegetables. Then you should drain, dry, and brush the vegetables with oil and salt (you can infuse the oil with fresh herbs, if you like). Roasting then takes place at 400° for 15 to 30 minutes, depending on the size and the vegetable. Roasted vegetables should be tested with a skewer to check for tenderness. You'll end up with a soft creamy interior and a crisp, browned crust.

SAUCE FIXES

For slow-cooked dishes like Osso Buco (page 176) and Red Wine Beef Stew (page 172), a rich, flavorful sauce is crucial. How does it taste? If the sauce, which began as the braising liquid, is thin or weak there are three ways to correct it:

The Thickening and Intensifying Fix: If your sauce is very soupy, remove the meat from the braising pan and reserve. Place the pan of vegetables and braising liquid over high heat and simmer to thicken the sauce and intensify its flavor. Stir occasionally and thoroughly so the sauce doesn't scorch on the bottom of the pan as it gets thicker. Adjust the seasoning with salt and pepper after it has been reduced, otherwise the seasoning may become too strong as the flavor of the sauce intensifies. This process may take 15 to 20 minutes, depending on the thickness of the original braising liquid. Be sure not to let it all reduce away or it will be too thick.

The Quick-Thickening Fix: When time is of the essence, a thin sauce can be corrected by adding a beurre manié: equal amounts of softened butter and flour, kneaded together into a paste. On a clean counter, combine 2 tablespoons softened unsalted butter and 2 tablespoons flour. Mix together with your fingertips, and then knead with the heel of your hand almost as you would a bread dough, until it is completely smooth. Drop a tablespoon at a time into the simmering sauce and stir in thoroughly. The sauce will thicken quickly, but allow the mixture to simmer for about 5 minutes to cook off the raw, starchy flavor of the flour. Drop in additional tablespoons of the beurre manié as necessary. The butter acts to distribute the flour evenly throughout the sauce, and adds flavor as well.

The *Glace de Viande* **Flavor-Fix:** To add flavor to a weak braising sauce, simply add a piece (1 to 2 tablespoons) of Meat Glaze (*Glace de Viande*, page 45). It will also enhance the flavor of a weak sauce, soup, stew, or gravy.

SAUTÉING AND SEARING

Sauté means "jump" in French. When we sauté, we cook a tender food quickly in a small amount of fat over direct, high heat, until it is done. The more expensive cuts of meat and seafood lend themselves especially well to this method of cooking, as do many vegetables.

To "sear" means to brown the surface of food, usually protein rather than vegetable or starch, over high heat. Then, the cooking process is finished at a lower heat on the stovetop, in the oven, or by a different, moist cooking method, such as braising. The goal is to caramelize the outer surface of a food, which, for any number of reasons (size, toughness) cannot be finished in the pan over high heat. So the simple difference between sautéing and searing is that sautéing is cooking something to completion, while searing is the first step before finishing the item through another cooking method.

Procedure for Searing and Sautéing

1. Bring meat to room temperature (this is not necessary for fish and seafood, unless they are very thick).

2. Dry the meat or seafood thoroughly with paper towels (this will prevent steaming).

3. Season the meat (but not seafood) with salt and pepper.

4. Choose a sauté pan that will hold all the food without overcrowding, or cook in batches. Place the pan over high heat until it is very hot. Test the temperature by sprinkling a few drops of water over the surface. If the water "jumps" in the pan, it is ready.

5. Add enough oil to coat the bottom of the pan by 1/8 to 1/4 inch. Heat the oil for 30 seconds. Carefully place the meat or seafood into the pan. Now you will sear the

exterior quickly, or sauté until done, depending on the thickness. The first side down is always called the "presentation side," because it receives the greatest burst of heat and will have the best color. Once the meat has caramelized, turn it over in the pan and sear or sauté the other side. Timing will depend on whether you're searing or sautéing and how thick the meat is.

6. If you are searing a thicker item, finish it in a 375° oven. Thinner items can be sautéed until done. Test for doneness using the touch method on page 22. Never cut into meat with a knife to check for doneness, as precious juices will be lost. Do not turn the meat over more than once. Sauté one side and then flip it over and finish the other side. If you continually flip the meat, it will become dehydrated and tough—the juice naturally travels away from the heat to the top of the meat, so if you keep flipping it back and forth, the juice on the top of the meat will be cooked away.

7. When the meat is done (whether it has been finished on the stovetop or in the oven), tip the pan to one side to allow the juices to flow away from the meat. If the meat sits in its own juice, the caramelized crust will become soggy. Transfer to a warm plate or platter, placing the meat on the rim to allow the juices to run off, and let stand, loosely covered with a piece of aluminum foil, for about 5 minutes. During the standing time, the juices are drawn inward and dispersed evenly. If the foil is sealed over the meat, a steam bath will be created and, again, the caramelized crust will melt.

STEWING

Stewing is very similar to braising (page 20), but in this case, the meat or poultry is cut into cubes, then seared, covered completely by a slowly simmering liquid, and cooked. (As opposed to braising, in which the meat is only covered by two-thirds with a liquid.)

Flouring the meat cubes before searing will thicken a stew (or a braise) and also provide a smoother tasting sauce—the starchiness of the flour will cook out during the long cooking process. You need to coat or dredge the meat with flour just before adding it to the pan. If the floured meat is left too long before searing, the flour will turn into a gluey mass.

The brown pan drippings left after searing add a wonderful flavor to the finished dish, but burned, black drippings will impart a bitter taste. Therefore, if you are cooking in batches using a small sauté pan, the brown drippings may burn. I recommend that you deglaze the pan after each batch, adding the deglazing liquid to the browned meat, then wipe the pan and add more oil for the next batch. Or, you could just use two pans.

Procedure for Stewing

1. Bring the meat to room temperature.

2. Dry the meat thoroughly with paper towels.

3. Season the meat with salt and pepper.

4. Follow the searing instructions through step 5 (pages 26–27). It is very important to cook the meat to a rich brown color. You don't want just a hint of color, nor do you want to burn it. The flavor created by correct browning will determine the final flavor of the dish.

5. Add your vegetables and enough liquid, preferably homemade stock, to just cover the meat. Let it simmer on the stovetop or place in a 325° oven, until the meat falls easily from the tines of a meat fork. Timing will depend on the meat, so check the recipe you're using. At the end, the liquid will have reduced, but should still cover the meat by half or two-thirds. Extra liquid, either stock, water, or wine, may be added if the liquid has reduced too much before the meat is done.

TEMPERING

Tempering is a simple method of helping two ingredients come together into one homogenous mixture. It is especially used to combine a hot item and a cold one, for instance, hot milk and beaten egg yolks in Basic Vanilla Custard Sauce (Crème Anglaise, page 222). A small amount of the hot milk is introduced into the egg yolks, which readies the yolks to accept the rest of the milk without being overly shocked. Without tempering, the eggs would curdle, thereby preventing the smooth incorporation that tempering provides.

WATER BATH (BAIN-MARIE)

A water bath, or *bain-marie* (Marie's bath) in French, is used for slow, moist cooking, and for keeping delicate foods and sauces hot. The French have a tale for just about everything. I was told, and this could be one of many versions, that the right temperature for a bain-marie is the temperature that Marie Antoinette liked in her bath. In any case, a bain-marie is basically a double boiler. One receptacle, containing the food, is placed inside another one containing hot water. A water bath is excellent for keeping sauces warm, melting chocolate, and softening icings. It is also used to protect delicate custards, such as Crème Caramel (page 241) and Crème Brûlée (page 243), from the direct heat of the oven, thereby preventing them from curdling.

To keep delicate butter sauces like White Wine Butter Sauce (page 59), Béarnaise Sauce (page 56), or Hollandaise Sauce (page 54) warm, place the pan of sauce inside another larger pot containing hot but not boiling water—you should be able to comfortably place your hand in it. Be sure that the inner pot sits high enough off the water that none will spill over the rim into the sauce. It is not advisable to hold one of these delicate sauces for more than 30 minutes if they contain egg. When using a water bath for cooking in the oven, the water must again be hot, not boiling. If it is boiling, it may curdle the food. If it is too cool, the cooking process will be slowed down.

Basic Recipes and Preparations

Bouquet Garni

Bouquet garnis are fresh herb packets used to add flavor to stocks, sauces, soups, braises, and stews. A bundle of fresh herbs, often including thyme, flat-leaf parsley, dried Turkish bay leaf, and peppercorns, is tied between 2 leek leaves or 2 stalks of celery. The bundle allows for easy removal and discarding at the end of cooking. Tying everything together also prevents peppercorns or loose herbs from being removed when skimming the surface of the liquid during the simmering process.

Toasting Nuts

Toasting brings out the flavor of nuts. To toast your almonds, hazelnuts, pecans, pine nuts, or any other kind of nut, preheat the oven to 350°. Spread the nuts on a rimmed baking sheet and bake until golden brown. Depending on the nut, the time will vary from 4 to 8 minutes. Sliced almonds and pine nuts will be in the 4-minute range, whole pecans and hazelnuts more like 8. Due to their high oil content, nuts burn easily, so you'll need to watch them carefully. Once they are golden brown, immediately turn the nuts onto a cold surface to prevent further cooking from the residual heat of the pan.

Peeling Tomatoes

I prefer to peel tomatoes with a Swiss peeler (page 18) because the fresh taste and texture of the tomato is preserved. The other option is to blanch the tomatoes, but you do lose a little bit of that freshness. To blanch, cut an X at the blossom end and drop the tomatoes into boiling water for 15 to 30 seconds. The skin will loosen quickly. Remove from the water with a fine-mesh skimmer and immediately place in a bowl of ice water. When cool enough to handle, starting at the X end, peel the skin down toward the stem end; it should come off easily.

Clarified Butter

Butter is made up of three components: water, milk solids, and fat. The process of clarifying butter removes the water and milk solids, leaving behind pure fat. Clarified butter has a wide range of uses, including sautéing meat and seafood, emulsifying sauces, and giving shine to chocolate icing. If you use whole butter in a hot sauté pan, the milk solids will burn almost immediately. The pure fat in clarified butter has a much higher smoking point, and therefore won't burn as easily. In emulsified sauces, such as Hollandaise (page 54), where butter is suspended in egg yolks, the sauce is much sturdier and holds together better when using pure fat rather than whole butter, which tends to break down the sauce. In Shiny Chocolate Icing (page 248), the clarified butter gives strength to the icing, again because the milk and excess water have been removed. The pure fat gives a shine to the icing; whole butter produces duller icing.

1. **You will lose one-fourth** to one-third of the butter in the clarifying process, so check how much your recipe calls for, and decide how much whole butter to start with. Cut a stick or 2 of unsalted butter into cubes and place into a small heavy saucepan over medium heat.

2. **Let the butter simmer briskly**, without stirring, until the mixture separates. After the water evaporates, you will see clouds of milk solids begin to fry in the clear golden butterfat. The solids should just begin to turn golden, which ensures clearer fat.

3. **Remove from the heat** and pass the butter through a fine-mesh strainer lined with damp cheesecloth into a heatproof container. (Dampening the cheesecloth allows every precious drop of fat to slide through the cloth, rather than being absorbed into it.) Cool before pouring into plastic storage containers, then refrigerate or freeze (I like to keep some in the fridge and some in the freezer). Clarified butter will harden upon storage, so keep it in shallow, wide, covered containers so it's easy to scoop. Deli containers work well. The containers should in turn be placed in ziplock plastic bags to prevent odor absorption in the refrigerator or freezer. Clarified butter can hold for 2 months in the refrigerator and 8 months in the freezer.

Crème Fraîche

Commonly found in Europe, crème fraîche is made of heavy cream mixed with a live culture that thickens the cream to the consistency of pudding. Crème fraîche is used in many recipes, including sauces, savory dishes, and desserts, to provide the richness of cream with a pleasant tang. I use buttermilk as my live culture—you must use it in its liquid form because the culture isn't alive in powdered buttermilk. You may also use plain yogurt in place of the buttermilk, but again make sure it contains live culture.

Don't be tempted to use sour cream in place of crème fraîche. In my opinion, sour cream is a poor substitute. Sour cream is often made of skim milk solidified with carrageenan and guar gum, and will always break down. Forty percent fat heavy cream can be used in place of crème fraîche.
🌿 MAKES 2-1/4 CUPS

2 cups heavy cream (at least 40 percent milk fat)

1/4 cup buttermilk (with live culture, not powdered)

1. **In a small bowl,** blend the cream and buttermilk together. Cover the bowl with plastic wrap and keep in a cupboard or warm room. The mixture will thicken and sour slightly after 12 to 36 hours, depending on the temperature of the room.

2. **When the crème fraîche** is solid with a pudding-like consistency, transfer to a jar with a lid and refrigerate until needed. It will keep in the refrigerator for 7 to 10 days.

Croûtons

Croûtons are slices of toasted bread, not cubes, that are used as a garnish for stews, to hold appetizers, or to top soups. 🌿 MAKES 6 TO 8 CROÛTONS

6 to 8 (1/4-inch-thick) slices French bread

1/3 cup melted unsalted butter or olive oil

2 cloves garlic, halved

1. **Preheat the oven to 350°.** Place the bread on a rimmed baking sheet and brush both sides of each slice liberally with the butter. Bake for 10 to 15 minutes, until pale golden in color. Remove from the oven and, while the bread is still warm, lightly rub both sides of each croûton with the cut side of the garlic. Use immediately or store at room temperature in an airtight container for up to 2 days.

Pesto

I use pesto in many different recipes—in freshly cooked pasta and soups, over poached salmon, or stuffed into chicken breasts. When adding pesto to pasta, stir the pesto with a tablespoon of hot water or heavy cream to loosen it up so it will spread into the pasta more easily. Although pesto is traditionally made with a mortar and pestle, I think that short bursts of power in a food processor work just fine. It might seem silly to dice the garlic before processing, but I've found that this double chopping helps to disperse the garlic flavor evenly. It is very important to adjust the salt when the pesto is finished. Depending on the Parmesan cheese used, the mixture may be very salty as it is.

Pesto can be held for a few days in the refrigerator, but the taste of freshly made pesto can never be equaled. Residing in a climate where the snow flies well before the plant dies, I always make a few large batches as soon as the first frost warnings appear on the news. If you make a large batch, freeze 1/4- to 1/2-cup scoops of pesto on baking sheets. Once hard, place the chunks in freezer bags for quick use. To freeze pesto, you need to make it without the Parmesan. When you want to use the pesto, just bring it back to room temperature, and then add the cheese. This recipe can easily be halved or doubled.

❧ MAKES 2 CUPS

1/3 cup pine nuts, toasted (page 30)

4 cloves garlic, finely diced

4 cups lightly packed fresh basil leaves

2 tablespoons unsalted butter, at room temperature

1 cup extra virgin olive oil

3/4 cup freshly grated Parmigiano-Reggiano cheese

1/2 cup freshly grated Romano or Pecorino cheese

Fine sea salt

1. **Combine the pine nuts** and garlic in a food processor and pulse 5 or 6 times. Add the basil and pulse 6 or 7 times, until coarsely chopped. (Alternately, use a mortar and pestle or a chef's knife to coarsely chop the ingredients.)

2. **Add the butter and oil** and pulse another 3 or 4 times, just until the ingredients are chopped, scraping down the bowl as necessary. Transfer the ingredients to a small bowl and mix in the cheeses. Taste, and add salt if necessary.

The Stages of Egg Whites

UNDERWHIPPED—TOO
LOOSE AND RUNNY

SOFT PEAK STAGE

FIRM PEAK STAGE

OVERWHIPPED—TOO
THICK AND LUMPY

Whipping Egg Whites

Before whipping, egg whites must be at room temperature, particularly for desserts or cheese soufflés, so they will blend to smoother consistencies and whip to higher volumes. I prefer to place eggs in warm water for a few minutes rather than wait an hour for them to come to room temperature.

Beating egg whites in a copper bowl will produce the strongest whites with the most volume. A natural chemical reaction occurs between whites and copper that strengthens the whites. The best whisk to use is a balloon whisk—a wide, bulbous shape. If you don't have a copper bowl, you should add cream of tarter to the whites, in a ratio of 1/8 teaspoon per white. A natural by product of grapes, cream of tarter lends some strength to the whites, but not nearly to the extent that copper does.

Overbeaten egg whites are one of the most common problems in baking and will always cause the failure of a cake. Think of the whites as bubble gum. You can only stretch the gum so far and fill it with so much air before it collapses. Once the whites are no longer holding the air, which creates the lightness or leavening, they are simply a heavy addition to the cake.

1. **Your copper bowl** must be properly cleaned no more than 10 minutes before using. Tarnish forms very quickly on copper, which impedes the whites from achieving great heights. Combine 2 tablespoons distilled white vinegar with 2 teaspoons table salt in the bowl that you're cleaning. Using a paper towel, rub the mixture around for 1 to 2 minutes, until the tarnish has been removed. Rinse in warm water and dry thoroughly with a paper towel. Though recommended by some people, you should never use lemon juice to clean your copper—it's an extravagant waste of a piece of good fruit!

2. **Pour the whites into** the clean copper bowl. Using a balloon whisk, tilt the bowl sideways a bit and begin whisking upward with circular, loop motions to break up the whites. If you are using a stainless steel, glass, or ceramic bowl, add the cream of tarter—1/8 teaspoon per white. *Do not add the cream of tarter if using a copper bowl.*

3. **Continuing with the same** whisk motion, whisk the whites to the soft peak stage. The soft peak stage is achieved when a slight curl exists at the top of the whites after you pull the whisk up and out. If you're making a dessert, at this stage add a tablespoon of sugar to tighten (strengthen) the whites. Continue to whisk for about 30 seconds, until the mixture begins to take on a shine and thickens to the firm peak stage—the tips of the whites should stand upright rather than curling. If you don't whisk enough, the whites will be too loose and liquidy looking. If you continue to whisk past the firm peak stage, you will deflate the whites and they will become lumpy and unusable.

Stocks

STOCKS ARE THE FUNDAMENTAL BASIS OF FINE CUISINE, and therefore are an important part of your *mise en place* (page x). Many stocks consist of nothing more than roasted or raw bones, fresh vegetables, and fresh herbs covered with water and simmered anywhere from 30 minutes for fish stock to 8 hours for beef stock. I never add salt because I have no idea how I will be using the stock, and salt can and should be added later. It is your job as the home chef to determine the amount of salt that should be added to a dish. Also, I use only sea salt (page 6), which I am quite certain is not used in canned products.

Some time ago, I taught the staff of an upscale local grocery store how to make stocks. Now they make beef, chicken, and fish stock and sell it frozen in 2-cup quantities. My students love the convenience, and the grocer tells me he can't keep enough in supply. I am not certain where all the bones in the world go, but I'd certainly like to see more high-quality stocks produced for home use. I've heard that there are some companies doing this, and I hope there will be more soon. If you must use store-bought stock, choose one without any added salt.

There is nothing difficult about making stock. It can be time-consuming, but requires very little attention. Stock should heighten the intrinsic flavor of the recipe. When you taste my Potato-Leek Soup (page 106) made with chicken stock, you will not be able to detect a chicken flavor. The stock enriches the flavor of the leeks and potatoes, but never overpowers the flavor of the vegetables. After all, it's Potato-Leek Soup, not chicken soup.

Canned stocks and bouillon cubes are, in my opinion, the epitome of the word "swill." They are nasty products made up of nothing but salt, monosodium glutamate, and a few other chemicals and preservatives. Cooking enhances ingredient flavors, therefore when you begin with a foul taste, you will have an enhanced foul taste after cooking (especially after reducing). It is much better to use plain old water than anything from a can or a foil-wrapped cube.

If you reduce 4 cups of my Brown Beef Stock (page 41) to 1/2 cup and then chill it, the result is a gelatinous dark brown mass called *glace de viande* (page 45), which means "glaze of meat." The texture comes from the natural gelatin in the bones. This highly flavored product is stored in the freezer for use in small amounts when a soup base, gravy, stew, or braise needs an extra burst of flavor. Canned beef stocks and bouillon cubes, however, never reduce to thick syrupy liquid. They simply produce a salty, bitter powder in the base of the pan. Canned stocks must be nothing more than heavily salted cow's bath water, for there is none of the cherished gelatinous consistency and certainly not a hint of roasted meat, fresh vegetable, or herb flavor!

To illustrate the amazing qualities of homemade stock, I have my students place 1/2 teaspoon of our *glace de viande* on their tongues and let it melt in their mouths. What do they taste? Caramelized beef, fresh vegetables and herbs, and a surprise ingredient—salt. Remember, the salt is not added, it is released naturally from the bones.

GENERAL STOCK RULES

After you add all the ingredients to the stockpot, bring the contents to a full boil over high heat. As soon as it reaches a boil, decrease the heat to low and maintain a slow simmer for the time indicated in the recipe. If a stock boils for any length of time, the fat will suspend within the liquid, resulting in a fatty, cloudy stock.

For long-cooking stocks (those other than fish or vegetable), it is important to occasionally skim off any impurities from the surface during the initial hour, after the stock has come to a boil and the temperature has been adjusted to a simmer. The impurities resemble a scum or foam that rises to the top of the stockpot.

When the stock has finished simmering, pour the liquid through a fine-mesh strainer into another large container. Cool the strained stock quickly by placing it in a sink filled with cold water, changing the water often. (You don't need to cool a vegetable stock quickly though, this is only for meat stocks for food safety.) *Never* cover a hot stock. Bacteria can grow in the drops of condensation that form on the underside of the lid and drip back into the stock, resulting in a sour taste. If you live in a cold climate, you can take the pot outside to cool (it is wise to cover the top with a piece of cheesecloth, which will allow the steam to escape yet prevent leaves or other mysterious objects from dropping in). Once the stock cools, a layer of fat will rise to the top and the stock will become gelatinous. Remove the fat and discard. For easy access, I store stock in 2- and 4-cup amounts in plastic containers or heavy-duty freezer bags. (Freezer bags work well for compact storage, but will require a bit of maneuvering when you want to remove the stock from the creased and frozen bag.)

If you have not made stock before, begin by making chicken stock. You will find that it will elevate your recipes to new heights, and soon making stock will be part of your repertoire.

Chicken Stock

This rich stock has many uses; it can be a base for soups, sauces, braises, and stews. If you don't have the meat itself for whatever reason, chicken stock can be made using only the bones, including necks and backs. Often you can get the bones for free at a butcher shop, especially if you give them some advance notice. Chicken feet, commonly found in Asian markets, provide a nice gelatinous consistency to the stock. Never use livers (residual blood will add unwanted color to the stock), although hearts and gizzards can be added. ✒ MAKES 4 TO 5 QUARTS

1 (2 1/2- to 3-pound) chicken, cut into pieces

4 leeks, white and light green parts only, 2 outer leaves reserved for the bouquet garni

6 pounds chicken bones (wing tips, necks, backs, and leftover bones)

2 onions, peeled and quartered

6 carrots, peeled and quartered crosswise

6 celery stalks, with leaves

4 cloves garlic, peeled

6 sprigs parsley

4 sprigs thyme

12 black peppercorns

1 Turkish bay leaf

1. **Rinse the chicken** well under cold running water. Tie loops of kitchen twine around each leek to prevent separation during the simmering process. Place the leeks, chicken, poultry bones, onions, carrots, celery, and garlic into a large stockpot. With kitchen twine, tie the parsley, thyme, peppercorns, and bay leaf between the reserved leek leaves to make a bouquet garni and add it to the pot. Add enough cold water to cover the contents by about 2 inches. Over high heat, bring just to a boil. Immediately lower the heat and adjust to a simmer. During the first hour, occasionally skim away the scum or gray foam from the surface with a fine-mesh skimmer. Do not allow the stock to boil.

2. **Simmer gently,** uncovered, for about 6 hours, skimming off impurities again if necessary.

3. **Pass the stock through** a large, fine-mesh strainer or chinois into another large pot or other nonreactive container and discard the solids. Cool to room temperature quickly by placing the pot into a sink filled with enough cold water to come halfway up the sides of the pot, changing the water occasionally to speed the cooling process.

4. **Refrigerate the stock** overnight. The next day, remove the fat layer that will have formed on the surface. Use immediately or freeze in 2- or 4-cup quantities for 6 to 8 months.

Brown Beef Stock

This important stock is always in good supply in our freezers. This recipe will yield 100 percent better results than anything you will find powdered or in a can on grocery store shelves. Though often scarce, veal bones soften the flavor of an assertive beef stock, but the stock will still be good if you can't find them. Turnip yields an earthy richness. If you do not have chuck steak, the stock may be made with only beef bones. It simply won't be as rich. But the most important point is, whatever you add to your stock should be fresh. Do not add old, lifeless vegetables, scraps of fatty meat, or dried herbs.

When browning the bones, it is very important to leave space in between them to allow air to circulate. Overcrowding the pan will result in steaming, not browning. If necessary, do the browning in batches or use several pans. It is wise to invest in a good roasting pan; it will serve many purposes in your kitchen. 🌿 MAKES 4 TO 6 QUARTS

2 pounds beef chuck, excess fat trimmed away and
    cut into large cubes

10 to 12 pounds beef bones, cut as small as possible

2 pounds split veal knuckle bones, if available

4 carrots, peeled and cut into thirds crosswise

4 onions, peeled and halved

Vegetable oil, for roasting

4 cups water

1 large turnip, peeled and cut into thirds

6 whole cloves

4 leeks, white and light green parts only, 2 outer
    leaves reserved for the bouquet garni

8 sprigs parsley

4 large sprigs thyme

2 Turkish bay leaves

6 celery stalks

4 cloves garlic, peeled

15 peppercorns

1. **Preheat the oven to 500°.** Thoroughly pat the beef cubes dry with paper towels. Place the beef and veal bones, beef chuck, carrots, and onions into 1 or 2 roasting pans (do not crowd the ingredients). Brush all the ingredients lightly with the oil. Decrease the oven temperature to 375°. Roast for 1 to 1 1/2 hours, turning each item once, until everything turns a rich, dark brown.

2. **Place the browned bones** and vegetables in a large stockpot. Discard the fat from the roasting pan by pouring off the excess and then dabbing the bottom of the pan with paper towels. Place the roasting pan on one burner (or over two if it is large) over high heat for 1 minute. Add the water to the pan and deglaze: bring the liquid to a boil, then loosen the drippings using a flexible metal turner. Let the drippings and water simmer for 2 minutes, then pour the entire mixture into the stockpot.

continued

3. **Stud each turnip section** with 2 cloves. Tie loops of kitchen twine around each leek to prevent separation during the simmering process. With kitchen twine, tie the parsley, thyme, and bay leaves between the reserved leek leaves to make a bouquet garni. Add the turnip, leeks, celery, garlic, peppercorns, and bouquet garni to the stockpot. Add enough cold water to cover the contents by about 2 inches. Place the pot over high heat and bring just to a boil. Immediately decrease the heat to low and adjust to a simmer. Cook, uncovered, for 6 to 8 hours (8 hours is best to ensure that as much flavor as possible is extracted from the bones). During the first hour of simmering, occasionally use a fine-mesh skimmer to remove any scum or impurities that rise to the top. Skim again occasionally during the cooking time, if necessary.

4. **Pass the stock through** a large fine-mesh strainer or chinois into another large pot or other nonreactive container and discard the solids. Cool to room temperature quickly by placing the pot into a sink filled with cold water to come halfway up the sides of the pot, changing the water occasionally to speed the cooling process.

5. **Refrigerate the stock overnight.** The next day, skim off the fat that will have risen to the surface. Use immediately or freeze the stock in 2- or 4-cup quantities for up to 1 year.

Variation

Brown Venison or Game Stock: Follow the above recipe, replacing half the beef bones with wild game bones, and half the beef chuck with the same variety of game meat. The addition of game yields a stronger flavor than pure beef stock.

Fish Stock

My students are amazed at the wonderful flavor of fish stock. The general perception seems to be that fish stock will be strong and overpowering—a nasty-tasting liquid. Just the opposite is true. Fish stock is sweet and very delicate. This versatile stock is used in sauces, seafood soups, and fish stews. This is an easy stock to make—it takes less than 1 hour total cooking time—so do not be tempted to use terrible-tasting clam juice.

Unlike other stocks, carrots are not added to fish stock because they give a sugary-sweet flavor. Wine cuts the strong character of fish and adds its own wonderful taste dimension. ✹ MAKES 1 QUART

2 pounds very fresh lean white fish with bones, or 3 pounds fish bones (do not use oily fish such as salmon, tuna, and mackerel)

3 tablespoons unsalted butter

1 onion, coarsely chopped

4 shallots, coarsely chopped

2 leeks, white part only, coarsely chopped, 2 outer leaves reserved for the bouquet garni

3 sprigs parsley

2 sprigs thyme

1 Turkish bay leaf

1 cup dry white wine or dry vermouth

10 black peppercorns

1. **Rinse the fish under cold running water.** Cut between the spine bones to create 3-inch sections and further break up the smaller sections with a chef's knife or heavy cleaver.

2. **In a large sauté pan,** melt the butter over medium heat. Add the fish, onion, shallots, and leeks. Sauté the mixture for 5 to 6 minutes, until the vegetables are softened but not browned. With kitchen twine, tie the parsley, thyme, and bay leaf between the reserved leek leaves to make a bouquet garni and add it to the pot. Add the wine and the peppercorns. Place the pot over high heat and bring to a boil. Decrease the heat to medium-high and cook for about 30 minutes, until the liquid is reduced by half.

3. **Pass the stock through a fine-mesh** strainer or chinois into another pot or a nonreactive container and discard the solids. Cool to room temperature quickly by placing the pot into a sink filled with cold water to come halfway up the sides of the pot, changing the water occasionally to speed the cooling process.

4. **Refrigerate the stock overnight.** The next day, skim off and discard the excess butter, which will have risen to the surface. Use immediately or freeze in 1- or 2-cup quantities for up to 6 months.

Vegetable Stock

A vegetable stock can be used in any soup or flour-based sauce recipe—even if it calls for beef or chicken stock. The taste will be different, but still good, so this is an essential recipe for vegetarians.

🌿 MAKES 4 QUARTS

1/4 cup extra virgin olive oil

1 onion, peeled and coarsely chopped

4 celery stalks, coarsely chopped

4 carrots, peeled and coarsely chopped

1/2 pound white button mushrooms, coarsely chopped

2 leeks, white and light green parts only, coarsely chopped, 2 outer leaves reserved for the bouquet garni

2 cloves garlic, peeled

4 sprigs parsley

4 sprigs thyme

1 Turkish bay leaf

1 parsley root, peeled and chopped (optional)

5 quarts water

8 black peppercorns

1. **In a large stockpot,** combine the oil, onion, celery, carrots, mushrooms, leeks, and garlic. Place over medium heat and sauté the vegetables, stirring occasionally, for about 5 minutes, until softened.

2. **With kitchen twine,** tie the parsley, thyme, and bay leaf between the reserved leek leaves to make a bouquet garni. Add to the pot along with the parsley root and water. Over high heat, bring the mixture just to a boil. Immediately decrease the heat to medium-low and simmer the stock for 45 minutes.

3. **Pass the stock through a fine-mesh** strainer or chinois into another pot or a large nonreactive container and discard the solids. Cool the stock to room temperature and refrigerate overnight. Remove any excess oil from the top of the chilled stock and use immediately or freeze in 2- or 4-cup quantities for up to 1 year.

Meat Glaze

(Glace de Viande)

This is a unique, highly reduced stock, which ends up very solid, gelatinous, and well-flavored. A small amount of glace de viande *may be added to a weak sauce, stew, gravy, or soup to heighten the flavor. When a classic Béarnaise sauce is served with a grilled steak, a teaspoon of* glace de viande *is often added to marry the flavor of the steak to the sauce.*

A glace, or highly reduced stock, may also be made from chicken and fish stocks. Any glace may be cut into small cubes and kept in freezer bags or a covered container in the freezer for 6 months. Glace may be reconstituted by dissolving in hot water, like (and yet completely unlike) a bouillon cube.

MAKES 1/2 CUP

1. **To make** *glace de viande,* cook 4 cups of Brown Beef Stock (page 41) over medium-high heat for about 20 minutes, until reduced to 1/2 cup. While reducing, skim off any impurities that rise to the surface (there will not be much as most of it should have been skimmed away when making the original stock). Watch the stock carefully near the end, as it can burn once it gets near the 1/2 cup amount. It will become thick and coat the back of a spoon.

2. **Pour the reduced liquid into** a 1/2-cup ramekin and allow it to cool on a wire rack at room temperature for 15 minutes. Refrigerate until the liquid has set into a gelatinous mass. Cut into small cubes and freeze. Four ounces of *glace de viande* added to 4 cups of water will become beef stock again.

Sauces

SAUCES ARE THE CORNERSTONES OF FRENCH COOKING, and they can make or break a meal. I have included three sauce categories in this chapter: flour-based, emulsified, and unstable emulsion. Each follows a different technique depending on the combination of ingredients. If you can make these sauces successfully, you are well on your way to becoming accomplished in your kitchen, for these are important and versatile additions to your recipe repertoire.

As in many French recipes, the building block theory applies to sauces. That is, you will first learn how to make a "mother" sauce, for example, Hollandaise (page 54). Then, with slight variations in the ingredients, you will make the relatives. If you add whipped cream to the Hollandaise Sauce, you've made Chantilly Sauce (page 55); simply add mustard for Mustard Sauce (page 55). And so it goes for all the sauces in this chapter.

Flour-Based Sauces

These classic sauces (also called roux-based) are still very much in my repertoire of recipes. Their uses are innumerable, and a well-made flour-based sauce can enhance and connect a wide range of recipes. These are not delicate sauces—they do not curdle like sauces containing egg yolks (Mornay Sauce is the one exception). The important point to remember about flour-based sauces is that any raw or "floury" taste will be cooked out during the long simmering at the end of preparation (so don't try to rush them!). These sauces should, when simmered gently, have a smooth flavor and a velvety consistency. Most flour-based sauces can be made in advance and re-warmed easily with no chance of curdling. If the sauce gets too thick after simmering or warming, it can easily be thinned with a little milk or cream before serving.

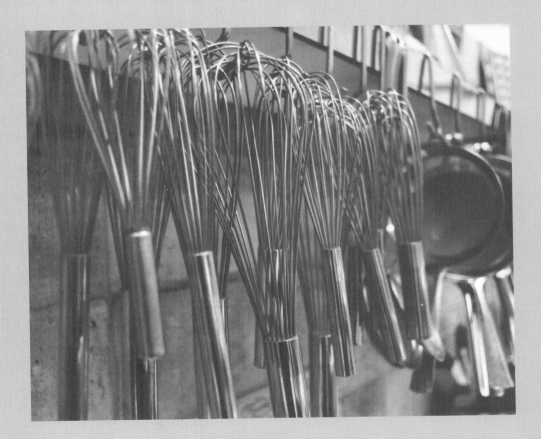

Béchamel Sauce

Béchamel is a milk-based sauce that starts with a classic roux: a thickener of equal parts flour and butter cooked over medium-low heat until it foams, without browning, for about 30 seconds. The goal is to cook the roux just long enough to remove the raw, starchy flavor of the flour, but not long enough to begin coloring the roux (which would also change the taste). The milk is infused with the flavor of onion, bay leaf, and peppercorns, giving what could be an ordinary sauce a much-enhanced flavor. (The infusion process may be eliminated if you are in a hurry, albeit with a consequential loss of flavor.) This versatile white sauce is made to a thinner consistency when it will be used as a base for a soup or for a cheese sauce. When it will be used as a sauce for vegetables or eggs, a medium roux is used. A thick roux is used to make the sauce base for a soufflé. Choose the appropriate roux for each purpose. ✴ MAKES 1 CUP

1 cup whole milk

1 (1/4-inch-thick) slice white or yellow onion

1 Turkish bay leaf

6 black or white peppercorns

1/4 teaspoon sea salt

1/8 teaspoon freshly grated white pepper

Pinch of freshly grated nutmeg

1 tablespoon cold unsalted butter (optional, for holding sauce)

THIN ROUX

1 tablespoon unsalted butter

1 tablespoon unbleached all-purpose flour

MEDIUM ROUX

1 1/2 tablespoons unsalted butter

1 tablespoon plus 1 1/2 teaspoons unbleached all-purpose flour

THICK ROUX

2 1/2 tablespoons unsalted butter

2 tablespoons plus 1 1/2 teaspoons unbleached all-purpose flour

1. **In a small saucepan,** bring the milk just to a boil over high heat, watching carefully. Add the onion, bay leaf, and peppercorns. Remove the pan from the heat and cover. Let the mixture infuse for 30 minutes.

2. **To make the roux** (choose either thin, medium, or thick as above): In another small saucepan, melt the butter over medium-low heat. Whisk in the flour and cook the mixture, stirring occasionally, for 1 to 2 minutes, until it foams. Continue to cook the roux for another 30 seconds, watching to be sure it does not brown. Remove from the heat and allow to cool.

continued

3. **Return the infused milk** mixture to high heat. As soon as it reaches a boil, pass the hot milk through a fine-mesh strainer into the pan of roux (off the heat), whisking the mixture well as you pour and continuing to whisk until the mixture is smooth. Discard the solids from the strainer.

4. **Bring the sauce just to** a boil over high heat, whisking constantly. Decrease the heat to achieve a simmer. Add the salt, pepper, and nutmeg. Simmer gently for about 5 minutes, stirring occasionally. At this point, you'll get varying degrees of thickness depending on which roux you used. Taste and adjust the seasonings with salt, pepper, and nutmeg.

5. **Serve immediately** or dot with butter to prevent the formation of a skin (place a tablespoon of butter at the end of a fork and dot gently over the surface of the sauce). Cover and refrigerate for up to 2 days before reheating gently.

Mornay Sauce

(A BÉCHAMEL SAUCE DERIVATIVE)

A well-aged cheese, such as a Gruyère, Emmenthal, Parmesan, or even a well-aged cheddar, is a fine choice for this sauce. The optional egg yolk adds richness to the sauce, while the Dijon gives a distinct flavor that would nicely complement a simple poached chicken. Mornay sauce made without the egg yolk is used to coat (nap) a vegetable gratin (the egg yolk would curdle under the heat of the broiler). This sauce is not a good candidate for reheating, since the cheese will get stringy and the yolk will curdle. However, the thin Béchamel sauce may be made ahead of time, and the yolk and cheese added to the reheated sauce just before serving time. ✒ MAKES 1-1/4 CUPS

1 large egg yolk (optional)

1 teaspoon Dijon mustard

1/4 cup finely grated cheese

1 tablespoon unsalted butter

1 cup thin Béchamel Sauce (page 49), hot

Sea salt and freshly ground white pepper

1. **Off the heat,** whisk the egg yolk, mustard, cheese, and butter into the hot béchamel sauce. Taste and adjust seasoning with salt and pepper. Serve at once.

Velouté Sauce

This sauce is similar to a Béchamel but is made with well-flavored stock instead of infused milk. I especially like to use chicken stock when serving a velouté with poached chicken. Often enriched with cream, velouté is served with poultry, fish, and veal. ✒ MAKES 1 CUP

1 1/2 tablespoons unsalted butter

1 tablespoon plus 1 1/2 teaspoons unbleached all-purpose flour

1 cup Chicken or Fish Stock (pages 40 and 43), at room temperature

Sea salt and freshly ground white pepper

1 tablespoon cold unsalted butter (optional, for holding sauce)

1. **In a small saucepan,** melt the butter over medium-low heat. Whisk in the flour and cook, whisking occasionally, for 1 to 2 minutes, until the roux is foaming. Cook for 1 minute more, until the roux is just beginning to brown. Immediately whisk in the cool stock.

2. **Bring the sauce to a boil** over medium-high heat, whisking constantly, and add a little pinch each of salt and pepper. (The sauce will concentrate during simmering, so it's best to adjust the seasoning at the end rather than risk over-seasoning.) Simmer, uncovered, whisking occasionally for 10 minutes, skimming off any scum or impurities from the surface, until the sauce reaches coating consistency (coats the back of a spoon and leaves a trail when your finger is drawn through it). Taste and adjust the seasoning, if necessary. All the starchy flour taste should be cooked out.

3. **Serve immediately** or dot with butter to prevent the formation of a skin (place a tablespoon of butter at the end of a fork and dot gently over the surface of the sauce). Refrigerate for up to 2 days before reheating gently.

Variations

DIJON MUSTARD VELOUTÉ SAUCE: Whisk 1 to 2 teaspoons Dijon mustard into the finished sauce.

HORSERADISH VELOUTÉ SAUCE: Add 1 tablespoon prepared creamed horseradish to the finished sauce.

VELOUTÉ CREAM SAUCE: Proceed with the recipe for Velouté Sauce through the end of step 2. Add 1/2 cup of heavy cream to the sauce and continue to simmer over medium-low heat for 10 minutes more, whisking occasionally, until the sauce reaches coating consistency (coats the back of a spoon and leaves a trail when your finger is drawn through it). Taste and adjust the seasoning with salt and freshly ground white pepper, if necessary.

Mushroom Sauce

(A Velouté Sauce derivative)

Mushrooms add an earthy tone to the Velouté, creating a sauce that nicely complements chicken, veal, and pork. ✍ MAKES 1-1/2 CUPS

1 cup Velouté Sauce (page 51), simmered for
    5 minutes in step 2, warm

1/3 cup chopped mixed wild mushrooms or white
    button mushrooms

Sea salt and freshly ground white pepper

1 tablespoon cold unsalted butter (optional,
    for holding sauce)

1. **After the basic velouté sauce** has simmered for 5 minutes in step 2, add the mushrooms. Continue to simmer over low heat, stirring occasionally, for an additional 10 to 20 minutes, until the sauce reaches coating consistency (coats the back of a spoon and leaves a trail when your finger is drawn through it). The sauce will take longer to thicken due to the liquid released from the mushrooms. Taste and adjust the seasoning with salt and pepper, if necessary.

2. **Serve immediately** or dot with butter to prevent the formation of a skin (place a tablespoon of butter at the end of a fork and dot gently over the surface of the sauce). Refrigerate for up to 2 days before reheating gently.

Variation

RICH CREAM MUSHROOM SAUCE: For an enriched version of the mushroom sauce above, add 1/2 cup heavy cream to the finished thickened sauce. Simmer over medium-low heat for an additional 10 minutes, again to a saucy coating consistency. Taste and adjust seasoning. Proceed as above.

Bruschetta, Roquefort with Walnuts on Toasted Croûtons, and Spicy Gruyère and Parmesan Cheese Crackers

(PAGES 97 AND 98)

French Onion Soup with a Cheese Crust

(PAGE 112)

Fresh Herb and Baby Greens Salad

(PAGE 123)

Spinach Gnocchi in Fresh Tomato Sauce

(PAGE 140)

Emulsified Sauces

To "emulsify" a sauce, you suspend one fat inside another. I tell students to imagine that they are painting each bubble of foamy egg yolks with a thin coating of butter. Thus, they create an emulsion by incorporating, or suspending, one fat (the clarified butter) into the other (the egg yolks). This process forms a luxurious, velvety sauce—a superb accompaniment to vegetables, seafood, and meats. I have included the most important basics here: Hollandaise and Béarnaise, along with several variations that will provide you with a versatile sauce repertoire. Hot emulsified sauces are fragile and cannot be refrigerated.

The most important thing to remember when making emulsified sauces is that too much heat will curdle the desired foamy, mousse-like mixture into scrambled eggs. There are three crucial steps: First, the egg yolk mixture must be cooked to the proper foamy consistency. At this time the sauce is removed from the heat. Second, the base of the pan must be cooled, otherwise the residual heat will continue to cook the eggs. Third, the clarified butter added to the eggs must be warm, not hot. So, remember that the enemy of egg yolks is heat. Too much heat will curdle the sauce.

Making the foamy base for the Hollandaise sauce is good practice. Get a dozen eggs and practice step 1 of the Hollandaise recipe (this way, you will not be wasting the other ingredients). Make several batches until you are confident that you have mastered getting the yolks to just the right consistency. Whole melted butter can be used to make the hot emulsified sauces, but clarified butter gives them more structure, helps prevent separating, and gives the sauces a wonderful sheen.

Emulsified sauces can be kept warm in a warm bain-marie (page 28) for up to 30 minutes before serving.

Hollandaise Sauce

One of the great classics of continental cuisine, Hollandaise and its derivatives serve many purposes in my kitchen. I have seen quite a few different versions of this recipe, many calling for a blender (supposedly to simplify the recipe). The blender method produces a thin sauce without the luxurious texture that we love so much. This simple sauce takes minutes to make, once mastered, and can be served with asparagus, eggs, artichokes, fish, or seafood.

Adding the lemon juice at the very end is one of the first methods I learned in France, and it makes the freshest-tasting Hollandaise I've ever come across.

✑ MAKES 1 CUP

3 tablespoons water

3 large egg yolks

Sea salt

Ice cubes, if needed

1/2 cup clarified butter (page 31), warm

2 to 3 teaspoons freshly squeezed lemon juice, or as needed

Freshly ground white pepper

1. **In a small heavy saucepan,** combine the water, egg yolks, and a pinch of salt. Whisk constantly over medium-low heat for 4 to 6 minutes, until the mixture is foamy and thick enough to form a ribbon when the whisk is pulled from the mixture. It should be pale yellow. *This is a very crucial stage. Once the mixture has thickened, it will* curdle if it continues to heat. Be ready to pull the pan off the heat and have an ice cube or two on hand. If the mixture goes beyond the thick and creamy stage and appears a little bit granular, immediately drop an ice cube into the mixture and whisk it in quickly. (This is the technique for saving the sauce.) When the mixture reaches the correct foamy consistency, cool the pan by tipping it to the side and carefully holding the base of the pan under cold running water for a few seconds.

2. **Off the heat,** begin adding the warm (not hot) clarified butter drop by drop, whisking all the time. Add the butter very slowly for about 30 seconds, then add the rest of the butter in a very thin, steady stream, whisking until it is all incorporated. (This is the process of emulsifying.) Whisk in 2 teaspoons of lemon juice and taste. You should be able to taste the lemon, but it should not overpower the delicate sauce or taste sour. Add more lemon juice bit by bit, if necessary, to achieve the perfect balance. Adjust the seasoning with salt and add a pinch of white pepper. Serve immediately or hold in a warm bain-marie (page 28) for up to 30 minutes.

Variation

MALTESE SAUCE: Replace the lemon juice with 2 to 3 tablespoons strained blood orange juice.

Chantilly Sauce

(A HOLLANDAISE SAUCE DERIVATIVE)

Serve this light and elegant sauce with fish, chicken, or vegetables. If you want to make the sauce ahead of time, proceed with the Hollandaise recipe as directed, to completion. Hold the Hollandaise in a warm bain-marie (page 28) for up to 30 minutes. Just before serving, fold in the whipped cream and adjust the seasoning. ✨ MAKES 1-1/2 CUPS

1/4 cup heavy cream

1 cup Hollandaise Sauce (page 54), warm

Sea salt and freshly ground white pepper

I. **In a chilled bowl**, whip the cream to soft peaks. Fold the whipped cream gently but thoroughly into the hollandaise sauce. Taste for seasoning, and adjust with salt and pepper if necessary. Serve immediately (this sauce can not be held in a warm water bath after the addition of the whipped cream).

Mustard Sauce

(A HOLLANDAISE SAUCE DERIVATIVE)

This classic Sauce Moutarde is especially good with eggs, chicken, and fish. ✨ MAKES 1 CUP

2 teaspoons Dijon mustard

1 cup Hollandaise Sauce (page 54), warm

Sea salt and freshly ground white pepper

I. **Whisk the mustard thoroughly** into the warm hollandaise sauce. Taste and adjust the seasoning with salt and white pepper. Serve immediately or hold in a warm bain-marie (page 28) for up to 30 minutes.

Béarnaise Sauce

A unique and popular sauce known for its assertive pepper and tarragon flavor. Served with grilled or sautéed steak, this sauce is a true classic. You may make the sauce without straining it, but you'll have to use chopped tarragon leaves and ground pepper in the reduction rather than the tarragon stems and crushed peppercorns specified below. (This shortcut may be the lazy way, but it still works beautifully with grilled steak.) ✍ MAKES 2/3 TO 3/4 CUP

3 tablespoons white wine vinegar

3 tablespoons dry white wine

2 tablespoons plus 1 1/2 teaspoons minced shallot

2 tablespoons coarsely chopped tarragon stems

10 black peppercorns, lightly crushed with the side of a chef's knife

3 large egg yolks

Sea salt and freshly ground white pepper

Ice cubes, if needed

1/2 cup plus 2 tablespoons clarified butter (page 31), warm

2 tablespoons finely chopped fresh tarragon leaves

1. **In a small saucepan**, combine the vinegar, wine, shallot, tarragon stems, and peppercorns. Place over medium-high heat and boil for 3 to 5 minutes, until reduced to about 2 teaspoons. Remove from the heat and cool the pan by tipping it to the side and carefully holding the base of the pan under cold running water for about 30 seconds.

2. **Thoroughly whisk in** the egg yolks and a good pinch each of salt and pepper. Return the pan to low heat and whisk constantly for 2 to 4 minutes, until the mixture is pale yellow in color and thickened. If the mixture begins to clump (scramble), immediately remove the pan from the heat and quickly whisk in an ice cube. (This is the technique for saving the sauce.) At this point the sauce should have the consistency of mayonnaise.

3. **Remove the pan** from the heat. Cool the bottom of the pan again. Begin whisking in the warm clarified butter, drop by drop at first, whisking all the time. After the first 30 seconds or so, you can add the rest of the butter in a very thin, steady stream, whisking until all the butter is emulsified.

4. **When all the butter** has been added, pass the sauce through a fine-mesh strainer. Add the chopped tarragon leaves. Taste for seasoning and adjust with salt and white pepper (Béarnaise should have a peppery bite). Serve immediately or hold in a warm bain-marie (page 28) for up to 30 minutes.

Sauce Choron

(A BÉARNAISE SAUCE DERIVATIVE)

This rosy sauce is good with eggs, and is especially nice with lamb. 🌿 MAKES 2/3 TO 3/4 CUP

1 tablespoon plus 1 rounded teaspoon tomato paste

1 tablespoon heavy cream (optional)

3/4 cup Béarnaise Sauce (page 56), warm

Sea salt and freshly ground white pepper, or ground cayenne pepper

1. **In a small bowl, whisk together** the tomato paste and heavy cream. Whisk this mixture into the warm béarnaise sauce in a saucepan. Taste for seasoning and adjust with salt and pepper if necessary. Warm over low heat for 1 to 2 minutes. Serve immediately or hold in a warm bain-marie (page 28) for up to 30 minutes.

Sauce Foyot

(A BÉARNAISE SAUCE DERIVATIVE)

Sauce Foyot is especially good served with grilled steak. In the classic tradition of refining and combining tastes that characterize French cuisine, glace de viande *is added to the Béarnaise in order to marry the flavor of the sauce to the meat being served. You will find the Béarnaise sauce is wonderful without the enhancement of the glace, but if you have made* glace de viande, *you must certainly try this sauce with steak.* 🌿 MAKES 2/3 TO 3/4 CUP

1 teaspoon Meat Glaze (*Glace de Viande*, page 45)

3/4 cup Béarnaise Sauce (page 56), warm

Sea salt and freshly ground white pepper

1. **Whisk the** *glace de viande* into the warm béarnaise sauce. The resulting sauce will have a light brown hue. Taste for seasoning and adjust with salt and pepper if necessary. Warm over low heat for 1 to 2 minutes. Serve immediately or hold in a warm bain-marie (page 28) for up to 30 minutes.

Unstable Emulsion Sauces

Unlike emulsified sauces that use egg yolks to bind the butter or oil into the sauce, *unstable* emulsions rely on whisking in a warm pan. These sauces are more difficult to hold, and should be made at the last minute or kept in a warm water bath/bain-marie (page 28) for a limited amount of time. Whole butter (as opposed to clarified butter) is used in these sauces because it is more flavorful. A few tablespoons of cream may be added to the reduction before adding the butter, to help bind the sauce, but as long as the correct technique is followed, these sauces are actually quite easy. (And the cream tends to mask the otherwise tangy bite of these classic sauces). The key to success with these sauces is the *on the heat/off the heat* method: simply make the reduction, carefully cool the bottom of the pan under running water so it is warm, not red-hot, then add several cubes of butter and whisk off the heat just until it melts. If the butter no longer melts from the warmth of the pan, return the pan to the heat for a few seconds. Continue adding cubes of butter and going back and forth, on and off the heat, until you have a sauce that is the consistency of heavy cream. If the pan is too hot or too much heat is used to warm the butter, the fat will separate from the whey in the whole butter. (See clarifying butter, page 31.)

One time-saving tip: the reduction can be made ahead and the whole butter whisked in just before serving.

White Wine Butter Sauce

(SAUCE BEURRE BLANC)

This sauce is very good with poached, steamed, or grilled fish. For a nice variation to serve with fish, add a few tablespoons of blanched julienned vegetables, such as leeks and carrots. A teaspoon or two of chopped tender fresh herbs, such as tarragon, chives, and flat-leaf parsley, may also be added to the finished sauce. MAKES 1 CUP

3 tablespoons white wine vinegar

3 tablespoons dry white wine

2 tablespoons plus 1 1/2 teaspoons minced shallot

8 to 10 tablespoons cold unsalted butter, cut into
   1/2-inch cubes

Sea salt and freshly ground white pepper

1. **In a small saucepan,** combine the vinegar, wine, and shallot. Place over medium heat and bring to a simmer. Simmer for 2 to 3 minutes, until reduced to about 1 1/2 teaspoons: just a loose glaze holding the shallots together. Cool the pan by tipping it to the side and carefully holding the base of the pan under cold running water for a few seconds. (At this point, you can set the reduction aside for up to a day before finishing the sauce. Be sure to keep the butter cold and rewarm the reduction very gently before continuing.)

2. **Whisk several cubes of the cold** butter into the pan (which should be warm, not hot). Whisk around in the pan until the butter no longer melts (emulsifies). Then place the pan over low heat and add several more cubes of cold butter and whisk around just until the butter begins to melt. It is important to use the *on the heat/off the heat* method here. The idea is that you need *some* heat to melt the butter, but if you leave the mixture on the heat it will simply separate the fat from the liquid and the sauce will be lost. Repeat the process of adding cold butter and moving on and off the heat as needed. The consistency of the finished sauce should be like heavy cream. You may not need to use all the butter—the sauce is finished when you have reached a coating consistency (coats the back of a spoon and leaves a trail when your finger is drawn through it). Pass the sauce through a fine-mesh strainer to remove the shallots. Add salt and pepper, taste, and adjust the seasonings as necessary. Serve immediately or hold in a lukewarm bain-marie (page 28) for up to 30 minutes.

Variation

RED WINE BUTTER SAUCE (SAUCE BEURRE ROUGE): The red color adds eye appeal and a tannic counterpoint to white fish. Simply replace the white wine with 1/3 cup dry red wine.

Citrus Butter Sauce

A refreshing citrus butter sauce will complement and enhance any mild-flavored fish, shrimp, or scallop recipe. MAKES 2/3 CUP

1/2 cup freshly squeezed blood orange juice or orange juice, strained to remove any pulp

1 tablespoon plus 1 teaspoon minced shallot

1 teaspoon freshly squeezed lemon juice, strained to remove any pulp

5 to 6 tablespoons cold unsalted butter, cut into 1/2-inch cubes

Sea salt and freshly ground white pepper

1. **In a saucepan,** combine the orange juice, shallot, and lemon juice. Place over medium-high heat and bring to a boil. Cook for 4 to 5 minutes, until reduced to about 1/4 cup, watching very carefully (fruit juice has a high sugar content and can burn easily once the liquid has reduced). When the reduction is thick and syrupy, immediately remove from the heat and cool the pan by tipping it to the side and carefully holding the bottom under cold running water for a few seconds.

2. **Whisk several cubes** of the cold butter into the pan. Whisk around in the pan until the butter no longer melts (emulsifies). Then place the pan over low heat and add several more cubes of cold butter and whisk around just until the butter begins to melt. Use the *on the heat/off the heat* method here. The idea is that you need *some* heat to melt the butter, but if you leave the mixture on the heat it will simply separate the fat from the liquid and the sauce will be lost. Repeat the process of adding cold butter and moving on and off the heat as needed. You may not need to use all the butter—the consistency of the finished sauce should be like heavy cream. Add salt and pepper, taste, and adjust the seasonings as necessary. Serve immediately or hold in a very warm bain-marie (page 28) for up to 30 minutes.

Tomato Butter Sauce

This rich butter sauce contains cream in the reduction, which helps to stabilize the sauce. The cream also decreases the acidity of the tomato paste, producing a delectable sauce that matches well with delicate fish and seafood like sole and scallops. You can even add a chiffonade of basil or some tarragon for some fresh herb flavor. ✧ MAKES 1 CUP

1/3 cup dry white wine or dry vermouth

2 shallots, minced

1/4 cup heavy cream

1 tablespoon tomato paste

6 to 8 tablespoons cold unsalted butter, cut into
    1/2-inch cubes

Sea salt and freshly ground white pepper

1. **In a small saucepan,** combine the vermouth and shallots. Place over high heat and bring to a boil. Cook for about 5 minutes, until the wine is reduced to about 2 teaspoons: just a loose glaze holding the shallots together.

2. **Whisk in the cream** and tomato paste until smooth. Decrease the heat to medium; cook for 2 to 3 minutes, until the sauce reaches coating consistency (coats the back of a spoon and leaves a trail when your finger is drawn through it).

3. **Immediately remove from** the heat and cool the pan by tipping it to the side and carefully holding the bottom under cold running water for a few seconds. Still off the heat, whisk in 2 cubes of cold butter. When the butter no longer melts (emulsifies), return the pan to low heat, still whisking. Add several more cubes of cold butter and whisk around just until the butter begins to melt. Use the *on the heat/off the heat* method. The idea is that you need *some* heat to melt the butter, but if you leave the mixture on the heat it will simply separate the fat from the liquid and the sauce will be lost. Repeat the process of adding cold butter and moving on and off the heat as needed. You may not need to add all of the butter—the consistency of the finished sauce should be like heavy cream. Pass the sauce through a fine-mesh strainer, capturing the liquid and discarding the solids. Add salt and pepper, taste, and adjust the seasonings as necessary. Serve immediately or hold in a very warm bain-marie (page 28) for up to 30 minutes.

Breads

BREAD BAKING HAS ALWAYS BEEN one of the most fascinating parts of cuisine for me. I have fond memories of a great aunt who lived on a cherry farm in Door County, Wisconsin. She was out of bed every morning by 4 A.M. and felt the rest of the world should be too. In the early mornings, cool, crisp breezes swept off the shores of Lake Michigan and kept us tucked into her warm homemade quilts. But the alluring scent of her freshly baked bread, topped with butter and red cherry jam, was incentive enough to get us gathered at the table for a typical breakfast of great food and conversation . . . by 7 A.M.! I continue to use this devious yet highly effective technique on my adult children when I want to get them out and about early in the day.

When I trekked off to France for the first time, I found a world of breads quite different from the American loaves I knew. I was enthralled by the wild yeast method of leavening breads and the seemingly endless regional varieties available. I have taken extensive bread baking courses in France and have perfected the art of creating superb loaves in professional bakeries as well as in the home kitchen. Professional bakeries use a foolproof method: they take the temperatures of both the air and the flour to determine what the temperature of the water should be. (This is because of something called the "friction factor," i.e. the amount of heat the mixer generates in the dough during the kneading process. By varying the water temperature, every element can be controlled. This is particularly important when the air temperature varies dramatically.) For home baking, I have developed more practical methods that work perfectly well. My intensive weekend bread course highlights many different techniques and recipes. Students go home with skills that always work and an armful of bread and sweet rolls.

This chapter describes two very different styles of bread baking. The first I call "straight doughs," those made with a large addition of yeast. Straight doughs take less time to rise, or proof, due to the higher yeast content, but this added yeast also causes them to stale faster.

The second style of bread are the levain, or wild yeast, breads. Many of these breads are made without added fat or sugar. Levain breads have a longer shelf life, without the need for preservatives. But most important, levain gives the loaves an earthy, slightly sour flavor. Several of the steps in the levain process take over a week, while you nurture the initial wild yeast starter, called the *chef*. This process cannot be rushed and is included in this book for dedicated bread bakers. I have had students who were so enthralled by the method that, after completing the course, they took home balls of dough and spent weeks perfecting the timing. One gentleman jokingly told me that he had to give up his day job, because the bread was ready to be baked at 2 A.M. Eventually he did get the timing situation under control and was able to keep his wild yeast starter alive and well.

We use three types of yeast at the school. Two—active dry yeast and fast-acting dry yeast—are dry and granulated. The third, compressed fresh cake yeast, is moist. I use dry yeast for the straight doughs and fresh cake yeast for the levain breads. Active dry yeast has been the standard for many years, and most recipes that call for dry yeast are referring to this product. Fast-acting dry yeast cuts the rising time of the dough in half, thus baking a fresh loaf of bread becomes a much faster project. There is a great debate as to whether or not there is a sacrifice in flavor when using fast-acting yeast. After much experimentation, I have decided that any breads that contain olive oil, fresh herbs, or spices suffer no loss of flavor whatsoever when made with fast-acting yeast. But in simpler breads, such as the French Baguette (page 80) or Buttery Dinner Rolls (page 73), I prefer to use regular-rise active dry yeast. Bread requires time to develop flavor. If a dough is pushed along too quickly, it develops a gassy taste. This is why it is not a good idea to put dough into a warm oven to speed the rising. Both fast-acting and regular-rise dry yeasts require water at around 115° for activation.

Compressed cake yeast is quite moist (about 70 percent water). It is perishable and should be stored in the refrigerator at all times. The shelf life is 8 weeks from packaging. When mixing a levain dough, I use barely warm water and fresh cake yeast. As a result, it takes some time to rise, but the flavor is fantastic. All good things come to those who wait.

"Proofing" yeast is a test to see if the yeast is living. A head of foam "proves" that the yeast is alive. To proof, place the yeast into a small custard cup and add a few table-spoons of very warm water and a pinch of sugar. If it foams and bubbles after about 5 minutes, it is alive.

I have found that both of America's widely available yeasts, Red Star and Fleis-chmann's, are quite trustworthy when used before the expiration date. Of course, even dry yeast must be stored in the refrigerator. Because I trust these two companies and store my yeast in the fridge, I never proof yeast anymore. The same goes for fresh cake yeast, which, again, is dated. Fresh yeast is more difficult to locate in some regions of the U.S., but can easily be obtained by your grocer or purchased for a few cents from a local bakery. It is always kept in a refrigerated case, possibly in the cheese or dairy case. It always seems to be hidden out of sight with no signage. The grocers say that nobody buys it, so they stop carrying it. (I say that the reason they do not sell it is that nobody can ever find it.) The packaged dried yeast is usually found in the baking aisle, but occa-sionally I find it in the refrigerated case.

Both unbleached all-purpose flour and bread flour can be used in straight dough and wild yeast breads. Flours have varying amounts of protein, and bread flour contains the most, somewhere between 12 to 14 percent. Unbleached all-purpose flour contains around 11 percent protein. Plain all-purpose flour has often been chemically treated with bleach and bromates, and contains 9 to 10 percent protein. Pastry and cake flour are in the 7 to 9 percent category. During the kneading process, when water is mixed with flour, the protein in the flour turns into gluten. In my analogy for the protein content of flour, I compare the flour to bubble gum. When you chew bubble gum, you can blow large bubbles, just like the strong high-gluten doughs that develop from high-protein flour and are capable of holding large bubbles of carbon dioxide. When you chew a piece of regular stick gum, you cannot blow a bubble, just as bleached all-purpose and cake flours don't contain enough gluten to hold the yeast's expelled gas, and thus produce breads with dense, heavy textures.

I use a 5-quart stand mixer (page 17) for all my breads. The mixing and kneading can, of course, be done by hand, but using the mixer makes the task a simple matter. I have developed a technique with the mixer that produces perfect breads—not over-floured or overworked. I never use a food processor or a bread machine to knead dough, because the results are never as good as when using the mixer or kneading by hand. Bread machines have only one purpose, to make bread, but they produce mediocre ones. Mixers can be used for hundreds of tasks and make the best bread. Which seems a better investment?

Plastic covers called pouring shields accompany some models of stand mixers or can be purchased separately. Supposedly, they prevent flour from being splashed out of the bowl during the initial kneading. I dislike these shields and actually find them annoying. I've found that a large towel placed over the top of the mixer bowl works much better, and gives me the freedom to get in and out of the bowl. (The producer/director and camera crew of my public television show are continually giving me a hard time during the tapings when I cover the bowl, telling me, "Yeah, Jill, we're really enjoying watching your towel out here in TV land!" My crew would much prefer action shots of flour or liquids flying from the bowl.)

The most important techniques I teach my students are how much flour to add to the straight dough breads, and that the firm but *never* stiff consistency of the dough should be achieved in the *first* few minutes of mixing. Trying to make a stiff dough encourages bakers to add way too much flour. The goal is to produce dough that is not wet and does not stick to your hands, but feels firm and pliable. It is critical that most of the flour, other than the small amount needed to get the kneading going, be added in the beginning of the mixing, not at the end when the dough hook is being used. The absorption of water into flour must take place early in the mixing process, or the dough will have an uneven texture.

Straight dough recipes often give a variable for the amount of flour needed. If the range is 5 to 5 1/2 cups, that means you may not need all 5 1/2. When it is extremely humid, flour will absorb moisture from the air. But in the dry winter months, the flour is also very dry, so the amount needed in a recipe will vary from month to month.

The method for levain breads requires exact amounts of flour so you don't have to worry about different absorption rates. But levain breads can also be affected by humidity. If your dough is exceptionally wet due to humidity, a small amount of flour can be added during the first minute after you've switched to the dough hook.

Dough rises twice: the first time in a bowl, and the second time as a shaped loaf. During these rising times, the yeast, which is a living organism, is actively feeding on the natural sugars and the flour. Yeast consumes so much food in such a short period of time that it begins to expel carbon dioxide or gas. The gas is captured within the walls of the kneaded dough, where the flour proteins have formed strong strands of gluten. The more gluten, the sturdier the bread. Sturdiness is good for the levain breads, which are usually free formed, but not for sweet rolls, which should have a more delicate structure.

For the first rise, always use a tall, lightly oiled bowl so the dough can grow upward, not outward. A typical mixing bowl is too wide and encourages the dough to spread out—this will result in a dry dough because of the larger surface exposed to the air. Allow the dough to double or slightly beyond; don't let it rise too much. There is no blue ribbon for a dough that rises to phenomenal heights. The gluten can only stretch so far before the strands give out and the air bubbles burst.

Dough likes to be proofed in a warm setting. The best method is to fill a large bowl one-third of the way with warm water and put the bowl of dough, covered with a damp cloth, into the water to make a warm bain-marie (page 28). This creates just enough heat to encourage the dough to get moving. Some people place the dough in a 100° oven (which you'd achieve by preheating and then turning off the oven), but I feel this is too much heat. It's also not constant enough and creates a gassy-flavored bread. In my early years of bread baking, I forgot to turn the oven off more times than I care to admit, and thus baked many loaves of bread at 100° for an hour or two.

Never allow a dough to be exposed to the air. Keep it covered with a damp towel or cloth at all times. Exposure to air kills the yeast, dries the dough, and even creates a crust, which will yield an uneven texture in the finished loaf.

After the first rising, the dough is punched down and then roughly shaped into ovals or rounds. The dough is then left to rest again, which lets the stressed gluten relax, allowing you to easily shape the dough without having it spring into an uncooperative mass.

I used linen-lined baskets for the second rise of the shaped loaves when I worked in professional bakeries, but this is really not practical for the home chef. These baskets are used for 12 to 14 hours, day after day, to ferment breads like the French Sourdough. Daily use provides a good environment for the wild yeast to grow, imparting flavor to the dough. But if you use these very expensive baskets only on an occasional basis, the wild yeasts that normally flourish with daily refreshments of new dough will die as the baskets dry out. For the home chef who doesn't bake every day, the only dough that should be placed in these baskets are those containing no butter or eggs, which could get rancid or breed salmonella or other food bacteria.

To bake bread, I place the loaves on heavy-duty aluminum baking sheets that conduct heat extremely well. Baking stones are okay, but I only use one when the oven will be free from other cooking tasks for a good while. These stones must be preheated in the oven, starting from cold, and then cannot be removed from the oven until they are cool. If you want to use a stone, you must place the shaped breads on a baking peel that has been coated with cornmeal, and then slide the loaves off the peel onto the hot baking stone with a well-calculated, short, sharp jerk of the peel.

It is very beneficial to give bread a little burst of steam during the very first seconds they are in the oven. The steam gives a little extra rise and makes a thicker crust. Professional ovens can provide an enormous burst of steam, then during the last half of the baking, vents are opened to release any excess steam and allow the breads to dry and crisp. To simulate this process, I throw a few tablespoons of water onto the oven floor (not on the coils). Or, you can use a squirt bottle with a straight stream and hit the side of the oven (not near the oven light). Some recipes suggest putting ice cubes in the bottom of a pie plate—a very bad idea. This method creates a lingering moistness—not a burst of steam—and thus a heavy, wet bread. The dough needs quick shot of steam, not a steam bath.

Lastly, and very importantly, never store bread in plastic bags on the counter. The plastic makes the bread gummy and destroys the crust within hours. When your bread comes out of the oven, you must allow it to cool before slicing. If you just cannot wait and want a slice of warm bread, then you should use a serrated bread knife to saw back and forth with a very gentle pressure. If you push down on warm bread with a knife or anything else, it will bond the steam to the dough and yield a gooey, wet bread. To store bread, I slice it and freeze it in plastic freezer bags. This allows me to take out a few pieces for toast or a sandwich without struggling with a whole loaf. Straight dough breads get stale within a day if stored out of the freezer, so I have made it a practice to freeze whatever is not eaten on the first day. Slices can go from freezer to toaster. If I want to serve a whole loaf of Crusty Bread, French Baguette, or Fougasse from the freezer, I simply sprinkle or spray them with tap water and put them on a baking sheet in a 350° oven for 5 to 6 minutes, until they feel crispy to the touch. Any of the levain breads can be left out for a few days. Either place the loaf on the counter, cut side down, put it in a paper bag, cover it with a dry heavy towel, or place it in a bread box.

Bread seems to be the common denominator linking most of the endlessly diverse cuisines of the world. Every country has its own specialty breads. Here, you can share mine.

Straight Dough Breads

Here are my proven steps for making straight dough breads with a stand mixer:

1. Fit the mixer with the paddle attachment. Put about 2 cups of the flour and the other dry ingredients, with the exception of the salt, into the bowl with the yeast. Add the hand-hot liquid. You should be able to immerse a finger in the water without feeling like you have to pull away quickly. On a thermometer, the goal is around 115°.

2. Mix the water and dry ingredients together for 30 seconds at low speed, stopping the mixer and scraping down the sides once, to make a "slurry." This will activate the yeast, bringing it back to life from its inactive dried state, and begin to form gluten. If herbs or citrus zest are added at this stage, the mixing action helps extract the natural oils, yielding a more uniform taste. Mix for another 2 minutes on medium speed.

3. Next, add the salt and 1/2 to 1 cup of flour and process on medium speed just until the flour is mixed in. Then stop the machine and repeat the flour addition and mixing until the dough begins to form. Do not over mix, you should add just enough flour to yield a dough that is firm, yet pliable, but not wet or sticky. This step should be accomplished in no more than 2 or so minutes. Most of the flour should be added at this point. At this stage, the dough will not be smooth; the surface will be quite ragged in appearance.

4. Now, switch to the dough hook. Lift the dough up slightly and throw 2 to 3 tablespoons of flour underneath (this is the big secret for success). Drop the dough back into the bowl and begin kneading the dough on low to medium-low speed. After about 30 seconds, the dough will begin to form a ball. If the dough begins to stick and gum up on the sides or bottom, add a tablespoon of flour with the mixer running. Sometimes you can add it to the side of the bowl, but if the dough has gotten into a swirled, gummy mass on the bottom, you'll have to stop the machine, lift the dough, and add the flour to the base of the bowl. Once the dough easily moves around the bowl in a ball, let the mixer knead for the remaining time called for in the recipe. If there seems to be a little sticking at the base or side of the bowl, just add a large pinch of flour. Just this small amount will be enough to keep the dough rolling around with the dough hook, without sticking to the bowl.

Crusty Bread

This is the recipe we use most often at the school; an all-purpose bread that is brushed with olive oil and covered with cheese. Or, if you prefer, flavored with fresh rosemary. If you want a very plain bread, eliminate the cheese and olive oil and brush the top of the bread with an egg white (see Variations). I strongly suggest that you read my detailed instructions on making bread dough on page 70.

MAKES 2 LOAVES; OR 20 DINNER-SIZED ROLLS

5 1/2 to 6 1/2 cups unbleached all-purpose flour

1 tablespoon sugar

2 envelopes (4 1/2 teaspoons) active dry yeast

2 1/2 cups hand-hot water (115°)

1 tablespoon sea salt

Coarse yellow cornmeal, for sprinkling

1/3 cup extra virgin olive oil

1 1/2 cups shredded Gruyère or freshly grated
   Parmesan cheese

1. **In the bowl of a stand mixer** fitted with the paddle attachment, combine 2 cups of the flour with the sugar and yeast. Add the warm water to the bowl and beat on low speed for 30 seconds, scraping down the sides of the bowl once. Increase the speed to medium and beat for 2 minutes.

2. **Add the salt** and the remaining flour in 1/2- to 1-cup increments, still on medium speed, to make a firm, pliable, but not stiff dough. Stop the machine when adding flour. The dough will appear ragged but should not feel wet or exceedingly sticky. This process should not take more than 2 minutes. Switch to the dough hook. Lift up the dough slightly and scatter about 2 tablespoons of flour underneath. Knead for about 5 minutes on low speed, or turn out onto a lightly floured surface and knead by hand until smooth and very elastic. The kneading process will take 3 to 4 minutes if using a mixer and 8 to 10 minutes by hand. Shape into a smooth ball. Lightly oil the same mixing bowl (no need to wash first) with a little olive or vegetable oil. Place the dough ball in the bowl and turn it once so that the entire ball is lightly oiled, keeping the smoothest side of the dough on top. Cover with a damp towel and set in a warm bain-marie (page 28) for about 2 hours, until doubled in size. (Quick-rise yeast will take approximately 1 hour to double the size of the dough.)

3. **Punch the dough down** with your hands to force out the air and shape into a rough oval. Let the dough rest on the counter, covered with a damp cloth, for about 5 minutes before shaping.

continued

4. **Divide the dough** and shape it into 20 rolls or 2 loaves, as follows: With the heel of your hand, shape the dough into a rough rectangle about 1 inch thick. Fold like a letter into thirds, overlapping the ends. Again with the heel of your hand, press and seal the edges together. Fold over in half so that the 2 short ends are facing you, and again press and seal the edges, but avoid pressing the middle of the dough. Turn the dough so the seam is on the bottom. Using both hands with firm presssure, roll the ends of the dough to form an oval loaf.

5. **Spread a generous layer** of cornmeal onto 1 or 2 large, rimmed baking sheets. Place the shaped loaves on the baking sheet, seam side down (leaving room for them to double in size without touching, if making 2 loaves). Cover with a damp towel and let rise in a warm place for 45 to 60 minutes, until doubled in size.

6. **Preheat the oven to 400°** and place a rack in the lower third of the oven. (If using a pure convec-tion oven (page 11), set it for 375° and bake on any shelf.) Using a very sharp knife, make 5 to 7 diagonal gashes along the center of the loaves 1/2 to 1 inch deep. If making rolls, cut a 1/2-inch-deep cross in the top of each. Brush the loaves or rolls generously with olive oil and scatter the grated cheese evenly over the tops. Bake loaves for 30 to 45 minutes, rolls for 20 minutes, until deep golden brown. The bread should sound hollow if you rap your knuckle on the bottom. Cool on wire racks and use within 24 hours or freeze in plastic bags for up to 1 month.

Variations

ROSEMARY BREAD: Add 3 tablespoons of finely chopped fresh rosemary to the flour, sugar, and yeast in step 1.

SHINY EGG WHITE GLAZE: Omit the cheese and olive oil. Whisk 1 tablespoon of water with 1 egg white, and use this glaze to brush the tops and sides of the risen loaves after they have been slashed.

Buttery Dinner Rolls

This is a great old recipe that will remind you of dinner at Grandma's house. These soft, chewy rolls are a favorite at my Thanksgiving table. I always start them off first thing on holiday mornings. My children used to eat so many that I had to start hiding them so there would be enough left for dinner. As my children grew older, their appetites increased. At that point, I started baking batches ahead of time and storing them in plastic storage bags placed inside a large paper bag labeled "fish heads." They never caught on. But I always baked at least one batch early in the morning of the holiday, so the wonderful aroma filled the house and the "starving" Prescott children had something to nibble on before the feast. I strongly suggest that you read my detailed instructions on making bread dough on page 70. ✇ MAKES 18 ROLLS

4 1/2 to 5 cups unbleached all-purpose flour

2 envelopes (4 1/2 teaspoons) active dry yeast

1 cup whole milk

1/2 cup sugar

1/2 cup unsalted butter, cut into 1/2-inch cubes

3 large eggs, at room temperature

2 teaspoons sea salt

1 large egg beaten with 1 tablespoon water,
    for the glaze

Poppy or sesame seeds, for topping (optional)

1. **In the bowl of a stand mixer** fitted with the paddle attachment, combine 2 cups of the flour and the yeast. In a small saucepan, heat the milk, sugar, and butter just until warm (115°), stirring constantly to melt the butter. Add to the dry ingredients and mix for 30 seconds on low speed. Add the eggs and beat on low speed for 30 seconds, scraping down the sides of the bowl once. Increase the speed to medium and beat for 2 minutes. Add the salt and beat for an additional 30 seconds.

2. **Add the remaining flour** in 1/2- to 1-cup increments, still on medium speed, to make a firm, pliable, but not stiff dough. Stop the machine when adding flour. The dough will appear ragged but should not feel wet: it may be slightly sticky due to the sugar content. This process should not take more than 2 minutes. Switch to the dough hook. Lift the dough up slightly and scatter about 2 tablespoons of flour underneath. Knead on low speed for 2 minutes or transfer to a lightly floured surface and knead by hand for 5 minutes. Shape into a ball. Lightly butter the same mixing bowl (no need to wash first). Place the dough ball in the bowl and turn over once to lightly coat the entire surface with butter. Cover with a damp towel and let rise in a warm bain-marie (page 28) for about 2 1/2 hours, until doubled in size. (Quick-rise yeast will take approximately 1 1/2 hours to double the size of the dough.)

continued

3. **Punch the dough down** to force out the air and turn out onto a lightly floured surface. Cover with a damp towel and let rest for 10 minutes.

4. **Divide the dough** into 3 pieces and separate each piece into 6 smaller chunks, for a total of 18 pieces. Shape each piece of dough into a 6-inch rope by rolling it back and forth with the palms of your hands on the counter. Make each rope into a U shape, then fold one end over the other to form a fish shape. Bring one end under and up through the hole in the center, and tuck the other end underneath the roll. Place the shaped rolls on the prepared baking sheet and cover with a damp towel. Let rise for 30 to 45 minutes in a warm place, until doubled in size.

5. **Preheat the oven to 350°**, lightly butter a baking sheet, and place a rack in the lower third of the oven. (If using a pure convection oven (page 11), set it for 325° and bake on any shelf.) Brush the rolls with the beaten egg and sprinkle with the poppy seeds. Bake for 10 to 12 minutes, until golden. Cool on a wire rack and use within 12 hours or freeze in plastic bags for up to 1 month.

Cinnamon Buns

I make these every Christmas morning and on snowy Wisconsin days. This basic sweet dough is used to make a variety of breakfast rolls. After the dough is rolled into a rectangle and spread with butter in step 3, you can then choose from several alternatives for filling: cinnamon and sugar, chocolate and orange, or chocolate and nut. I always make a double batch and freeze one after it has cooled, but before frosting. Be sure to wrap the extra batch tightly in foil; it can be frozen for up to a month. To serve, place in a pre-heated 350° oven for 10 to 15 minutes, and then frost as directed.

This recipe showcases the importance of using freshly ground, high-quality spices. And I strongly suggest that you read my detailed instructions on making bread dough on page 70. ✢ MAKES 12 BUNS

DOUGH

4 1/2 to 5 1/2 cups unbleached all-purpose flour

1 envelope (2 1/4 teaspoons) active dry yeast

1 cup whole milk

1/4 cup granulated sugar

1/4 cup unsalted butter, cut into 1/2-inch cubes

2 large eggs, at room temperature

1 teaspoon sea salt

FILLING

1/2 cup unsalted butter, at room temperature

1/2 cup granulated sugar

1 tablespoon best-quality ground cinnamon

ICING

1 1/2 cups confectioners' sugar

4 to 6 tablespoons heavy cream

1 teaspoon vanilla extract

1. **In the bowl of a stand mixer** fitted with the paddle attachment, combine 2 cups of the flour with the yeast. In a saucepan, heat the milk, sugar, and butter just until warm (115°), stirring to dissolve the sugar and melt the butter. Add the milk mixture to the flour and mix on low speed for 1 minute, scraping down the sides of the bowl once. Add the eggs with the machine off and beat on medium speed for 2 minutes.

2. **Add the salt** and the remaining flour in 1/2- to 1-cup increments, still on medium speed, to make a firm, pliable, but not stiff dough. Stop the machine when adding flour. The dough will appear ragged but should not feel wet or sticky. This process should not take more than 2 minutes. Switch to the dough hook. Lift up the dough slightly and scatter about 2 tablespoons of flour underneath. Knead for 2 to 3 minutes on low speed, or turn out onto a lightly floured

continued

surface and knead by hand for 7 to 8 minutes, until smooth, pliable, and very elastic. Shape into a ball. Lightly butter the same mixing bowl (no need to wash it). Return the dough to the bowl and turn over once to lightly coat all sides with the butter. Cover the bowl with a damp towel and let the dough rest in a warm bain-marie (page 28) for about 2 1/2 hours, until doubled in size. (Quick-rise yeast will take approximately 1 1/2 hours to double the size of the dough.)

3. **Punch the dough down** to force out the air and shape into a rough rectangle. Place on a flat surface, cover with the damp towel, and let rest for 10 minutes.

4. **Roll the dough out into** a 14 by 18-inch rectangle with one long edge parallel to the edge of the counter. With an offset spatula or the back of a large spoon, spread the softened butter evenly over the rectangle. In a small bowl, mix together the sugar and cinnamon and sprinkle the mixture evenly over the butter. Starting with one long side, roll the rectangle into a log. With a serrated knife, cut the log crosswise into thirds, using light pressure to avoid squeezing the filling out. Cut each third into four slices, to yield 12 pieces.

5. **Arrange the buns,** cut side down, into a deep 9 by 12-inch baking pan (see bakeware, page 13). Cover the pan with a damp towel and let the buns rise in a warm place for 30 to 60 minutes, until doubled in size.

6. **Preheat the oven to 350°** and place a rack in the lower third of the oven. (If using a pure convection oven (page 11), set it for 325° and bake on any shelf.) Bake the buns for 20 to 30 minutes, until golden brown. The buns should not be doughy in the center.

7. **While the rolls are baking,** make the icing: combine the confectioners' sugar, 2 tablespoons of the cream, and the vanilla in a bowl. Whisk the mixture briskly to remove all the lumps. Add more cream, 1 tablespoon at a time, until the mixture has a thick, fluid coating consistency. You may need slightly more than 4 tablespoons, depending on the sugar.

8. **Remove the buns** from the baking pan and cool on a wire rack, bottom side up. Immediately drizzle the icing over the hot buns so that it seeps and melts into the crevices. Serve warm.

Variations

CHOCOLATE AND ORANGE: Omit the cinnamon-sugar filling. Mix together the finely grated zest of 2 oranges, 1/4 cup sugar and 1/2 cup chopped bittersweet chocolate, and use this for the filing. For an orange icing, substitute freshly squeezed orange juice for all but 1 tablespoon of the cream.

CHOCOLATE AND NUT: Omit the cinnamon from the filling, cut the amount of sugar to 2 tablespoons, and add 1/3 cup chopped chocolate and 1/3 cup chopped walnuts or pecans. Lift the edges of the dough slightly when rolling so that the ingredients are not squeezed out.)

Fougasse

Fougasse, a specialty flatbread from the south of France, is one of my all time favorite breads. In this straight dough version (don't be confused, I also include a levain version on page 93), I use olive oil and fresh rosemary. Two nice variations, detailed below, include chopped cured olives or Parmesan, or you could combine the two. I use kosher salt instead of sea salt for topping here, because I think its milder flavor doesn't compete with the other seasonings. I strongly suggest that you read my detailed instructions on making bread dough on page 70.

☙ MAKES 2 LOAVES

6 to 6 1/2 cups unbleached all-purpose flour

3 tablespoons sugar

3 tablespoons finely chopped fresh rosemary

1 envelope (2 1/4 teaspoons) active dry yeast

1 1/2 cups hand-hot water (115°)

1/3 cup extra virgin olive oil, plus extra for brushing

2 large eggs

1 teaspoon sea salt

Coarse yellow cornmeal, for sprinkling

1 to 2 teaspoons kosher salt (page 7)

1. **In the bowl of a stand mixer** fitted with the paddle attachment, combine 2 cups of the flour with the sugar, rosemary, and yeast. Add the warm water and olive oil to the bowl and mix on low speed for 1 minute, scraping down the sides of the bowl once. Add the eggs with the machine off, increase the speed to medium-low, and mix for 2 minutes. Add the sea salt, increase the speed to medium, and mix for 15 seconds more.

2. **Add the remaining flour** in 1/2- to 1-cup increments, still on medium speed, to make a firm, pliable, but not stiff dough. Stop the machine when adding flour. The dough will appear ragged but should not feel wet or sticky. This process should not take more than 2 minutes. Switch to the dough hook. Lift up the dough slightly and scatter about 2 tablespoons of flour underneath. Knead for about 5 minutes on low speed, or turn out onto a lightly floured surface and knead by hand until smooth and very elastic. The kneading process will take 2 to 3 minutes if using a mixer and about 6 minutes by hand. Shape into a smooth ball. Lightly oil the same mixing bowl (no need to wash it) with a little olive or vegetable oil. Place the dough ball in the bowl and turn it once so that the entire ball is lightly oiled, keeping the smoothest side of the dough on top. Cover with a damp towel

continued

and set in a warm bain-marie (page 28) for 1 to 2 hours, until doubled in size. (Quick-rise yeast will take approximately 1 hour to double the size of the dough.)

3. **Punch the dough down** to force out the air and let it rest for 5 minutes, covered with a damp towel.

4. **Dust 2 large baking sheets** liberally with the cornmeal. Divide the dough in half and, on a flat surface, roll each half out to about 1 inch thick, to form a 12 by 14-inch oval. Place each oval onto one of the prepared baking sheets. With the tip of a sharp knife, cut a long gash all the way through, down the center of each loaf, leaving about 2 inches uncut on each end. Spread the 2 halves apart by about 4 inches. Cut 3 to 5 smaller gashes in each half to resemble the veins of a leaf, spreading the cuts wide apart so they won't close up when the loaves are baked.

5. **Cover both loaves** with slightly damp towels, and leave to rise again in a warm place for about 45 minutes, until doubled in size.

6. **Preheat the oven to 425°** and place one rack in the lower third of the oven and another in the upper third. (If using a pure convection oven (page 11), set it for 400° and bake on any shelf.) Brush the loaves very generously with olive oil, so that the oil actually runs down into all the gashes and pools slightly on the baking sheets. Sprinkle with Kosher salt, holding your hand about 18 inches above the loaves to ensure an even distribution of the salt. Bake for 20 to 25 minutes, until deep golden brown. The bread should sound hollow if you rap a knuckle on the bottom. Cool on wire racks and use within 1 day or freeze in plastic bags for up to 1 month.

Variations

CURED BLACK OLIVES: Toss 1/2 cup of chopped cured black olives with a tablespoon of flour to stop them from clumping together. Add the olives to the dough during the last few minutes of kneading. Don't worry if it looks messy. Just transfer the contents to the counter, flour your hands well, and knead the olives into the dough.

PARMESAN CHEESE: Sprinkle 1/2 cup freshly grated Parmesan over the shaped and risen loaves after they have been brushed with olive oil.

Cheese Flatbread

Traveling through the Normandy countryside, I came upon this wonderful cheese flatbread. It is made with a very thin yeast batter, which is poured into a cake pan with crème fraîche and a soft-rinded cheese like Brie. It is marvelous with a salad or to accompany a rustic menu. I strongly suggest that you read my detailed instructions on making bread dough on page 70.

✿ MAKES 1 LOAF

1 cup unbleached all-purpose flour

1 envelope (2 1/4 teaspoons) active dry yeast

1 large egg, lightly beaten

1 teaspoon sugar

1 cup whole milk

1/4 cup melted unsalted butter, cooled

1/2 teaspoon sea salt

4 ounces Brie cheese, rind removed and cut into 1/2-inch cubes

2 tablespoons crème fraîche (page 32) or 1 tablespoon heavy cream

1 tablespoon unsalted butter, diced

1 to 2 teaspoons kosher salt (page 7)

1/8 teaspoon freshly ground black pepper

1. **In the bowl of a stand mixer** fitted with the paddle attachment, combine the flour, yeast, egg, and sugar. In a small saucepan, heat the milk just until warm (115°). Add the milk to the mixer bowl and mix for 30 seconds on low speed. Add the melted butter and sea salt; mix for 2 minutes more. Cover the bowl with a slightly damp towel and let rise in a warm bain-marie (page 28) for about 1 1/2 hours, until the batter doubles in size. (Quick-rise yeast will take approximately 45 minutes to double the size of the dough.)

2. **Butter and flour** an 8-inch round cake pan. Stir the batter to deflate it slightly and pour into the prepared cake pan. Drop the cheese cubes evenly over the batter and dot with the crème fraîche and diced butter.

3. **Cover the pan with** a slightly damp towel, and leave to rise again in a warm place for about 20 minutes, until puffy.

4. **Preheat the oven to 375°** and place a rack in the lower third of the oven. (If using a pure convection oven (page 11), set it for 350° and bake on any shelf.) Sprinkle with the kosher salt and pepper and bake for 30 minutes, until golden brown. Serve immediately.

Variation

ROSEMARY-CHEESE FLATBREAD: Replace the melted butter with olive oil and add 1 teaspoon finely chopped fresh rosemary to the batter.

French Baguette

This bread is raised with a fermented starter called "poolish sponge," a more liquid relative of the wild yeast starter, levain. This starter gives the bread a springier texture than the levain. The initial 8-hour resting time of the sponge gives a slightly sour taste to the bread. Quick-rise yeast can be used for this bread (and would cut the rising time in half), but the longer fermentation of regular-rise yeast will provide a more intense sourdough flavor. I strongly suggest that you read my detailed instructions on making bread dough on page 70. *MAKES 4 LOAVES*

SPONGE

1 cup unbleached all-purpose flour

1 envelope (2 1/4 teaspoons) active dry yeast

1 cup hand-hot water (115°)

1 1/4 cups hand-hot water (115°)

2 teaspoons sea salt

4 1/2 to 5 cups unbleached all-purpose flour

Olive oil, for brushing

Coarse yellow cornmeal, for sprinkling

1. **To prepare the sponge starter,** in a tall, narrow (not wide) bowl, mix together the flour, yeast, and water with a whisk. Transfer to a 1-quart glass jar or similar container and cover with plastic wrap. Store in a warm place for 8 hours.

2. **Transfer the sponge to the bowl** of a stand mixer fitted with the paddle attachment. Add the yeast and 1/4 cup of the warm water and beat on low speed for 10 seconds. Let the mixture stand for 20 minutes, until bubbly. Add the remaining 1 cup warm water and the salt and mix for 30 seconds on low speed. Add the remaining flour in 1-cup increments, still on medium speed, to make a firm, pliable, but not stiff dough. Stop the machine when adding flour. The dough will appear ragged but should not feel wet or sticky. This process should not take more than 2 minutes. Switch to the dough hook. Lift up the dough slightly and scatter about 2 tablespoons of flour underneath. Knead for 2 to 3 minutes on low speed, or turn out onto a lightly floured surface and knead by hand for about 6 minutes until smooth and very elastic.

3. **Shape into a smooth ball.** Lightly oil the same mixing bowl (no need to wash it) with a little olive or vegetable oil. Place the dough ball back into the bowl and turn it once so that the entire ball is lightly oiled, keeping the smoothest side of the dough on top. Cover with a damp towel and set in a warm bain-marie (page 28) for 1 1/2 to 2 hours, until doubled in size.

4. **Punch the dough down** to force out the air and let it rest for 5 minutes, covered with a damp towel.

5. **Divide the dough into 4 pieces.** With the heel of your hand, shape the dough into a rough rectangle about 1 inch thick. Fold like a letter into thirds, overlapping the ends. Again with the heel of your hand, press and seal the edges together. Fold over in half so that the 2 short ends are facing you, and again press and seal the edges, but avoid pressing the middle of the dough. Turn the dough so the seam is on the bottom. Starting in the center with slightly cupped hands, gently roll the dough back and forth, working your hands out toward the ends of the dough, using firm pressure to stretch the dough into a loaf 14 to 16 inches long.

6. **Sprinkle 2 rimmed baking sheets** generously with cornmeal and place 2 shaped loaves on each, leaving room for them to double in size without touching each other. Cover the loaves with a slightly damp towel and let rise for 30 minutes to 1 hour, until doubled in size.

7. **Preheat the oven to 425°** and place one rack in the lower third of the oven and another in the upper third. (If using a pure convection oven (page 11), set it for 400° and bake on any shelf.) With a very sharp knife, slash the tops of the loaves diagonally about 7 times, 1/2 inch deep. Brush the tops and sides of the loaves generously with olive oil and sprinkle them lightly with cornmeal. Bake for 20 to 30 minutes, until browned. The bread should sound hollow if you rap your knuckle on the bottom. Cool on wire racks and use within 8 hours or freeze in plastic bags for up to 1 month.

Wild Yeast Breads

CHEF AND LEVAIN

There are two ways of obtaining a *chef*. One is to create your own from scratch by fermenting organic raisins and spring water together for 5 to 7 days. Then, you mix the strained juice with flour and allow that to ferment, then add more flour and water to ferment again. The good news is that this very long process will only need to be done once. All future *chefs* will be based on this first one.

Once the above process is complete, you must make one full recipe of the French Sourdough Bread dough (page 85) and divide it into 1/2-cup balls. (The balls can be kept in the refrigerator for 4 to 5 days or frozen for up to 2 months.) Each 1/2-cup portion can be made into a *chef* by covering and fermenting it on the counter for 1 day (or for up to 5 days in the refrigerator). A levain is then made from this fermented piece of dough by adding more flour, water, and yeast. The levain is the leavening that will make another dough for French Sourdough Bread (or any of the other wild yeast breads in this chapter) in a sort of self-feeding cycle. In a professional bakery, a portion of sourdough is always held back from the day's baking to be fermented and used to make the next day's levain.

Think of the levain as the equivalent of yeast. It is the main leavening for the breads, along with a small amount of compressed fresh cake yeast. Levain is used in many classic French hearth breads. It yields an excellent flavor and an extended shelf life. The levain must ferment and rise for 5 to 7 hours, until it has doubled, in a covered, tall container that will allow it to spread upward, not outward. The rising time will depend on the temperature of the air and the virility of the wild yeasts. It is much less predictable than bread made with dried yeast. Once it has risen, the levain then has a 2-hour window in which it must be used. After that, it will begin to flatten and sour and will be unusable. I recommend that you follow my theory of *mise en place* (page x) to prepare all the breads you want to bake. Get them prepped and ready to bake so that you can mix one dough after another if you are going to make several batches.

MAKING THE *CHEF*

Day 1

Combine 1 cup organic raisins and 1 cup spring water (or enough to cover the raisins by at least 1/2 inch) in a tightly sealable jar with at least 3 inches of headspace. Press a piece of parchment paper down onto the raisins to keep them submerged in the water. Cover tightly with the lid, then cover with a towel to block out all light, and store at room temperature for 5 to 7 days. When ready, the water will ferment and become very frothy and bubbly.

Day 5 or 7

1. **Pass the mixture through a strainer** into a bowl, pushing hard on the raisins to extract at least 3 tablespoons of liquid. Reserve 3 tablespoons of the liquid. Discard the raisins and any remaining liquid.

2. **Add 1/3 cup bread flour and** 1/8 teaspoon fresh cake yeast to the fermented water and mix together with a wooden spoon or by hand until the mixture forms a ball. Transfer the dough to a tightly sealable jar that will allow the dough to double and still leave a few extra inches of air space. Cover tightly with the lid and set aside at room temperature for 3 to 5 hours, until doubled in size.

3. **Transfer the dough to a bowl** and add 2 tablespoons water, 1 pinch fresh cake yeast, and 1/3 cup bread flour. Mix by hand until the dough comes together. Turn out onto a lightly floured surface and knead by hand for 2 to 3 minutes, until smooth and elastic.

4. **If you plan to bake the following day:** place the *chef* in a container, cover, and let rise at room temperature for 1 day. If baking within 4 days: place the *chef* in a covered container in the refrigerator. When ready to bake, bring the *chef* to room temperature, cover, and let rise for 1 day before proceeding to the next step, turning the *chef* into a levain.

THE NEXT STEP: MAKING THE LEVAIN

The following recipe will yield slightly less than 1 pound of levain: enough to make approximately 2 batches (or 4 loaves) of bread.

1. **In the bowl of a stand mixer** fitted with the paddle attachment, combine 3/4 cup lukewarm spring water, 1/2 cup *chef,* a large pinch of fresh cake yeast, and 2 cups plus 1 rounded tablespoon bread flour. Mix on low speed until the ingredients come together. Switch to the dough hook and knead for 1 1/2 to 2 minutes on low speed, or turn out onto a lightly floured surface and knead by hand for 3 minutes, until smooth and elastic.

2. **Lightly oil the same mixing bowl** (no need to wash it) with a little olive or vegetable oil. Place the dough ball in the bowl and turn it once so that the entire ball is lightly oiled. Cover with a damp cloth and let stand for 5 to 7 hours, until doubled in size. This is your levain.

AT A GLANCE PROCEDURE FOR WILD YEAST BREADS

1. **Ferment raisins** and water for 5 to 7 days.

2. **Add flour** and a little yeast and ferment for 3 to 5 hours.

3. **Add water,** flour, and yeast and ferment for 24 hours to create the *chef.*

4. **Mix the *chef* with water,** flour, and a little yeast and proof for 5 to 7 hours, until doubled, to make a levain. Once risen, the levain has only a 2-hour window in which it can be used.

Once a levain has been used to make a recipe of French Sourdough Bread (page 85), future *chefs* can be made from the dough in the following way:

1. **Make one recipe** of French Sourdough Bread dough and divide into 1/2-cup portions.

2. **Wrap and refrigerate** the portions if you plan to use them within a few days, or freeze for future use.

3. **Note that the balls must ferment** for at least 24 hours at room temperature before you proceed to making the levain, as above.

4. **Use the thawed** and risen *chef* to make the levain that is needed for any of the breads in this section.

French Sourdough Bread

Called pain de campagne *in France, this wonderful country bread is chewy with a thick crust. It is excellent served with imported Italian hams and cold cuts, assertive cheeses, and pâtés. This is a sourdough bread containing no fat or sugar, with a wonderful nutty flavor. When baked in a professional bakery, this bread contains no added yeast. Due to the lack of controlled fermentation in a home setting, however, I have added fresh compressed cake yeast to give it a boost.*

French Sourdough Bread is made with a levain and a long fermentation. The second proofing period of 8 to 18 hours, which takes place after the shaping of the loaves, determines the degree of sourness in the final product. The longer the fermentation, the more sour the taste. Due to the long and complicated process, I recommend that this dough be made and sectioned into balls to make future chefs. *All of the other levain breads that follow can be made from this base.* ✒ MAKES 1 LOAF

1 cup lukewarm water

2 tablespoons wheat germ

1 teaspoon fresh cake yeast

1 cup levain (pages 83–84)

3 cups bread flour

2 teaspoons sea salt

Coarse yellow cornmeal, for sprinkling

1. **In the bowl of a stand mixer** fitted with the paddle attachment, combine the lukewarm water, wheat germ, and yeast and mix on low speed until the yeast is almost dissolved. Turn the mixer off and add the levain and the flour all at once. Mix on low speed for 1 minute until the dough comes together.

2. **Switch to the dough hook** and knead for 5 minutes on low speed. Or, turn the dough out onto a lightly floured surface and knead by hand for 7 to 8 minutes, until smooth and elastic. Add the salt and knead for another 3 minutes.

3. **Lightly oil the same mixing bowl** (no need to wash it) with a little olive or vegetable oil. Place the dough ball in the bowl and turn it once so that the entire ball is lightly oiled. Cover with plastic wrap and allow it to ferment for at least 12 hours in the refrigerator.

4. **Punch the dough down** to force out the air. This is a very heavy dough. (At this stage, the dough can be sectioned into balls and frozen as a *chef* to make future levains or you can continue with the recipe to baking. If you are making loaves, I recommend removing at least two 1/2-cup balls from the dough first, to freeze as *chefs*, otherwise you will always have to start the process of fermenting raisins and water from scratch. Place the reserved balls into 1-cup

continued

containers that can be tightly sealed. When using frozen *chef*, it is important to give it at least 24 hours to thaw, then double in size before making the levain. Plan ahead.)

5. **Liberally dust a rimmed** baking sheet with cornmeal. After punching down the dough, shape into an oval or round loaf according to the instructions in step 4 on page 72. Place on the prepared baking sheet. Cover the loaf loosely with plastic wrap and leave to rise in a cool place, ideally at 55 to 60°, for 8 to 18 hours, until doubled in size. The longer you let it rise, the more sour the bread will be. (Or, the dough can be covered tightly and refrigerated for 4 to 5 days. Bring it back to room temperature, form the loaves, and let rise as above before baking.)

6. **Preheat the oven to 425°** and place a rack in the lower third of the oven. (If using a pure convection oven (page 11), set it for 400° and bake on any shelf.) With a sharp knife, cut a 1/2-inch-deep slash down the length of the loaf. Bake for 30 minutes, until browned. The bread should sound hollow if you rap your knuckle on the bottom. Cool on a wire rack and use within 3 to 4 days or freeze in plastic bags for up to 1 month.

Raisin Walnut Bread

A chewy bread packed full of raisins and nuts; walnuts or pecans are both great choices. This bread contains no added fat and a very small amount of sugar, especially compared to some of my straight dough breads and rolls. This bread is excellent served alone or as toast and is spectacular with goat cheese and red wine!

It is imperative to use organic raisins and fresh nuts in this recipe. I am amazed at the difference between the nasty little shriveled common raisins and the plump, juicy, and sweet organic raisins available at health food stores and upscale markets. Nuts should be fresh and whole. Fresh nuts have a sheen, look plump, and taste rich and sweet. Avoid nuts that look dry, shriveled, and dark: these will have a bitter taste. It takes only a few seconds to chop nuts with a chef's knife. ✒ MAKES 2 LARGE LOAVES

1 1/2 cups lukewarm water

2 1/2 tablespoons sugar

2 tablespoons crumbled fresh cake yeast

1 1/2 cups levain (pages 83–84)

4 1/4 cups plus 1 tablespoon bread flour

2 teaspoons sea salt

1 1/4 cups chopped walnuts or pecans

1 3/4 cups organic raisins

Coarse yellow cornmeal, for sprinkling

1. **In the bowl of a stand mixer** fitted with the paddle attachment, combine the lukewarm water, sugar, and yeast and mix until the yeast is almost dissolved. Turn the machine off and add the levain and the flour all at once. Mix on low speed for 1 minute until the ingredients come together.

2. **Switch to the dough hook** and knead for 3 minutes on low speed until the dough is smooth. Or, turn the dough out onto a lightly floured surface and knead by hand for 5 minutes, until smooth and elastic. Add the salt and knead for 1 minute.

3. **Add the nuts and raisins** and knead on very low speed just to work in the ingredients. When the dough can no longer absorb any more of the nuts or raisins, turn it out onto a flat surface and knead the obstinate nuts and raisins into the dough. Just push the ingredients in with the heel of your hand. Lightly coat the same mixing bowl (no need to wash it) with a little butter or vegetable oil. Place the dough in the bowl and turn over to coat all sides lightly. Cover the bowl with a damp towel and leave to rise in a warm bain-marie (page 28) for 1 to 1 1/2 hours, until doubled in size.

continued

4. **Punch the dough down** to force out the air and let it rest on the counter for 5 minutes, covered with the towel. Generously dust a rimmed baking sheet with cornmeal. Divide the dough into 2 pieces and shape each into an oval loaf according to the instructions in step 4 on page 72. Place on the prepared baking sheet, leaving room for the loaves to double without touching each other. Again, cover with a damp cloth and let rise for 30 minutes to 1 hour more, until doubled in size.

5. **Preheat the oven to 400°** and place a rack in the lower third of the oven. (If using a pure convection oven (page 11), set it for 375° and bake on any shelf.) With a sharp knife using light pressure, make 3 to 5 diagonal slashes, 1/2 inch deep, across the width of the bread. Bake for 30 to 40 minutes, until the crust is a deep rich brown. The bread should sound hollow if you rap your knuckle on the bottom. Cool on wire racks and use within 4 days hours or freeze in plastic bags for up to 1 month.

Caramelized Onion Bread

This bread is outstanding for toasted sandwiches stuffed with Gruyère or fontina cheese and a few slices of fresh tomato. The slippery onions are difficult to incorporate into the dough, so you'll need to do the folding and flattening technique detailed in step 4 several times. ✒ MAKES 2 LOAVES

3 tablespoons unsalted butter

3 onions, sliced

2 tablespoons unbleached all-purpose flour,
plus extra for sprinkling

1 2/3 cups lukewarm water

2 tablespoons crumbled fresh cake yeast

1 1/2 cups levain (pages 83–84)

3 1/2 cups bread flour

1 3/4 cups plus 1 rounded tablespoon medium-ground rye flour

2 1/4 teaspoons sea salt

Coarse yellow cornmeal, for sprinkling

1. **In a large heavy sauté pan,** melt the butter over medium heat. Add the onions and cook for about 10 minutes, stirring occasionally, until softened. Increase the heat to medium-high and continue cooking for 15 to 20 minutes, until the onions turn a cinnamon color, scraping the bottom of the pan and turning constantly. It's important to use a flat metal spatula (page 17) to scrape up the browned bits, otherwise they will stick. If there is a spot on the pan that

simply can't be scraped up and it is getting too dark, drizzle a few tablespoons of water over the spot and the caramelized onion sugars will dissolve. Add just enough liquid to dissolve the darkened spot—too much liquid will slow down the entire caramelization process. Remove the onions from the heat and let cool completely. When cool, chop the onions coarsely, just to break them up a bit. Sprinkle the onions with the all-purpose flour and toss to coat each strand of onion evenly (this will help the onions mix into the dough instead of clumping together in a buttery mass).

2. **In the bowl of a stand mixer** fitted with the paddle attachment, combine the lukewarm water and yeast and mix until the yeast is almost dissolved. Turn the machine off and add the levain, bread flour, and rye flour all at once. Mix on low speed for 1 minute until the ingredients come together into a supple dough.

3. **Switch to the dough hook** and knead for 3 minutes on low speed. Or, turn the dough out onto a lightly floured surface and knead by hand for 6 minutes, until smooth and elastic. Add the salt and knead for 1 minute more.

4. **Transfer the dough** to a lightly floured surface and press down to flatten it into a rectangle approximately 10 by 14 inches. Spread the floured

continued

onions evenly onto the surface and, with floured hands, use the heels of your palms to press the onions into the dough. Fold the dough over into thirds and press down again to flatten and spread the dough, gradually working the onions deeper into the dough. Repeat the process until the onions are evenly distributed, then continue kneading by hand for about 1 minute. Lightly oil the same mixing bowl (no need to wash it) with a little olive or vegetable oil. Place the dough in the bowl and turn over to coat all sides lightly with oil. Cover with a damp towel and leave to rise in a warm bain-marie (page 28) for 1 to 1 1/2 hours, until doubled in size.

5. **Punch the dough down** to force out the air and let it rest on the counter for 5 minutes, covered with the towel. Generously dust a rimmed baking sheet with cornmeal. Divide the dough into 2 pieces and shape each into an oval loaf according to the instructions in step 4 on page 72. Place on the prepared baking sheet, leaving room for the loaves to double without touching each other. Again, cover with a damp cloth and let rise for 30 minutes to 1 hour more, until doubled in size.

6. **Preheat the oven to 400°** and place a rack in the lower third of the oven. (If using a pure convection oven (page 11), set it for 375° and bake on any shelf.) Using a fine-mesh strainer, dust the tops of the loaves with a little unbleached flour. With a sharp knife using light pressure, make 3 to 5 diagonal slashes, 1/2 inch deep, across the width of the bread. Bake for 30 minutes, until the crust is a deep rich brown. The bread should sound hollow if you rap your knuckle on the bottom. Cool on wire racks and use within 3 to 4 days or freeze in plastic bags for up to 1 month.

Olive Bread

This tasty somewhat salty bread is good with assertive cheeses, such as goat cheese, and fresh tomato slices.

MAKES 2 LOAVES

1 2/3 cups lukewarm water

2 tablespoons crumbled fresh cake yeast

1 1/2 cups levain (pages 83–84)

3 1/2 cups bread flour

1 3/4 cups plus 1 rounded tablespoon medium-ground rye flour

2 1/4 teaspoons sea salt

1 cup finely chopped cured black olives

2 tablespoons unbleached all-purpose flour

Coarse yellow cornmeal, for sprinkling

1. **In the bowl of a stand mixer** fitted with the paddle attachment, combine the lukewarm water and yeast and mix until the yeast is almost dissolved. Turn the machine off and add the levain and flours all at once. Mix on low speed for 1 minute, until the ingredients come together.

2. **Switch to the dough hook** and knead for 3 minutes on low speed. Or, turn the dough out onto a lightly floured surface and knead by hand for 5 minutes, until smooth and elastic. Add the salt and knead for 1 minute more.

3. **Transfer the dough** to a lightly floured surface. In a bowl, toss the olives with the 2 tablespoons flour to coat evenly. With floured hands, flatten the dough into a 10 by 14-inch rectangle. Spread on the olives evenly and reflour your hands.

Press the olives into the dough. Fold the dough in half and press down to flatten and spread it, gradually working the olives deeper in. Repeat until the olives are evenly distributed, then continue kneading by hand for about 2 minutes. Lightly oil the same mixing bowl (no need to wash it) with a little olive or vegetable oil. Place the dough in the bowl and turn it over to coat all sides lightly with oil. Cover with a damp towel and leave to rise in a warm bain-marie (page 28) for 1 to 1 1/2 hours, until doubled in size.

4. **Punch the dough down** to force out the air and let rest on the counter for 5 minutes, covered with the towel. Generously dust a large baking sheet with cornmeal. Divide the dough into 2 pieces and shape each into an oval loaf according to the instructions in step 4 on page 72. Place on the prepared baking sheet, leaving room for the loaves to double without touching. Cover with a damp cloth and let rise for 30 minutes to 1 hour more, until doubled in size.

5. **Preheat the oven to 400°** and place a rack in the lower third of the oven. (If using a pure convection oven (page 11), set it for 375° and bake on any shelf.) Using a strainer, dust the tops of the loaves with unbleached flour. With a sharp knife, make 3 to 5 diagonal slashes, 1/2 inch deep, across the width of the bread. Bake for 30 minutes, until the crust is a deep rich brown. The bread should sound hollow if you rap your knuckle on the bottom. Cool on wire racks and use within 2 to 4 days or freeze in plastic bags for up to 1 month.

Tuscan Bread

This is a thin crisp-crusted bread with a hint of the nutty flavor of barley. The wild yeast fermenting process produces a soft dough and a bread full of holes. This is a superb sandwich loaf, which may be served with meats, cheeses, and fresh tomatoes and greens. Malted barley is found in health food stores or in establishments that cater to the home beer-maker.

MAKES 1 LARGE OR 2 SMALL LOAVES

1 1/2 cups lukewarm water

2 tablespoons barley malt

1 tablespoon crumbled fresh cake yeast

1 1/2 cups levain (pags 83–84)

3 3/4 cups bread flour

2 teaspoons sea salt

Coarse yellow cornmeal, for sprinkling

1. **In the bowl of a stand mixer** fitted with the paddle attachment, combine the lukewarm water, malt, and yeast and mix until the yeast is almost dissolved. Turn the machine off and add the levain and the flour all at once. Mix on low speed for 2 minutes, until the ingredients come together into a smooth dough.

2. **Switch to the dough hook** and knead on low speed for 3 minutes. This is a very soft dough and may be too sticky to knead in the mixer. If so, turn out onto a lightly floured surface and knead by hand for 5 minutes, until smooth and elastic. Add the salt and knead for 1 minute more.

3. **Lightly oil the same mixing bowl** (no need to wash it) with a little olive or vegetable oil. Place the dough in the bowl and turn it over to coat all sides lightly with oil. Cover with a damp towel and leave to rise in a warm bain-marie (page 28) for 2 hours, until doubled in size.

4. **Turn the dough out** onto a lightly floured surface. It will be very soft and loose. Punch the dough down, but handle carefully to preserve as much air as possible. Form 1 ball or divide into 2 pieces for 2 loaves, tucking the outer edges under to form smooth balls. Generously dust a large baking sheet with cornmeal. Place on the prepared baking sheet, leaving room for the loaves to double without touching each other, if making 2 loaves. Cover the loaves with damp towels and let rise for 1 hour more, until doubled in size.

5. **Preheat the oven to 425°** and place a rack in the lower third of the oven. (If using a pure convection oven (page 11), set it for 400° and bake on any shelf.) With a sharp knife, cut 2 curved gashes, 1/2 inch deep, across the top of the bread. Cut another 2 gashes, crisscrossing over the first 2, to form a grid. Sprinkle each loaf evenly with about 1 tablespoon cornmeal. Bake for 30 minutes, until the crust is a deep rich brown. The bread should sound hollow if you rap your knuckle on the bottom. Cool on wire racks and use within 2 to 3 days or freeze in plastic bags for up to 1 month.

Wild Yeast Fougasse

This is the levain version of the Fougasse on page 77. It is a more classic and flavorful bread. Some of my favorite variations on this specialty Provençal flatbread are made with black olives, Parmesan, or bacon. I have even tasted this bread made with orange flower water and orange zest, which was very good. I like to make several batches of bread and freeze the baked loaves. At serving time, put the frozen bread, unwrapped, into a preheated 350° oven for 10 to 15 minutes, until the loaves are crisp.

✄ MAKES 2 LOAVES

1 1/2 cups lukewarm water

2 tablespoons fresh cake yeast

1/3 cup extra virgin olive oil

1/3 cup finely chopped fresh rosemary

1 3/4 cups levain (pages 83–84)

5 3/4 cups bread flour

2 1/2 teaspoons sea salt

Coarse yellow cornmeal, for sprinkling

Olive oil, for brushing

Kosher salt, for sprinkling

1. **In the bowl of a stand mixer** fitted with the paddle attachment, combine the lukewarm water, yeast, oil, and rosemary and mix until the yeast is almost dissolved. Turn the machine off and add the levain and the flour all at once. Mix on low speed for 2 minutes, until the ingredients come together into a smooth dough.

2. **Switch to the dough hook** and knead on low speed for 3 minutes. Or, turn the dough out onto a lightly floured surface and knead by hand for 5 minutes, until smooth and elastic. Add the sea salt and knead for 1 minute more.

3. **Lightly oil the same mixing bowl** (no need to wash it) with a little olive or vegetable oil. Place the dough in the bowl and turn it over to coat all sides evenly with the oil. Cover with a damp towel and leave to rise in a warm bain-marie (page 28) for 2 hours, until doubled in size.

4. **Punch the dough down** to force out the air and let it rest on the counter for 5 minutes, covered with the towel. Generously dust 2 large baking sheets with cornmeal. Divide the dough into 2 pieces and shape each into an oval. Using a French rolling pin (page 16), roll out to 12 by 14 inches and 1 inch thick, maintaining the oval shape. Place on the baking sheets. Cover both loaves with slightly damp towels and leave to rise again for 30 minutes to 1 hour, until doubled in size.

5. **Preheat the oven to 400°** and place one rack in the lower third of the oven and another in the upper third. (If using a pure convection oven (page 11), set it for 375° and bake on any shelf.) Generously brush the loaves with olive oil, and sprinkle them evenly with kosher salt. Bake for about 30 minutes, until golden brown and cinnamon colored. Cool on wire racks and use within 1 day or freeze in plastic bags for up to 1 month.

Appetizers and First Courses

IN MY OPINION, AN APPETIZER SHOULD BE nothing more than a tease or temptation for the main course. They are meant to awaken the palate, not fill the stomach, so I design appetizers to be small servings. This chapter features a few of my favorites. Several of these dishes may be served as a main course. In particular, the Pizza Margherita, both quiches, and the Buckwheat Crepes are quite lovely served with just a simple salad.

Tapenade

All the salty things—olives, anchovies, and capers—go into this Provençal specialty. Tapenade may be used in potato salads, on croûtons, in deviled eggs, as a topping for pizza, spread thinly on bread for a sandwich, or in pasta sauces such as Puttanesca (page 143) or even, for a change of pace, Fresh Tomato Sauce (page 139).

Whole cured olives are easily pitted by laying them flat and pressing with the side of a chef's knife. The olive meat will then separate easily from the pit. An olive/cherry pitter also works well. Don't even consider using the common grocery store olives, sold in a tin can and labeled "ripe." To me, these are not olives at all. ✒ MAKES ABOUT 1-1/2 CUPS

1 pound large plump cured black olives, pitted

2 ounces anchovies, salt-cured or packed in oil (page 1)

1 large clove garlic, minced

1 to 2 teaspoons capers, drained

1/4 cup extra virgin olive oil

1/8 teaspoon freshly ground black pepper

1. **Place the pitted olives** into the bowl of a food processor and process to a fine, but not completely smooth paste. If you don't have a food processor, you can chop the olives with a chef's knife, and then crush the resulting paste with the side of the knife blade, smearing the olives against the cutting board.

2. **Coarsely chop the anchovies** and add them to the food processor, along with the garlic, capers to taste, olive oil, and pepper. Pulse the machine quickly on and off, scraping down the bowl as necessary, until the mixture forms a slightly coarse paste.

3. **Use immediately or transfer** to small jars and refrigerate for up to 2 months.

Roquefort with Walnuts on Toasted Croûtons

(SEE PHOTO INSERT)

An Ecole de Cuisine favorite to accompany a spicy red wine from the Rhône Valley. The croûtons can be prepared hours in advance, as can the Roquefort butter, for assembly just before baking. ☙ SERVES 6

5 tablespoons unsalted butter, at room temperature

7 ounces Roquefort cheese, crumbled

2 tablespoons Cognac or brandy

1/8 teaspoon freshly ground black pepper

1 cup coarsely chopped walnuts

18 croûtons (page 32), warm

1. **Preheat the oven to 350°.** In a bowl, combine the butter, Roquefort, Cognac, and pepper. Whisk just until the contents are blended, but still quite lumpy. Fold in the walnuts.

2. **Spread the cheese mixture** onto the warm croûtons. Place on a rimmed baking sheet and bake for 2 to 3 minutes, just to warm the cheese. Transfer to a platter and serve immediately, allowing 3 croûtons per person.

Bruschetta

(SEE PHOTO INSERT)

A simple, fresh, flavorful quick appetizer this is one of those perfect finger foods that everyone loves. ☙ SERVES 8

1 tablespoon balsamic vinegar

2 tablespoons coarsely chopped fresh basil

1 tablespoon coarsely chopped fresh flat-leaf parsley

Sea salt and freshly ground black pepper

1/4 cup extra virgin olive oil

2 pounds plum tomatoes, peeled, seeded, and diced

16 croûtons (page 32)

1. **In a bowl, whisk together** the vinegar, basil, and parsley and season with salt, and pepper. Drizzle in the oil, whisking all the time.

2. **About 15 minutes before serving,** add the tomatoes to the dressing and toss together until evenly coated. Top each croûton with a dollop of the tomato mixture and serve at once.

Spicy Gruyère and Parmesan Cheese Crackers

(SEE PHOTO INSERT)

A perfect appetizer with red wine or beer. The crackers can be kept at room temperature for up to 1 week or covered in the freezer for up to 1 month—that is, if you can resist the temptation to nibble on them!

MAKES 18 (1-INCH) CRACKERS

3/4 cup unbleached all-purpose flour

1/8 teaspoon finely ground black pepper

1/8 teaspoon ground cayenne pepper

6 tablespoons unsalted butter, cool but not cold

3/4 cup freshly grated Parmesan cheese (use the finest holes of the grater)

1 large egg lightly beaten with 1/4 teaspoon salt

1/3 cup finely shredded Gruyère cheese

1/3 cup finely chopped walnuts

1. **On a flat surface or a pastry board,** combine the flour and black and cayenne peppers in a pile.

2. **Cut the butter into several pieces** and then cut it into the flour mixture using a plastic scraper. Keep cutting and scraping the flour and butter together until the mixture resembles fine fresh bread crumbs.

3. **Add the Parmesan and smear** the dough against the surface with the heel of your hand until the cheese is incorporated, kneading lightly until the dough forms a smooth soft ball. Press the dough into a flat disk and wrap with plastic wrap. Chill the dough for at least 45 minutes, or up to 2 days (you may also freeze the dough for up to 2 months).

4. **Preheat the oven to 375°** and place a rack in the middle. Lightly butter a baking sheet. Roll the dough out to 1/4 inch thick. Cut into 1- or 1 1/2-inch rounds or squares with a cookie cutter (make several different sizes and shapes, if desired). Or, cut with a knife into small squares or rectangles. Place the shapes on the prepared baking sheet, and brush the tops lightly with the egg glaze. Sprinkle each cracker with a little Gruyère and some chopped walnuts. Place in the oven and bake for about 15 minutes, until the crackers are a nice golden brown. Watch the crackers carefully—some may be done before others, and you don't want them to burn. As they are done, remove with a metal spatula and transfer to a wire rack to cool. Continue baking until all the crackers are done. Serve at room temperature on a platter.

Pizza Margherita

Making homemade pizza is deceptively simple, and always popular with children and guests. This simple pizza, named after a queen, is my favorite. It's important to spread only a thin layer of sauce over the pizza—too much sauce will weigh it down and make the pizza soggy and limp. The sauce should be considered an enhancement to the pizza crust, rather than an ingredient on its own. *SERVES 6*

OLIVE OIL PIZZA CRUST

3 1/2 cups unbleached all-purpose flour, or as needed

1 1/4 cups water at 115 to 120°

1/4 cup olive oil

Pinch of sugar

2 envelopes (4 1/2 teaspoons) active dry yeast

1 teaspoon sea salt

1 tablespoon finely chopped fresh rosemary (optional)

3/4 cup coarse cornmeal

Extra virgin olive oil, for drizzling

1/2 cup chopped fresh basil

1 1/2 cups Fresh Tomato Sauce (page 139)

1/2 cup freshly grated Parmesan cheese

1. **In a stand mixer** fitted with the paddle attachment, combine 1 cup of the flour and the water, olive oil, sugar, yeast, salt, and rosemary. Mix for 3 minutes on medium speed. (Or, mix by hand with a sturdy wooden spoon.) A little at a time, add just enough of the remaining flour to make a dough that is firm but not stiff. It should feel supple but not sticky. This process should not take more than 3 minutes.

2. **Switch to the dough hook** and knead the dough on low speed for 2 to 3 minutes, until it feels smooth. Or, knead the dough by hand for 6 to 7 minutes. Lightly coat the inside of a large clean bowl with a little olive oil. Place the dough in the bowl and turn over, so that both sides have a light film of oil. Cover with a damp cloth and let rise in a warm bain-marie (page 28) for 1 to 2 hours, until doubled in size.

3. **Preheat the oven to 425°.** Punch the dough down to force out the air, and again let it rest, covered, for about 10 minutes. Generously scatter cornmeal on 3 rimmed baking sheets. Divide the dough into 6 equal pieces and form each one into a smooth ball. On a lightly floured surface, roll each ball out to 1/8 to 1/4 inch thick and 6 inches in diameter. As they are done, transfer them to the baking sheets.

4. **To assemble the pizzas,** brush the crusts generously with the extra virgin olive oil and sprinkle with basil. Spread on a thin layer of sauce. Scatter the sauce with the Parmesan.

5. **Bake the pizzas,** in batches if necessary, for about 20 minutes each, until the crusts are well browned and the topping is bubbling slightly. Serve immediately.

Buckwheat Crepes with Mushroom Stuffing

In the Brittany region of France, a famous crepe called a galette is made with buckwheat flour. In my recipe, the crepe is made with a mixture of plain flour and buckwheat flour, and then filled with a wild mushroom, leek, and spinach mixture. This recipe has three parts: the crepes, the filling, and the butter glaze. It may sound complex, but there are several very easy make-ahead steps.

MAKES ABOUT 16 CREPES; SERVES 8

CREPES

3/4 cup water

1/2 cup whole milk

2 tablespoons clarified butter (page 31)

2 large eggs

3/4 cup unbleached all-purpose flour

1/4 cup buckwheat flour

1 tablespoon finely chopped fresh dill

1/4 teaspoon sea salt

1/2 cup clarified butter (page 31), melted and warm, for cooking the crepes

Sprigs of dill, for garnish

DILL-BUTTER GLAZE

1/2 cup unsalted butter

1 tablespoon finely chopped fresh dill

MUSHROOM STUFFING

6 tablespoons unsalted butter

4 leeks, white and light green parts only, quartered lengthwise and cut into 1/4-inch pieces

4 green onions, white and light green parts only, sliced crosswise into 1/4-inch pieces

2 cloves garlic, minced

1/2 pound mixed wild mushrooms, finely chopped

1/2 pound fresh flat-leaf spinach, stemmed

1/2 cup heavy cream or crème fraîche (page 32)

1/2 teaspoon sea salt

1/8 teaspoon freshly ground black pepper

1. **To prepare the crepe batter,** in a bowl, blender, or food processor, combine the water, milk, the 2 tablespoons clarified butter, and eggs. Whisk or process just to combine. Add the all-purpose and buckwheat flours, dill, and salt and whisk or process just until smooth. Let the batter rest, covered, for at least 30 minutes, at room temperature. It should be the consistency of heavy cream. The batter can be made up to 8 hours in advance, kept covered and refrigerated. Bring back to room temperature for 10 to 15 minutes before making the crepes.

2. **To prepare the butter glaze**, combine the butter and dill in a small saucepan and place over medium heat. Bring to a simmer, then remove from the heat. Let stand for 30 minutes, uncovered, so the dill flavor infuses into the butter.

3. **To prepare the filling**, melt 4 tablespoons of the butter in a sauté pan over medium heat. Add the leeks and green onions and cook, stirring occasionally, for 3 to 4 minutes, until they begin to soften. Add the garlic and continue cooking for 1 minute more. Add the mushrooms and cook, stirring occasionally, for 5 to 6 minutes, until tender and the juices have evaporated. Remove from the heat and set the pan aside.

4. **In another sauté pan**, melt the remaining 2 tablespoons butter over medium heat. Add the spinach and cook, tossing occasionally, for 3 to 4 minutes, until it is wilted and cooked through. If any liquid remains after cooking, press the spinach between double layers of paper towels to thoroughly dry. Transfer the spinach to a cutting board and chop it finely. Add the spinach and the cream to the pan with the mushroom mixture and place over medium-high heat. Cook, stirring, for 5 to 8 minutes, until the mixture has thickened. Stir in the salt and pepper, taste, and adjust the seasoning if necessary. Let the filling cool slightly.

5. **To prepare the crepes**, heat a 5-inch crepe pan (page 14) over medium heat. Brush the pan lightly with the warm clarified butter. Pour about 1 ounce of the batter on one side of the crepe pan and swirl the pan around until the batter coats the base evenly. If the batter does not spread easily on the crepe pan, add a few teaspoons of water to the remaining batter to thin it. As the crepes cook, the batter will appear to dry. After 1 to 2 minutes, the bottom will be browned, with a lacy appearance. Using a flat metal spatula, turn the crepe over and cook the underside for a few seconds more, just long enough to dry (do not brown the second side). As the crepes are finished, transfer them to a platter, slightly overlapping. Proceed immediately with the recipe, or wrap the platter with plastic wrap and refrigerate for up to 2 days before filling.

6. **To assemble the crepes**, preheat the oven to 350°. Butter a large baking dish. Place 1 rounded tablespoon of the mushroom filling in the center of the pale side of a crepe (be sure that the lacy side is on the outside—it's much prettier). Spread the filling to within 1/2 inch of the edge and fold the crepe in half. Fold in half again to form a triangle. Place the crepe in the prepared baking dish and continue making crepes in the same manner until you have used all the ingredients, overlapping them in the pan as they are assembled. Brush the tops of the crepes with the dill-butter glaze. (At this point the baking dish can be covered with plastic wrap and refrigerated for up to 4 hours before heating and serving.) Place in the oven for about 10 minutes, until heated through. (If the crepes have been refrigerated, they will take about 5 minutes longer to heat through.)

7. **Serve 2 crepes per person**, garnished with a sprig of dill.

Alsatian Onion Quiche

This is a simple dish—onions are cooked in cream and milk until they seem to melt together into a homogeneous filling. For a heartier and authentic Alsatian meal, try crumbling 3 slices of crispy cooked bacon into the filling. I sometimes turn this into tiny appetizers by baking the crust and filling in one-inch tins.

SERVES 8 AS AN APPETIZER, 4 AS A MAIN COURSE

1/4 cup unsalted butter

3 large onions, thinly sliced

2 tablespoons unbleached all-purpose flour

1/2 cup heavy cream

1/2 cup whole milk

3 large eggs, lightly beaten

1/2 teaspoon sea salt

1/8 teaspoon freshly ground white pepper

1/8 teaspoon freshly grated nutmeg

1 (9-inch) Flaky Butter Crust (page 210), baked and cooled

1. **Melt the butter** in a heavy sauté pan over medium-high heat. Add the onions and cover the pan. Decrease the heat to low and cook, stirring occasionally, for 15 to 20 minutes, until the onions are very soft, but not brown. Remove the lid and increase the heat to medium-high. Cook, stirring frequently, for about 5 minutes, to evaporate any excess liquid. Continue cooking for 5 to 8 minutes, until the onions turn a light golden color. Do not allow the onions to brown.

2. **Preheat the oven to 375°.** Add the flour to the onions and cook for 3 minutes more, stirring constantly. Add the cream and milk and bring to a boil, again stirring constantly. Cook, stirring occasionally, for 3 to 5 minutes, until the mixture thickens. Remove the pan from the heat and stir in the eggs, salt, pepper, and nutmeg.

3. **Pour the filling into** the cooled crust. Place the quiche on a rimmed baking sheet (to catch any spillovers) and bake for 30 minutes, until the filling is set and golden brown. Serve hot, warm, or at room temperature, cut into wedges.

Roquefort and Onion Quiche

The assertive flavors of the Roquefort and onion actually cook together to create a mellow, rich, earthy flavor for this quiche. Even students who tell me they generally don't like blue cheeses love this preparation.
❧ SERVES 8 AS AN APPETIZER, 4 AS A MAIN COURSE

2 tablespoons unsalted butter

3 large onions, thinly sliced

1 teaspoon finely chopped fresh thyme

1/2 cup crumbled Roquefort cheese

1 (9-inch) Flaky Butter Crust (page 210), baked
    and cooled

1 large egg

2 large egg yolks

1/2 cup heavy cream

1/4 cup whole milk

1/2 teaspoon sea salt

1/8 teaspoon freshly ground black pepper

Pinch of freshly grated nutmeg

1. **Preheat the oven to 375°.** Melt the butter in a heavy sauté pan over medium heat. Add the onions and thyme and cover the pan. Decrease the heat to low and cook, stirring occasionally, for 15 to 20 minutes, until the onions are very soft, but not brown. Remove the lid and increase the heat to medium-high. Cook, stirring frequently, for about 5 minutes, to evaporate any excess liquid. Add the Roquefort and stir over low heat just until the cheese has melted and the mixture is smooth. Spread the onion and cheese mixture evenly into the cooled crust.

2. **In a bowl, combine the egg**, egg yolks, cream, milk, salt, pepper, and nutmeg. Whisk just until thoroughly combined. Pour the custard filling over the onion mixture and place on a rimmed baking sheet (to catch any spillovers).

3. **Bake for 30 minutes,** until the filling is set and the top is puffed and browned. Serve hot, warm, or at room temperature, cut into wedges.

LESSON SIX

Soups

THE BEST SOUPS ALWAYS BEGIN WITH HOMEMADE STOCK (lesson two, page 37) and the freshest vegetables and herbs. Contrary to some people's belief, soup is not a good destination for tired and limp produce. Fresh ingredients will give the soup a bright, fresh taste.

Correct consistency is crucial for cream soups. If the soup is too thin, you can simmer it over high heat to evaporate some of the liquid and thicken the consistency. If a soup is too thick, a little bit of cream, milk, stock, or even water will thin it down slightly. Never settle for the wrong consistency—fix it!

It is also important to add sufficient salt to the soup, particularly when using homemade stocks, which are not salted. My students are often surprised at the amount of salt added at the end of cooking. I remind them that the salt we put into a soup is probably half what goes into a processed soup. At the school, we have done side-by-side taste tests using canned stock and homemade stock to construct the same vegetable soup. It is no surprise to me that you can taste the vegetable itself (and the cream) in the soup made with homemade stock, while the soup made with canned stock tastes like salt and monosodium glutamate.

Potato-Leek Soup

True comfort food. This soup may be made with water rather than stock, but the stock yields a superb flavor and body. Leek is one of my favorite vegetables. Its mild onion flavor blends perfectly with potatoes and numerous other foods where an onion would be too strong. 🌿 SERVES 4 TO 6

6 large leeks, white and light green parts only

1/4 cup unsalted butter

6 large baking potatoes, peeled and cut into
    1-inch chunks

6 cups Chicken Stock (page 40), or as needed

1 1/2 to 2 cups heavy cream or crème fraîche
    (page 32)

2 teaspoons sea salt

1/2 teaspoon freshly ground white pepper

1. **Trim away the root ends** of the leeks and cut lengthwise into quarters. Rinse thoroughly under cold running water to remove any sand and grit. Cut crosswise into 1/2-inch slices.

2. **In a heavy pan** or Dutch oven, melt the butter over medium heat. Add the leeks and cook, stirring frequently, for 5 minutes, until softened. Do not allow to brown.

3. **Add the potatoes** and enough stock to cover the vegetables by about 1 1/2 inches. Bring the stock to a simmer and cook gently for about 15 to 20 minutes, until the potatoes are quite tender.

4. **Pass the soup through** the finest disk of a food mill. Rinse the original pan, wipe with a paper towel, and return the soup to the pan.

5. **Stir in 1 1/2 cups** of the cream and simmer gently for 3 to 5 minutes, until the soup thickens to a creamy consistency. If the soup is too thick, add a little more stock, cream, or water. If too thin, simmer for a few minutes to evaporate some liquid and reduce slightly. Stir in the salt and pepper and taste for seasoning. Adjust if necessary. Divide among individual bowls and serve at once.

Pesto Minestrone

A hearty winter soup with white beans and vegetables, given a delicious zing with pesto. For this soup, I like to make the pesto without garlic, but if you have garlicky pesto in the freezer, you should certainly use it. Just let the pesto mellow in the simmering soup for a few minutes before serving, to tame the garlic.

SERVES 6 TO 8

1/4 cup olive oil

2 carrots, peeled and diced

2 onions, diced

4 celery stalks, diced

2/3 cup dried white kidney beans, soaked in water to cover by 4 inches for at least 8 hours or overnight

4 cloves garlic, minced

12 cups Chicken or Vegetable Stock (pages 40 and 44), or water

1 Turkish bay leaf

4 leeks, white and light green parts only, chopped

12 green beans, cut into 1/2-inch pieces

2 teaspoons sea salt

1/2 teaspoon freshly ground black pepper

1 small head cauliflower, divided into florets

1/3 cup small macaroni

2 zucchini, cut crosswise into 1/2-inch pieces

3 plum tomatoes, peeled, seeded, and chopped

1 cup pesto (page 33), made without the garlic

1. **In a large heavy pan** or Dutch oven, heat the olive oil over medium-high heat. Add the carrots, onions, and celery and sauté, stirring frequently, for 3 to 4 minutes to soften the vegetables. Drain the kidney beans. Stir in the garlic and cook for 1 minute more. Add the stock, bay leaf, and kidney beans and bring up to a boil. Adjust the heat so the soup maintains a slow simmer for 15 to 20 minutes.

2. **Add the leeks,** green beans, salt, and pepper. Increase the heat to achieve a brisk simmer for 5 minutes. Add the cauliflower and macaroni and continue simmering for 10 to 14 minutes, until the pasta is al dente.

3. **Add the zucchini** and tomatoes and simmer for 5 minutes. Retrieve and discard the bay leaf and stir in the pesto. Taste for seasoning and adjust with salt and pepper, if necessary. Ladle into individual bowls and serve.

Cream of Tomato Soup

Fresh, ripe, fleshy tomatoes, such as Roma, are the best choice for this soup. I always squeeze the seeds and juice from the tomatoes to drastically cut the cooking time. This also produces a fresher, brighter tomato taste that a longer simmering period would take away. ✿ SERVES 6

1/2 cup unsalted butter

4 yellow onions, thinly sliced

1 teaspoon finely chopped fresh thyme

4 pounds plum tomatoes, seeded and coarsely
    chopped

2 cloves garlic, minced

1 to 2 teaspoons sugar, if necessary

4 cups Chicken Stock (page 40)

2 cups heavy cream

1 1/2 teaspoons sea salt

1/4 teaspoon freshly ground white pepper

1/2 cup heavy cream whipped to soft peaks with
    1/4 teaspoon salt, for garnish (optional)

Finely chopped fresh chives or basil, or
    a combination, for garnish

1. **In a large heavy pan** or Dutch oven, melt the butter over very low heat. Add the onions and thyme and soften for 10 to 15 minutes, stirring occasionally, until the onions are very soft.

2. **Add the tomatoes** and garlic and increase the heat to medium. Cook for about 10 minutes, until the tomatoes are soft and falling apart. Taste the mixture; if it is too tart, add sugar to taste (tomatoes vary enormously in acidity depending on season and place of origin.)

3. **Add the stock** and bring just to a boil over high heat. Decrease the heat and adjust to maintain a brisk simmer. Cook, uncovered, for about 10 minutes, until the mixture has reduced by one-third.

4. **Pass the mixture through** the finest disk of a food mill or cool slightly and purée the soup, in batches if necessary, in a blender or a food processor. (Never place a very hot liquid into a blender or food processor, or the top will explode and the soup will be on the walls rather than in the bowls!) Rinse the original pan and wipe with a paper towel. Add the cream to the pan and place it over high heat. Bring the cream to a boil and let it boil for 1 minute. Return the puréed tomato mixture to the pan. Simmer the soup over medium heat, stirring occasionally, for 20 to 25 minutes, until it reaches a thick, creamy consistency. Stir in the salt and pepper and taste for seasoning. Adjust if necessary.

5. **Ladle the soup into** individual bowls and garnish with a dollop of whipped cream and a little of the chopped chives.

Cream of Mushroom Soup

Cream produces a rich taste and texture in this soup and enhances the flavor of the mushrooms themselves. If you prefer, milk, or a combination of milk and cream, also makes a nice soup. Be sure to adjust the consistency of the soup as directed in step 4. No matter what is used as the base for the soup, the final consistency is critical. ✿ SERVES 4 TO 6

7 tablespoons unsalted butter

1/2 cup finely chopped onion

1/2 pound white button or cremini mushrooms, stemmed and finely chopped

1/4 cup unbleached all-purpose flour

4 cups Chicken or Vegetable Stock (pages 40 and 44)

2 cups heavy cream

1 teaspoon sea salt

1/8 teaspoon freshly ground white pepper

1/4 pound shiitake mushrooms, stemmed and finely chopped (optional)

1. **In a heavy pan** or Dutch oven, melt 6 tablespoons of the butter over medium heat. Add the onion and mushrooms. Cook, stirring frequently, for 5 minutes, until softened and only a few tablespoons of liquid remain. Do not allow the vegetables to brown.

2. **Stir in the flour and cook,** stirring constantly, for 2 minutes, to cook off the raw taste of the flour. Do not allow the flour to brown; adjust the heat if necessary.

3. **A little at a time,** whisk in the stock. Bring to a boil, then immediately decrease the heat to medium. Stir constantly for about 5 minutes, until the soup thickens. Pass the soup through the finest disk of a food mill, or cool slightly and purée the soup, in batches if necessary, in a blender or food processor. (Never place a very hot liquid into a blender or food processor, or the top will explode and the soup will be on the walls rather than in the bowls!) Rinse the original pan and wipe it with a paper towel. Return the soup to the pan.

4. **Stir the cream into** the soup and place the pan over high heat. Bring the soup just to a boil, then adjust the heat to maintain a brisk simmer. Cook the soup, uncovered, for about 15 minutes, until it reaches a thickened, creamy consistency. If the soup is too thick, add a little water, milk, or cream. If too thin, adjust the heat to medium-high and simmer the soup, stirring occasionally, for a few minutes to evaporate some moisture and reduce to a thicker consistency. Add the salt and pepper and taste for seasoning. Cover and set aside while you finish the mushroom garnish.

continued

5. **Melt the remaining** 1 tablespoon butter in a small sauté pan over medium-high heat. Add the shiitake mushrooms and cook, stirring, for about 5 minutes, until all the juices have evaporated. Swirl the mushroom mixture into the soup and taste for seasoning. Adjust with salt and pepper if necessary. Ladle into individual bowls and serve.

Variation

ASSORTED VEGETABLE SOUPS: Omit the chopped mushrooms in step 1. Simmer 2 to 3 cups of one of the following: trimmed broccoli florets, trimmed cauliflower florets, chopped carrots, trimmed asparagus, celery, or corn kernels, in the flour-thickened stock in step 3. Simmer until tender before puréeing and finishing the soup as above, with or without the shiitake mushroom garnish.

Cream of Root Vegetable Soup

Do not turn past this recipe! For some reason, root vegetables like turnips tend to strike terror into the hearts of even the most dedicated cooks. Other root vegetables, such as parsnip or rutabaga, can be added or substituted. The earthy, hearty soup is perfect for a chilly autumn or winter evening. SERVES 4

1/2 cup unsalted butter

2 small carrots, peeled and finely chopped

1 small turnip, peeled and finely chopped

2 baking potatoes, peeled and cut into 1-inch chunks

2 plum tomatoes, peeled, seeded, and chopped

4 cups Chicken or Vegetable Stock (pages 40 and 44)

4 ounces fine French green beans (haricots verts), or standard green beans, trimmed and cut on the diagonal into 1/2-inch lengths

1 cup heavy cream or crème fraîche (page 32)

2 teaspoons sea salt

1/4 teaspoon freshly ground white pepper

2 tablespoons finely chopped fresh flat-leaf parsley or chives, for garnish

1. **In a large saucepan,** melt the butter over medium heat. Add the carrots and decrease the heat to low. Sauté, stirring occasionally, for 3 to 4 minutes, until softened. Add the turnip, potatoes, tomatoes, and stock and increase the heat to medium-high. Bring the mixture up to a boil, then adjust the heat to achieve a simmer. Cook, uncovered, for 30 minutes, stirring occasionally until all the vegetables are very tender. Let cool for 20 minutes.

2. **Bring a small saucepan** of lightly salted water to a boil. Add the green beans and cook until they have lost their raw crunch but are still firm, about 4 minutes for haricots verts, 5 for standard green beans, Drain the beans in a colander and run under cold water to stop the cooking process and preserve their color. Set aside.

3. **Purée the soup,** in batches if necessary, by passing it through the smallest disk of a food mill or pulsing in a food processor or blender. (Never place a very hot liquid into a blender or food processor, or the top will explode and the soup will be on the walls rather than in the bowls!) Rinse the original pan to remove any chunks of vegetable. Return the soup to the pan and stir in the cream. Place the pan over high heat and bring just to a boil. Immediately decrease the heat to medium and adjust to maintain a simmer. Cook uncovered, stirring occasionally, for 8 to 10 minutes, until the soup has a thick, creamy consistency. Add the green beans and simmer for 1 minute to warm them through. Stir in the salt and pepper, taste for seasoning, and adjust if necessary. Ladle the soup into individual bowls and garnish each with some of the chopped parsley.

French Onion Soup with a Cheese Crust

(SEE PHOTO INSERT)

This classic soup is served in every region of France, and there are many imitators here in the States. But when you have tasted this recipe made with home-made stock, you will know the true meaning of French onion soup!

Caramelizing the onions correctly is very important to the final taste of this recipe. Don't be tempted to use anything but common yellow onions. Once, when catering a special event in the South, I was shocked by the strange, sugary flavor of my usually delicious French onion soup. I suspected someone had mistakenly added sugar instead of salt—but no, in fact the staff had bought sweet Vidalia onions, which are excellent raw but overwhelmingly sweet when caramelized. ✒ SERVES 6

1/2 cup unsalted butter

4 to 5 large yellow onions, thinly sliced

3 tablespoons unbleached all-purpose flour

2 teaspoons sea salt

1/4 teaspoon freshly ground black pepper

6 cups Brown Beef Stock (page 41)

1 to 2 teaspoons Cognac (optional)

6 croûtons (page 32)

1 1/2 cups shredded Gruyère cheese

1. **In a large heavy sauté pan,** melt the butter over medium heat. Add the onions and cook for about 10 minutes, stirring occasionally, until softened and the juice has been released. Increase the heat to medium-high and continue cooking, scraping the bottom of the pan and turning constantly, for 15 to 20 minutes, until the onions turn a cinnamon color. It's important to use a flat metal spatula (page 17) to scrape up the browned bits, otherwise they will stick. (Be careful not to chop up the onions with the spatula.) If there is a spot of caramelized sugar on the pan that simply can't be scraped up and it is getting too dark, drizzle a few tablespoons of beef stock over the spot and it will dissolve. Add just enough liquid to dissolve the darkened spot—too much liquid will slow down the entire caramelization process.

2. **Add the flour and cook,** stirring constantly, over medium-high heat for 1 minute.

3. **Add 1/2 teaspoon** of the salt and a few grinds of pepper to begin flavoring the soup (you will add more later). Add the stock and stir to combine. Adjust the heat to a simmer and cook, uncovered, for 30 minutes, until the soup has thickened and the flour taste has cooked out. Add the remaining salt and pepper and the Cognac. Taste for seasoning, adjusting if necessary. Increase the heat to medium-high and continue to cook for 1 minute to incorporate the seasonings.

4. **Preheat the broiler.** Ladle the soup into 6 heat-proof bowls, scooping up plenty of the onions. Float a croûton on top of each one and press down very gently to moisten with the soup. Divide the cheese evenly among the croûtons, covering the surface of the bread completely. Place the bowls on a baking sheet and place under the hot broiler until the cheese is bubbling and golden. Watch carefully to avoid burning and serve immediately.

Salads and Salad Dressings

MY DEFINITION OF A SALAD GREEN is certainly not the pale, round, flavorless balls called iceberg that are found in every chain restaurant. Thankfully, many interesting greens, such as mesclun mix, are appearing in American markets. Often used in Provence, each leaf in the mesclun mix is small, usually no larger than 3 inches. Although the mix may seem expensive, there is no waste, since nothing needs to be trimmed away. A good mesclun should consist only of small individual leaves, and should look fresh and bright, with a variety of colors and textures. I also like to add several tablespoons of chopped fresh herbs, such as tarragon, chervil, mint, or the feathery tops of fresh fennel to mesclun or any other tender greens.

When it comes to dressing salad greens, I find that bottled dressings (or worse yet, dry packets that need to be reconstituted) have an acrid taste and scent, undoubtedly due to all the added preservatives. Homemade dressings are preferable as their freshness matches that of your greens. Be sure to pair your greens with the appropriate dressing: use lighter dressings like vinaigrettes for tender greens, such as mesclun, and save creamy dressings like Roquefort for the sturdier leaves, such as romaine.

I am particularly fond of the vinegars from Orleans, in France. Although they contain a higher level of acidity than some other vinegars, they are made from wine and aged in wooden barrels, which imparts an exceptional dimension of taste. The common grocery store brands of vinegar are made from grain and have a very harsh flavor compared to wine vinegars (in spite of reduced acidity!). Balsamic vinegar is the "must" or unfermented juice from sweet, ripe grapes. It has an intense, full, almost caramel-like flavor. The best balsamics are aged for at least seven years in wooden barrels. I have a bottle of 100-year balsamic, which is used in Italy as an after dinner drink. As with anything popular, there are many balsamic "frauds" on the market that are nothing more than caramelized sugar added to bad vinegar. It is best to purchase any vinegar, particularly balsamic, from a reputable business where the staff can explain the differences to you.

I like to use safflower, sunflower, and extra virgin olive oil as the "base" oil in my vinaigrettes. My favorite is a sweet oil made from ripe olives in the south of France but, unfortunately, I can only find it at the source. A few years ago, I bought a gallon of this prized oil while visiting Provence. Much to my despair, on its journey from Paris to Chicago, the container leaked, and my entire wardrobe was coated with oil. Losing the clothing was bothersome. Losing the olive oil was disastrous.

Specialty and nut oils, like citrus, sesame, hazelnut, walnut, and peanut, are stronger tasting, and small amounts of them can be mixed with one of the "base" oils so that just a hint of flavor comes through.

Invest in a good, sturdy salad spinner. This essential tool has a basket that holds the greens for washing under cold running water. More important, the centrifugal force of the spinner removes all water from the leaves. Dressing does not adhere to wet, soggy greens—it just pools on the bottom of the bowl.

Pasta with Kale and Spicy Italian Sausage

(PAGE 147)

Poached Salmon with Pesto

(PAGE 150)

Coquilles St. Jacques

(PAGE 158)

Herb-Roasted Rack of Lamb with Béarnaise Sauce

(PAGE 166)

Traditional Vinaigrettes

I find many vinaigrettes too acidic, so I tend to give a range in the amount of oil to add to the recipe. The common ratio of oil to vinegar (acid) is one-to-three, or one-to-four. I prefer to let the taste of flavorful greens shine through, rather than overwhelming their flavor with acid. The final ratio depends on the vinegar itself and on your personal preference.

Make a large quantity of Simple Vinaigrette and keep it in the refrigerator in a tightly covered bottle—it'll hold for 2 to 3 months. An hour or so before serving, you can add flavor with your choice of freshly chopped chervil, tarragon, chives, parsley, basil, shallots, or garlic.

The following recipes are traditional vinaigrettes: *Simple Vinaigrette, Sweet Sherry Vinaigrette,* and *Raspberry Vinaigrette.*

Simple Vinaigrette

This vinaigrette is the simplest of the emulsified dressings, with the emulsifying agent being Dijon mustard. It's an all around good salad dressing, going well with just about any green or vegetable. For a variation on the simple vinaigrette, replace the vinegar with an equal amount of freshly squeezed lemon juice. ❧ MAKES ABOUT 1/2 CUP

2 tablespoons wine vinegar (use red or white wine, sherry, or any flavored wine vinegar)

1 teaspoon Dijon mustard

1/4 teaspoon sea salt

1/8 teaspoon freshly ground black pepper

1/4 to 1/3 cup safflower, sunflower, or extra virgin olive oil

1. **In a small bowl,** combine the vinegar, mustard, salt, and pepper. Whisk together thoroughly. Wrap a damp dish towel around the base of the bowl to stabilize it, allowing you to add drops of oil with one hand while whisking with the other.

2. **Begin adding the oil** drop by drop, whisking all the time. After the first tablespoon or so is added, add the remaining oil in a slow, thin stream, whisking constantly. Taste and adjust the seasoning with salt and pepper.

3. **Serve immediately** or cover tightly and store in the refrigerator for up to 1 month.

Sweet Sherry Vinaigrette

The slightly sweet taste of the sherry mixed with a little sugar goes particularly well with a mesclun salad featuring large amounts of fresh chopped herbs such as fennel, tarragon, basil, flat-leaf parsley, and mint. ❧ MAKES ABOUT 1/2 CUP

2 tablespoons sherry vinegar

1/2 teaspoon Dijon mustard

1/4 teaspoon sea salt

1/8 teaspoon freshly ground white pepper

2 to 3 teaspoons sugar

1/4 to 1/3 cup safflower, sunflower, or extra virgin olive oil

1. **In a small bowl,** combine the vinegar, mustard, salt, pepper, and 2 teaspoons of the sugar. Whisk together thoroughly. Wrap a damp dish towel around the base of the bowl to stabilize it, allowing you to add drops of oil with one hand while whisking with the other.

2. **Begin adding the oil** drop by drop, whisking all the time. After the first tablespoon or so is added, add the remaining oil in a slow, thin stream, whisking constantly. Taste and adjust the seasoning with sugar, salt, and pepper.

3. **Serve immediately** or cover tightly and store in the refrigerator for up to 1 month.

Raspberry Vinaigrette

Raspberry vinaigrette appeared on virtually every menu in the 1980s—boring! But it actually makes a nice addition to summer salads that include grapes, kiwis, and raspberries. ❧ MAKES ABOUT 3/4 CUP

2 tablespoons Raspberry Vinegar (page 121)

1 tablespoon sherry vinegar

1/2 teaspoon Dijon mustard

2 teaspoons sugar (optional)

1/2 teaspoon sea salt

1/8 teaspoon freshly ground black pepper

1/3 to 1/2 cup safflower, sunflower, or extra virgin olive oil

1. **In a small bowl,** combine the raspberry and sherry vinegars, mustard, sugar, salt, and pepper. Whisk together thoroughly. Wrap a damp dish towel around the base of the bowl to stabilize it, allowing you to add drops of oil with one hand while whisking with the other.

2. **Begin adding the oil** drop by drop, whisking all the time. After the first tablespoon or so is added, add the remaining oil in a slow, thin stream, whisking constantly. Taste and adjust the seasoning with salt and pepper.

3. **Serve immediately** or cover tightly and store in the refrigerator for up to 1 month.

Basil and Fresh Tomato Vinaigrette

This dressing tastes especially good over thick slices of tomatoes and fresh mozzarella cheese, or a mixed garden vegetable salad. ❧ MAKES ABOUT 1 CUP

2 tablespoons red wine vinegar

2 tablespoons balsamic vinegar

20 fresh basil leaves

1 clove garlic, peeled

1 shallot, peeled

3/4 cup extra virgin olive oil

2 ripe plum tomatoes, peeled and seeded

1/2 teaspoon sea salt

1/8 teaspoon freshly ground black pepper

1. **In a blender or food processor,** combine all the ingredients. Process for about 30 seconds, until the ingredients are all incorporated and a thick, emulsified consistency is reached. Taste and adjust the seasoning with salt and pepper.

2. **Serve immediately** or transfer to a container and refrigerate for up to 1 week. Return to room temperature before serving.

Lavender Vinaigrette

The scent of lavender always speaks to me of Provence. There, it scents the air and flavors many of the south of France's signature dishes. The first time I had this magnificent dressing was in Nice, my favorite town on the French Riviera. If you come across a nice yellow olive oil from France, try it in this recipe. The lighter-colored oils are made from ripe olives and have a sweet, mild flavor. Dried lavender is available at specialty herb shops, but as always, fresh is a step above the dried variety. The flower head should be at the stage where it has just barely bloomed—but don't use flowers from a florist, which may have been treated with chemicals—ideally, use lavender you've picked yourself. Lavender honey is another specialty of southern France. Serve this dressing over a delicate mix of tender greens such as mesclun, Bibb, or Boston lettuce. It's also great over tomatoes. ✢ MAKES ABOUT 1 CUP

6 whole fresh lavender flower heads or 1 teaspoon dried lavender

2/3 cup extra virgin olive oil, preferably a yellow French oil

1/4 cup white wine vinegar

1 generous tablespoon lavender honey

1/4 teaspoon sea salt

1/8 teaspoon freshly ground black pepper

1. **In a blender or food processor**, combine all the ingredients and process for 30 seconds, until the mixture is completely blended and smooth.

(This dressing can be made without a blender or food processor, but it is very important that you chop the lavender extremely fine. In a small bowl, combine the chopped fresh lavender, vinegar, honey, salt, and pepper. Whisk together well. Wrap a damp dish towel around the base of the bowl to stabilize it, allowing you to add drops of oil with one hand while whisking with the other. Begin adding the oil drop by drop, whisking all the time. After the first tablespoon or so is added, add the remaining oil in a slow, thin stream, whisking constantly.)

2. **Taste and adjust** the seasoning with salt and pepper. If not used immediately, the dressing can be stored in the refrigerator, tightly covered, for up to 1 week.

Raspberry Vinegar

There are many good raspberry vinegars available commercially, but I have included this recipe because it demonstrates how infusing can create exceptional flavors without the use of extracts. If you use distilled white vinegar made from grains instead of white wine vinegar, the acidity will be quite mild. This vinegar is used for my Raspberry Vinaigrette (page 119) and in the Strawberry-Spinach Salad (page 127).

MAKES ABOUT 2 CUPS

3/4 **pound ripe red raspberries, blackberries or a combination**

1 1/4 **cups distilled white or white wine vinegar**

1/4 **cup sugar**

1/4 **cup Cognac or grain alcohol**

1. **In a bowl,** crush half of the berries with the back of a ladle. Pour the vinegar over the berries and crush 5 or 6 times more. Cover and set aside for 24 hours at room temperature.

2. **Pass the mixture through** a fine-mesh strainer or chinois into a medium bowl, pushing the fruit gently with the ladle to extract some of the juices. Discard the berry pulp.

3. **Add the remaining berries** to the strained liquid and slightly crush them with the back of a ladle. Cover and set aside for another 24 hours at room temperature. Repeat step 2.

4. **In a saucepan or the top** of a large double boiler over barely simmering water, combine the juice-infused vinegar, sugar, and Cognac. Stir to dissolve the sugar completely.

5. **Place the saucepan into** a warm bain-marie (page 28; a roasting pan half filled with water, placed over high heat, works well). Bring the bain-marie water just to a boil. Decrease the heat so the vinegar maintains a shimmer (page 20) and maintain the temperature so that the vinegar stays at a constant shimmer for 1 hour (you will have to watch carefully). Occasionally add more hot water to the bain-marie if it evaporates to less than a few inches.

6. **Pass the vinegar through** a fine-mesh strainer into a bowl and let cool. Store the vinegar in very clean covered canning jars or decorative bottles in the refrigerator for up to 6 months.

Roquefort-Cream Salad Dressing

The salt content of Roquefort, a sheep's milk cheese, varies greatly, so don't add salt to this recipe until the end. Depending on the cheese, you may not need to add any at all. Creamy dressings work best with greens that will support the heaviness of the dressing, like romaine. They should be tossed thoroughly so that the dressing coats the leaves only lightly. I like to leave some of the crisp white base of the romaine leaf: remove 1/4 inch from the stem end and make a "V" cut into the base of the leaf to remove the hard center if necessary. Blue cheese made from cow's milk may be substituted. ✍ MAKES 1 CUP

3 ounces Roquefort cheese, at room temperature, crumbled

1 tablespoon red or white wine vinegar, or freshly squeezed lemon juice

1/2 cup heavy cream

2 tablespoons finely chopped fresh chives

1/8 teaspoon freshly ground white pepper

Sea salt (optional)

1. **In a small bowl**, combine the cheese and vinegar and whisk until well blended but still slightly chunky. Add the cream and continue whisking until the mixture is creamy and smooth, breaking up the chunks a little with the whisk.

2. **Stir in the chives** and pepper and taste for seasoning. Add a little salt if necessary. Or, place all the ingredients except the chives in a blender or food processor and blend for 2 to 3 seconds only (over-blending will turn the cream to butter). Stir in the chives.

3. **Serve immediately** or store the dressing in the refrigerator, tightly covered, for up to 3 weeks.

Fresh Herb and Baby Greens Salad

(SEE PHOTO INSERT)

Mesclun, a mix of tender small greens, or Bibb lettuce is enhanced by chopped fresh herbs, fortunately available coast to coast. The first time I observed a fresh herb salad being made was in a professional kitchen in France. With such a large amount of herbs, I thought the salad would have a strong and overwhelming taste, but the flavor was magnificent. The herbs can be a combination of "tender" herbs, including tarragon, chervil, basil, chives, mint, and fresh fennel ferns. If using mint, note that there are two available in markets—spearmint and peppermint—but they are usually not labeled. For this recipe, you can use spearmint or peppermint, with the later being used judiciously as it is quite strong. All of the following herbs can be combined or any may be omitted.
🌿 SERVES 4

10 cups mesclun salad greens (about 5 ounces),
   or 2 heads Bibb lettuce

2 tablespoons finely chopped fresh mint

2 tablespoons finely chopped fresh tarragon

2 tablespoons finely chopped fresh flat-leaf parsley

2 tablespoons finely chopped fresh chervil

1 tablespoon finely chopped fresh basil

1/3 cup finely chopped fresh fennel tops

1 recipe Sweet Sherry Vinaigrette (page 118) or
   Lavender Vinaigrette (page 120)

1/3 cup pine nuts, toasted (page 30)

1. **Toss the greens and herbs** in a large salad bowl. Add the vinaigrette and pine nuts and toss well until all the greens are coated with dressing. Serve immediately on individual salad plates.

Cucumber Salad with Crème Fraîche and Chervil

Cucumbers bring a wonderfully cool, refreshing taste and a nice crunch to this salad. Once you have tried this combination, you will have sampled one of the great and simple salads of France. ✿ SERVES 4

4 cucumbers, peeled and halved lengthwise

1 1/2 teaspoons sea salt

1/2 cup crème fraîche (page 32) or sour cream

1 teaspoon Dijon mustard

1/2 teaspoon freshly squeezed lemon juice

1 tablespoon finely chopped fresh chervil or flat-leaf parsley

1/8 teaspoon freshly ground white pepper

1. **Scrape the seeds out** of the cucumber halves with a spoon, running it down the channel in a long scooping action. Slice the cucumbers 1/8 inch thick.

2. **In a bowl,** combine the cucumbers and the salt. Toss together until the salt is distributed evenly. Cover and refrigerate for 2 hours (the salt will draw the excess moisture out of the cucumbers and will be rinsed off later).

3. **In a small bowl,** mix together the crème fraîche and mustard. Add 1/4 teaspoon of the lemon juice and taste the dressing. It should not taste sharp or acidic—just have a hint of lemon. Adjust the lemon juice to taste. Add the chervil and pepper and whisk to combine.

4. **Place the cucumbers** in a large colander and rinse very thoroughly under abundant cold running water. Press down on them with your hands or a large flat spoon to squeeze out the excess moisture. Transfer the cucumbers to paper towels and pat them dry with more paper towels, then transfer them to a salad bowl.

5. **Add the dressing** to the cucumbers and toss to coat evenly. Taste for seasoning, adding salt if necessary (since the salad will be served cold, the dressing can be a little saltier than normal). Cover and refrigerate the salad for at least 30 minutes or up to 2 hours, until chilled.

6. **Remove the salad** from the refrigerator 10 to 15 minutes before serving so that it will be cool, not cold.

Hot Goat Cheese Salad

(SALADE DE CHEVRE CHAUD)

In my opinion, the best goat cheese salad in all of France is made at the Thoumieux Restaurant in Paris, where a raw goat milk cheese called Cabecou is used. Raw milk cheeses are illegal in the United States, which truly amazes me. Our "food police" consider raw milk cheese dangerous due to the use of unpasteurized milk, but they allow copious amounts of colored, chemically infused junk food on our grocery store shelves. I have never stepped over a raw milk-cheese fatality in the streets of Europe. In Europe, the artisanal cheese makers produce cheese in a time-honored and perfectly safe (if time-consuming) fashion. Here, we make the product for profit, not for taste. So steps are skipped to save time (and money), and the result is inferior. Once you have eaten cheese in Europe, you will understand what it really is. Unfortunately, before an imported cheese enters the U.S.'s pristine world (of food coloring and chemicals), it must be pasteurized. There are, however, a group of artisans in this country working diligently to change the procedure and laws so that we can have the same good cheese that is produced in Europe. This particular recipe is usually made with frisée lettuce in France, but the varieties available here are too rough and prickly to serve on their own, so I add mesclun. 🌿 SERVES 6

6 cups mesclun salad greens, including frisée (about 3 ounces)

6 (1/4-inch-thick) slices French bread

Melted butter or olive oil

6 (1/2-inch-thick) rounds goat cheese, about 1 ounce each

1/2 cup pine nuts, toasted (page 30)

1/2 cup Simple Vinaigrette (page 118)

1. **Preheat the oven to 350°.**

2. **Thoroughly wash the salad greens** and dry them in a salad spinner. If they are large, tear them into bite-sized pieces.

3. **Place the bread on** a rimmed baking sheet and brush thoroughly on both sides with the melted butter. Toast in the hot oven for 5 to 8 minutes, turning once halfway through, until pale golden.

4. **Preheat the broiler.** Place a slice of goat cheese in the center of each slice of bread. Broil until the cheese has melted or is warmed and turns a light golden brown (depending on the age and moisture content of the cheese). Toss the salad greens with the dressing and divide among 6 plates. Place a warm cheese croûton on top of each individual salad and serve immediately.

Warm Vegetable Salad with Balsamic Vinegar and Honey

A colorful salad composed of sautéed vegetables and fresh greens. Haricots verts are slim little French green beans found in better markets. They have a sweet, bright flavor. To remove the leaves from watercress, hold the leaf and tender stem end in one hand, the thicker stem end in the other, and then twist the tender portion off. Watercress must be washed well, as sand tends to cling to the leaves. SERVES 6

1/2 pound haricots verts (fine French beans) or standard green beans

Sea salt

2 tablespoons extra virgin olive oil

1 yellow bell pepper, cored, seeded, and julienned

1 small head red cabbage, cored and thinly sliced

1 Belgian endive, halved, cored, and julienned

6 green onions, white and light green parts only, sliced 1/2 inch thick on the diagonal

2 tablespoons balsamic vinegar

2 tablespoons honey

1/2 cup tender leaves and stems of watercress

1 head Bibb lettuce, torn into bite-sized pieces, 6 whole outer leaves reserved for garnish

1/4 teaspoon freshly ground black pepper

1. **Haricots verts may be left whole.** If using standard green beans, trim off the stem ends and cut crosswise into thirds. Bring a large saucepan of water to a boil over high heat and add 1 teaspoon of salt. Add the beans to the pan and adjust the heat so the beans are simmering. When the beans are al dente, or just firm to the bite, drain in a colander (about 4 minutes for haricots verts, 6 minutes for green beans). Rinse thoroughly with cold running water until the beans are no longer hot (this stops the cooking and preserves the green color). Drain thoroughly and set aside.

2. **Place a large sauté pan** over medium-high heat. When the pan is very hot, add the olive oil and heat for 30 seconds. Add the bell pepper and sauté for 1 minute, stirring occasionally. Add the cabbage, endive, and green onions and sauté for about 1 1/2 minutes, just until all the vegetables are slightly wilted. Add the reserved green beans, vinegar, and honey. Toss the vegetables so that they are well coated with vinegar and honey.

3. **Add the watercress** and lettuce to the pan, toss together quickly, and remove from the heat. Add 1/3 to 1/2 teaspoon of salt and the pepper, taste and adjust the seasoning if necessary.

4. **Lay 1 whole lettuce leaf** on each individual plate, divide the salad among the plates, and serve immediately.

Strawberry-Spinach Salad

Though this may come as a surprise, a magical
match occurs between spinach and fresh strawberries.
Although both are in season in the late spring and
summer months, this salad would brighten any holiday table! Use flat-leaf spinach, as the flavor is much
sweeter and milder than the curly leaf variety. This
dressing is also excellent with a mixed fruit salad.
✒ SERVES 4

STRAWBERRY DRESSING

1 pint strawberries, sliced

2 tablespoons Raspberry Vinegar (page 121)

2 tablespoons sugar

1/2 cup safflower, sunflower, or extra virgin olive oil

1/4 teaspoon sea salt

1/8 teaspoon freshly ground black pepper

10 ounces fresh flat-leaf spinach, stemmed, washed,
and well dried

2 pints strawberries, sliced

1 small jicama bulb, peeled and julienned

1. **To prepare the dressing**, combine all the ingredients in a blender or food processor. Process
for about 15 seconds, until completely blended
and slightly thickened.

2. **Pass the dressing through** a fine-mesh strainer
to remove the seeds, pressing down on the fruit
pulp to extract all the juices.

3. **In a salad bowl**, combine the spinach, strawberries, and jicama. Add the dressing and toss to
coat evenly. Taste for seasoning and adjust with
salt and pepper if necessary. Serve immediately.

LESSON EIGHT

Pasta

IN THIS CHAPTER, I HAVE INCLUDED a few homemade egg pastas, some of my favorite sauces, and some great pasta and sauce combinations. I use egg pasta for all flat noodles, and I always use a hand-crank pasta machine. Electric pasta machines extrude the pasta using heat through a variety of templates and are advertised as easier, but in reality, all that heat yields a tough product. Homemade pasta—especially spinach, beet, and tomato—is superb, but that doesn't mean dried, store-bought pasta is inferior. There are two exceptional brands on the market, both Italian: De Cecco and Barilla. If you like fresh pasta but don't want to make your own, there are pasta shops springing up around the country where you can buy freshly made pasta. However, avoid the "fresh" pasta sold in sealed plastic containers in the refrigerated sections of supermarkets. That pasta is about as fresh as your doormat.

In Italy, pasta is served as a *primo piatto,* the traditional first plate that starts off every family meal. Like many Americans, I prefer to serve pasta as a main course with a leafy green salad and crusty bread. Italians also traditionally pair certain shapes of pasta with specific sauces, but for the purpose of teaching (both on my public television show and in this book), I have included pasta sauces that will work with any of the flavored egg pastas.

Pasta makes a simple meal, but there are a few tricks to cooking it correctly. Remember that the pasta serves as a "vehicle" for the sauce. The starch on the outside of the noodle should absorb the sauce, and there are some steps to follow to ensure the proper texture and "holding power."

Pasta Cooking Notes

Have you ever drained a pot of cooked pasta in a colander and found it glued together in a solid lump before you could add the sauce? This is what happens if the pasta is not cooked in enough water. The starch is released from the pasta into the boiling water and creates something like wallpaper paste. For the first pound of pasta to be cooked, bring 6 quarts of water to a boil, adding 3 quarts of water for each additional pound of pasta. Once the water is boiling, add 1 tablespoon of fine salt or 2 tablespoons of coarse salt to the water. You will not be consuming all that salt, because it will be drained away—it simply serves to flavor the pasta. Pasta cooked without salt will be quite bland.

Put the pasta in the boiling, salted water and stir it once or twice. Adding oil to the boiling water is one of the worst techniques I have ever heard of. The supposed reasons are two-fold: to prevent the pasta strands from sticking together and to keep the water from boiling over. In fact, the oil coats the pasta and prevents the sauce from being absorbed into it, or even sticking to it. And if you use the right size pot, you don't need to worry about the water boiling over.

When pasta is cooked correctly, it will be al dente or firm to the bite—not hard and not mushy. Never rinse cooked pasta in a colander, which supposedly prevents the pasta from sticking together. If enough water is used in cooking, the pasta will not stick together. Rinsing pasta chills it quickly and washes away the starch on the outside of the noodles. Some of the starch must be left on the pasta to help it absorb the sauce.

If you have leftover sauce, do not mix it with leftover pasta. Pasta should be cooked fresh for each use.

Always toss your pasta thoroughly with the sauce before serving. I'm always amused by television commercials and ads showing a bright red sauce parked in the middle of a large pile of naked pasta. Sauce should be absorbed into the pasta uniformly. It is also important to not have too much sauce, so that the pasta is swimming in a pool of it. A balance between sauce and pasta is the key.

Homemade Fresh Egg Pasta

Fresh egg pasta is great with a variety of sauces, but it can also be added to chicken or beef soups. These simple pasta recipes use a hand-crank pasta machine that does the rolling for you. If you do not want to invest in a pasta machine, the dough can be rolled out with a rolling pin to 1/16 to 1/8 of an inch, depending on the use.

For storing, fresh pasta must be well air-dried for about an hour before being sealed in plastic food storage bags. Some water will evaporate as it dries, which can cause molding if allowed to occur within a bag. Freeze fresh pasta in plastic containers that will offer the fragile noodles some protection in the freezer. If you live in a humid climate, I recommend that you always freeze fresh pasta—the humidity can prevent the pasta from ever drying completely, leading to molding.

When you start using fresh pasta as opposed to store-bought dried, you'll find that the weight equivalencies aren't exact. Dried pasta is sold by its dry weight, but it absorbs water as it cooks. A one-pound package of dried pasta actually yields more than one pound of cooked pasta. With fresh pasta, however, the water absorption rate is much less. Even if you allow fresh pasta to dry before cooking, it will only gain back a little more than the water weight it lost during drying. Therefore, if you're using a 1-pound package of dried pasta, I recommend removing 2 to 3 ounces for any recipe that calls for a pound of pasta. Don't get too obsessed with every little ounce, though. I include this information only so you will have a reference point and understand the differences between fresh and dried pasta.

❧ SERVES 3 TO 4 AS A FIRST OR MAIN COURSE

MAKES 1/2 POUND FOR A FIRST COURSE

1 1/3 cups unbleached all-purpose flour

2 large eggs

MAKES 1 POUND FOR A MAIN COURSE

2 cups unbleached all-purpose flour

3 large eggs

1. **Place the flour in a mound** on a large cutting board or a flat counter surface. Use the base of a measuring cup to make a large well in the center. Place the eggs inside the well. Using a fork, mix the eggs together and then begin to slowly incorporate the flour from the inner rim of the well, whisking 1 to 2 teaspoons of flour into the egg each time you stir, always taking the flour from the lower part of the rim. Push some of the flour off to the side and just whisk in enough so that the dough is not wet.

2. **Once the mixture becomes fairly solid,** scrape it up with a dough scraper and pull it together with your hands. Scrape the work surface, gathering enough flour to make a stiff but not dry dough. Once the dough feels stiff yet still pliable, do not work in any more flour. Scrape up all the excess flour and pass it through a fine-mesh strainer or tamis to remove any lumps.

3. **Wash, dry, and flour your hands.** Knead the dough mixture, continuing to incorporate just a

continued

little more of the sifted flour until the dough is no longer wet or sticky. Knead the dough for 2 to 3 minutes, working in small shakes of the flour a little at a time. The amount of flour left over will vary. The dough should be smooth and elastic, never stiff or dry. Cover the dough with plastic wrap and allow to rest at room temperature for 10 minutes. Now you are ready to start kneading it by machine. If you are making a portion of pasta with more than 2 eggs, divide the dough into 2 pieces for easier handling.

4. **Set the rollers of the pasta machine** at the widest setting. With the palm of your hand, flatten the ball of dough into a disk that will fit between the rollers.

5. **Pass the dough through the rollers**, cranking it through with one hand while you guide it out with the other. Fold the ends of the dough together to meet in the center, forming a rectangle, and press it firmly with the heel of your hand so that the layers are compressed and no air remains between them. Lightly flour both sides of the dough and pass through the rollers again. Repeat the rolling, folding, and flouring process 10 times at the widest setting.

6. **Now you are ready to stretch** and shape the dough for cutting. Each time you prepare to run the dough through the rollers, dust it lightly with flour to prevent it from sticking inside the machine. Pass the dough through the rollers, this time adjusting the rollers down 1 notch after each pass-through, until the desired thickness is reached, usually the second-to-last or the last notch, depending on the noodle style selected. (The second-to-last is used for standard pastas, the last for angel hair.) At this point, the pasta will be quite long, and it is helpful to have an extra set of hands to support it as it goes through the rollers. Cut the strips into 3 to 4 pieces and flour each lightly. Finally, pass each strip through the cutting attachment of the machine to achieve the desired size of noodles. Spread out the finished pasta on dry towels or a wooden rack until cooking (you can let it rest for a few minutes or use immediately).

7. **In a large pot, bring 6 quarts of water** to a boil for 1 pound of pasta, adding 3 quarts of water for every additional pound, and add 1 tablespoon fine sea salt or 2 tablespoons coarse sea salt. Add the pasta and stir once or twice to distribute. Cook for 2 to 3 minutes, until al dente (see Pasta Cooking Notes on page 130). Drain well, without rinsing, and immediately combine with a sauce and serve.

Spinach Pasta

Nothing can equal the visual appeal of pasta made with fresh spinach. The color is strikingly bright and the fresh taste comes through in the pasta itself. This pasta works well with a variety of sauces and preparations.

Spinach is extremely gritty and needs to be washed several times. Fill a sink with cold water and add the spinach leaves. Swirl the leaves around to shake the grit loose. Allow the grit to settle for a minute, and then lift the spinach from the water. Empty and rinse the sink. Repeat the process twice more to ensure the spinach is free of any grit.

❧ SERVES 3 TO 4 AS A MAIN COURSE

1 pound fresh spinach, stemmed

3 large eggs

2 1/4 to 2 1/2 cups unbleached all-purpose flour

I. **Bring a generous amount of** lightly salted water to a boil in a large pot. Add the spinach and cook for 5 to 6 minutes, until tender. Drain in a colander and run cold water over the spinach to stop the cooking process and preserve the bright green color. With your hands, press down hard on the spinach in the colander to remove as much moisture as possible. Spread the spinach between doubled layers of paper towel and continue to squeeze between the towels until completely dry (the spinach will resemble a fruit leather or roll-up). Remove the paper towels and, using a large chef's knife, chop the spinach very fine. Then, mash it with the side of the knife in a smearing action against the cutting board. Gather the spinach together in a small pile and repeat at least 20 times, until a smooth, velvety paste is formed—you should have about 1/4 cup.

2. **In a small bowl,** whisk together the eggs and spinach until well blended.

3. **Proceed from step 1** on page 131 in the master recipe for egg pasta, using the spinach-egg mixture in the center of the well of flour in place of the plain eggs.

Red or Orange Pasta

Beets will make a finished pasta that is light pink, while tomato paste produces a pale orange pasta. You will have to cook more beets than needed in order for the food processor to purée the beets fine enough for making a dough—use the leftover puréed beets as a side vegetable, as an addition to risotto (for the pink color), or in a salad dressing.

🌿 SERVES 3 TO 4 AS A MAIN COURSE

4 or 5 small beets (for beet pasta), or 1 1/2 heaping tablespoons tomato paste (for tomato pasta)

3 large eggs

2 1/4 to 2 3/4 cups unbleached all-purpose flour

1. **If you are making tomato pasta,** proceed to step 2. To prepare the beet purée: Leave at least 1 inch of the beet stems and all of the root ends intact, so that the beets will retain their juice. In a saucepan, combine the whole beets with enough water to cover them by 2 inches. Over medium-high heat, bring the water to a boil. Adjust the heat to achieve a simmer and cook the beets, uncovered, for about 15 minutes. When the beets are tender and easily pierced with a knife, transfer to a bowl and cool slightly. Peel the beets and place in the bowl of a food processor or blender. Add a spoonful or so of water and pulse on and off, scraping down the sides of the bowl, until you have a very fine, thick purée with no lumps. Add a little bit of extra water to help the purée move in the proces-

sor, if necessary. Transfer the purée to a fine-mesh strainer set over a bowl and allow the excess water and juice to drain out for about 10 minutes. Measure 3 heaping tablespoons of the beet purée for making the pasta, and reserve the remaining purée for another use.

2. **In a small bowl,** whisk together the eggs and the beet purée until well blended. If making orange pasta, whisk together the eggs and tomato paste.

3. **Proceed from step 1** on page 131 in the master recipe for egg pasta, using the beet-egg mixture or the tomato paste–egg mixture in the center of the well of flour in place of the plain eggs.

Potato Gnocchi

These simple potato-cheese dumplings complement many main courses. Every European country has their variation of the potato dumpling—this is the French version. Rather than baking it with cheese, gnocchi can also be served as a pasta; it goes well with a variety of sauces. ✒ SERVES 4 TO 6 AS A SIDE DISH

1 pound large baking potatoes, scrubbed

2 tablespoons unsalted butter, at room temperature

1 large egg, lightly beaten

1 cup unbleached all-purpose flour

3/4 cup freshly grated Parmesan cheese

1/2 teaspoon plus 1 tablespoon sea salt

1/4 teaspoon freshly ground white pepper

1/8 teaspoon freshly grated nutmeg

2 tablespoons unsalted butter, melted

1. **Preheat the oven to 400°.** Place the potatoes on a rack over a baking sheet, in the middle of the oven. Bake for 1 hour, until tender and easily pierced with a knife.

2. **Holding each hot potato** with a folded towel or potholder, halve the potatoes and immediately scoop out the pulp into a bowl, so that the steam evaporates. Discard the skins. Pass the potato through the coarse disk of a food mill or a potato ricer into a bowl.

3. **While the potatoes are still very hot,** add the softened butter and egg and beat until very smooth with a heavy wooden spoon. The heat of the potato will thicken the egg slightly. Beat in the flour with the spoon or work in with your hands until the dough is soft and slightly sticky. Mix in 1/2 cup of the Parmesan and add the 1/2 teaspoon salt, the pepper, and nutmeg. Let the mixture stand for 20 minutes, uncovered, so the flour can absorb the egg and butter.

4. **Flour your hands** and lightly flour a baking sheet. Cut off about a cup of the dough and form it into a rope, about 3/4 inch in diameter, by rolling it back and forth on a counter or wooden cutting board, using the palms of your hands. Cut the rope crosswise into 3/4-inch lengths. Roll each length in your palm to round the edges. Place a piece of dough on your fingertips and roll it off your fingers using the tines of a fork. Repeat with the remaining pieces of dough, placing the finished dumplings in a single layer on the floured baking sheet. Form more ropes and gnocchi until all the dough has been used.

5. **Preheat the oven to 400°.** Butter a large baking dish. Bring a large sauté pan of water to a boil and add the 1 tablespoon salt. Cook the gnocchi in batches, without overcrowding them in the pan. Adjust the heat under the pan as you cook,

continued

to keep the water just barely simmering (if the water boils too briskly, the gnocchi cook on the outside but stay raw on the inside). The gnocchi will sink to the bottom then rise to the surface. After they come to the surface, let them simmer for 1 to 2 minutes more. To test for doneness, remove one from the water and cut open—it should just be cooked through with no raw dough visible. With a fine-mesh skimmer or slotted spoon, remove the gnocchi from the pan, shaking off any excess water, and place them in the prepared baking dish. Continue until all the gnocchi are cooked.

6. **Sprinkle the gnocchi evenly** with the melted butter and remaining 1/4 cup Parmesan. (The gnocchi can be covered with plastic wrap and refrigerated for up to 8 hours at this point. The baking time will be slightly longer if they are coming from the refrigerator.) Bake in the oven for about 20 minutes, until they are warmed through and the top is lightly browned. Serve immediately.

Shaping Potato Gnocchi

Cut the dough ropes into 3/4-inch lengths

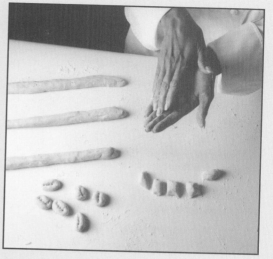

Roll in your palm to round the edges

Roll off your fingertips using the tines of a fork

Spaetzle

I love to serve these tiny Alsatian dumplings, cooked in butter until crispy, alongside Sautéed Veal Chops with a Parmesan Crust (page 175). You can also add spaetzle to chicken soup, to create a comforting chicken dumpling soup. ⚜ SERVES 4 TO 6 AS A SIDE DISH

2 1/2 cups plus 2 tablespoons unbleached
   all-purpose flour

Sea salt

3 large eggs, lightly beaten

1 1/4 cups whole milk or water, or as needed

2 tablespoons melted unsalted butter, for serving

Freshly ground white pepper

1. **In a large bowl,** whisk together the flour, a pinch of salt, and the eggs. Whisking all the time, add the milk, adding just enough to create a consistency similar to a very thick pancake batter. Let the batter rest for 15 minutes at room temperature.

2. **Bring a large saucepan** of generously salted water to a boil and place a large bowl of cold water next to the stovetop. Put the batter into a flat-bottomed colander with large holes (at least 1/4 inch in diameter) or a spaetzle maker. Using a plastic pastry scraper, push the batter through the device directly into the boiling water, using a sweeping motion. Scrape 1- or 2-inch lengths of batter off the bottom of the pan with a knife as they extrude. Or, transfer some of the batter to a plate and tip it slightly over the boiling wa-

ter (be careful not to burn your arm in the steam). Push about a tablespoon of batter to the edge of the plate with a damp knife and cut on the edge of the plate, letting the strips fall into the water (this method will produce larger dumplings). When the dumplings are cooked, they will float to the surface. This will take 30 seconds to 2 minutes, depending on size.

3. **Preheat the oven to 350°.** Using a fine-mesh skimmer, transfer the dumplings to the bowl of cold water. Let cool for 2 minutes. Again using the skimmer, remove the dumplings from the cold water, shake off any excess water, and transfer to a serving dish or saucepan. Add the melted butter. Continue making the dumplings in the same manner until all the batter is used. Stir the dumplings gently as you transfer them to the serving dish so that they are evenly coated with the butter. (The spaetzle can be covered with plastic wrap and refrigerated for up to 8 hours at this point. The baking time will be slightly longer if they are coming from the refrigerator.)

4. **To serve, bake the buttered** spaetzle for 5 to 8 minutes, until hot throughout. (Or, to make crispy, browned spaetzle, melt 1 tablespoon butter in a sauté pan over medium-high heat, add the spaetzle, and cook until crispy.) Taste for seasoning and adjust with additional salt and some pepper, if necessary.

Fresh Tomato Sauce

A simple sauce to serve with pasta, to top a pizza, or to use in stews or soups. Whenever I see lots of fresh, ripe tomatoes I make a large batch and freeze it in 1- or 2-cup containers. The secret is to squeeze the seeds and excess liquid from the center of the tomato. If the seeds and liquid are not discarded, it takes more than three times as long to reduce the tomatoes to a sauce consistency and the freshness in taste is lost. Italian plum, or "Roma," tomatoes are oblong in shape and meatier than round slicing tomatoes. They are always the appropriate choice for cooking and making sauces. Slicing tomatoes have a higher water content, and therefore yield a watery sauce. You may, if you choose, use canned tomatoes for this sauce, but be sure to get canned plum tomatoes packed in sauce.

The enriched version of this recipe is also good to have on hand. It's particularly nice in braised dishes like Osso Buco (page 176), or to add to soups like Minestrone (page 107). ✇ MAKES 2 TO 3 CUPS

4 pounds plum tomatoes

4 cloves garlic, peeled

1/2 cup extra virgin olive oil

20 fresh basil leaves, coarsely chopped (dried basil is not acceptable here)

2 teaspoons sea salt

1/4 teaspoon freshly ground black pepper

1. **Cut off the stem end of each tomato,** then cut each in half crosswise. Hold the tomatoes, cut-side down, over a sink and squeeze and rotate until the seeds and juice come out. Coarsely chop the tomatoes.

2. **Slightly crush the garlic cloves** with the side of a large knife. In a heavy pan or casserole, combine the garlic and olive oil. Over medium heat, cook for 1 minute. Add the tomatoes, cover, and cook, stirring occasionally, for about 5 minutes, until the tomatoes are softened. Keep an eye on them to make sure they don't scorch. Uncover the pan and continue cooking for 20 to 30 minutes, until the liquid has evaporated.

3. **Pass the tomato mixture through** the finest disk of a food mill. If the sauce is too thin, return it to the pan and simmer for a few minutes, until the sauce has thickened. Add the basil, salt, and pepper, taste for seasoning, and adjust if necessary. Use at once or cool, cover, and chill for up to 3 days. Or, the sauce can be frozen in small containers for up to 6 months.

Variation

ENRICHED TOMATO SAUCE: Before adding the tomatoes, add the following to step 2:

2 carrots, peeled and finely chopped

1 onion, finely chopped

2 celery stalks, finely chopped

Cook over medium heat for about 10 minutes, until all the vegetables are softened.

Spinach Gnocchi in Fresh Tomato Sauce (SEE PHOTO INSERT)

A wonderful taste of summer that can be easily served throughout the year if you've made the sauce in advance. Spinach gnocchi is best mixed in a food processor, which provides a better blend of the ingredients. If you do not have a processor, be sure to chop the spinach very fine. ❧ SERVES 8 AS A FIRST COURSE, 4 TO 6 AS A MAIN COURSE

GNOCCHI

1¼ pounds fresh flat-leaf spinach, stemmed

1½ cups whole-milk ricotta cheese

1½ cups freshly grated Parmesan cheese (use the fine holes of the grater)

¾ cup unbleached all-purpose flour

2 large eggs, lightly beaten

6 tablespoons olive oil

1 teaspoon sea salt

¼ teaspoon freshly ground black pepper

¼ teaspoon freshly grated nutmeg

6 cups Fresh Tomato Sauce (page 139)

15 fresh basil leaves, finely chopped

2 cups drained and shredded fresh mozzarella

1. **Bring a generous amount** of lightly salted water to a boil. Add the spinach and cook for 5 to 6 minutes, until tender. Drain in a colander and run cold water over the spinach to stop the cooking process and preserve the bright green color. With your hands, press down hard on the spinach in the colander to remove as much moisture as possible. Spread the spinach in between doubled layers of paper towel and continue to squeeze between towels until completely dry (the spinach will resemble a fruit leather or roll up). Place the spinach in the bowl of a food processor and process until a smooth velvety paste is formed.

2. **Place the spinach, ricotta,** ½ cup of the Parmesan, flour, eggs, 2 tablespoons of the olive oil, salt, pepper, and nutmeg, in the bowl of a food processor. Process until completely uniform in color and texture: it should be soft and thick. Cover the bowl and refrigerate for at least 2 and up to 8 hours, until the mixture is stiff and cold.

3. **Preheat the oven to 350°** and lightly flour a baking sheet. Bring a large saucepan of salted water to a boil over high heat. Remove the pasta dough from the refrigerator. Dip 2 soup spoons into a bowl of cold water. Scoop up 1 rounded spoonful of the mixture with 1 spoon and shape with the interior of the other spoon. Pass the

mixture back and forth between the spoons until an elongated oval is formed. Continue shaping the gnocchi, placing them on the prepared baking sheet as they are done. You should have about 24 dumplings.

4. **Working in several batches**, drop the gnocchi into the boiling water. The gnocchi will sink to the bottom of the pan, then rise to the top. Allow the gnocchi to simmer for 1 minute after they rise to the surface. Remove the gnocchi with a fine-mesh strainer, shake off any excess water, and place in a bowl. Cook the remaining gnocchi in the same way.

5. **Mix the tomato sauce** and basil together. Pour a generous portion of the tomato sauce into individual baking dishes. Place the dishes on 1 large or 2 small baking sheets. Arrange 3 gnocchi on top of the sauce in each dish for a first course, or 4 to 6 gnocchi for a main course. (You can hold the gnocchi at this point for several hours before baking.) Sprinkle evenly with the remaining 1 cup Parmesan and scatter with the mozzarella. Drizzle the remaining 4 tablespoons olive oil evenly over all and bake for 10 to 15 minutes, until the sauce bubbles and the cheese begin to melt. Cool for 5 minutes and serve.

Pasta with Fresh Tomato Sauce, Prosciutto, Onion, and Pecorino

A quick but delicious dinner that can be whipped up in no time, especially if you've made your tomato sauce ahead. A nice variation for this dish is to omit the prosciutto and onion and add 1 1/2 cups cubed fresh mozzarella cheese. SERVES 6 AS A FIRST COURSE, 4 AS A MAIN COURSE

3 tablespoons extra virgin olive oil

1 onion, cut into 1/4-inch dice

3 cups Fresh Tomato Sauce (page 139)

1/2 pound prosciutto, cut into 1/4- to 1/2-inch pieces

1/2 cup chopped fresh basil

Sea salt and freshly ground black pepper

1 pound Homemade Fresh Egg, Spinach, or Orange Pasta (pages 131, 133, and 134), or 14 ounces dried fettuccine

1/2 cup freshly grated Pecorino cheese

1. **In a large saucepan**, heat the olive oil over medium heat and add the onion. Cook, stirring occasionally, for 3 minutes, until softened. Add the tomato sauce, prosciutto, and basil. Taste and adjust seasoning with salt and pepper, if necessary. Bring the sauce to a simmer and cook for 5 minutes to allow the flavors to marry.

2. **Bring 6 quarts of water** to a boil in a large pot and add 1 tablespoon fine sea salt or 2 tablespoons coarse sea salt. Add the pasta and stir once or twice to distribute. Cook until al dente (see Pasta Cooking Notes on page 130). Homemade fresh pasta will take 3 to 4 minutes to reach the al dente stage. Drain well, without rinsing, and immediately add to the sauce. Add 1/4 cup of the Pecorino and toss to combine.

3. **Divide the pasta among** individual warmed plates or bowls. Sprinkle a little of the remaining cheese over each portion and serve at once.

Penne alla Puttanesca

Puttanesca loosely translated means "lady of the night." (Presumably, she is as hot and spicy as this recipe.) This is my favorite pasta sauce; it's bright and fresh, with a lively combination of ingredients.

Anchovies packed in salt are preferable for this recipe, but canned anchovies may be substituted, and in a pinch you could even use 1 tablespoon of anchovy paste.

If you like, to simplify this already simple recipe, use a few tablespoons of Tapenade (page 96), an olive spread from the south of France. The tapenade already contains olives, capers, and anchovies, so those ingredients don't need to be added.

☙ SERVES 4 AS A MAIN COURSE

1 cup olive oil

10 cloves garlic, minced

4 large jalapeño peppers, stemmed, seeded, and minced

4 pounds plum tomatoes, peeled, seeded, and cut into 1/2-inch dice

32 large cured black olives, pitted and chopped

2 tablespoons capers, rinsed

2 teaspoons dried oregano

1/4 teaspoon freshly ground black pepper

16 whole salt-cured anchovies, rinsed, boned (page 1), and finely chopped

1 pound dried penne pasta

1/4 cup finely chopped fresh flat-leaf parsley, for garnish

1. **Heat the olive oil** in a large sauté pan over low heat. Add the garlic and jalapeños and cook, watching carefully and stirring occasionally, for 1 to 2 minutes, until slightly softened and the aroma is released. Do not let the garlic brown. Add the tomatoes, olives, capers, oregano, and pepper and increase the heat to medium-high. Cook, uncovered, for 3 to 4 minutes, stirring occasionally, until the tomatoes are cooked through.

2. **Add the anchovies** and cook for 1 minute more to blend the flavors. Taste and adjust the seasoning with salt and pepper if necessary (capers, olives, and anchovies are all very salty, so the sauce may not need any additional salt). Cover and set aside.

3. **Bring 3 quarts of water** to a boil in a large pot and add 1 1/2 teaspoons fine sea salt or 1 tablespoon coarse sea salt. Add the penne and stir once or twice to distribute. Cook according to package instructions, until al dente (see Pasta Cooking Notes on page 130). Drain well, without rinsing, and immediately add to the sauce. Toss together thoroughly, so that each strand of pasta is coated with sauce. Taste and adjust seasoning with salt and pepper, if necessary.

4. **Divide the pasta** among individual warmed plates or bowls. Sprinkle the parsley evenly over each portion and serve at once.

Fettuccine with Pesto and Cream

This is a truly elegant and simple first course. It is subtly rich from just a little cream and has the bright, fresh flavor of pesto. The starch on the cooked noodles absorbs the cream, with a luscious result. A nice serving variation is to pair it with salmon—either poached or sautéed: just serve the finished salmon over the sauced fettuccine, and dollop another spoonful of pesto on top of the salmon.

SERVES 6 AS A FIRST COURSE OR SIDE DISH, 4 AS A MAIN COURSE

1/2 cup pesto (page 33)

1/2 pound Homemade Fresh Egg or Spinach Pasta (pages 131 and 133), or 7 ounces dried thin fettuccine

1/4 cup heavy cream

Salt and freshly ground white pepper

1. **In a small bowl,** combine the pesto with 1 tablespoon of hot water. Whisk together to loosen the pesto, so it will combine easily and evenly with the pasta.

2. **Bring 3 quarts of water** to a boil in a large pot and add 1 1/2 teaspoons fine sea salt or 1 tablespoon coarse sea salt. Add the fettucine and stir once or twice to distribute. Cook according to package instructions for dried pasta, until al dente (see Pasta Cooking Notes on page 130). Homemade fresh pasta will take 3 to 4 minutes to reach the al dente stage.

3. **Drain the pasta well,** without rinsing. Immediately transfer to a warmed serving bowl and add the cream. Toss to thoroughly combine, letting the cream absorb into all the strands of pasta evenly. Add the pesto mixture and toss again, until thoroughly blended. Taste and adjust the seasoning with salt and pepper, if necessary.

4. **Divide the pasta** among individual warmed plates or bowls. Serve immediately.

Fettuccine Alfredo

A very simple and classic pasta dish that makes a satisfying first course; it's generally too rich for a main course. Proper reduction of the cream is the key to this recipe—you want it to achieve a creamy, not milky, consistency. My students are always hesitant to boil cream and cringe when I turn up the heat.

✍ SERVES 4 AS A FIRST COURSE

1 1/2 cups heavy cream

3 tablespoons unsalted butter

1/2 pound Homemade Fresh Egg, Spinach, Red,
    or Orange Pasta (pages 131, 133, and 134),
    or 7 ounces dried thin fettuccine

2/3 cup freshly grated Parmigiano-Reggiano cheese,
    plus extra for serving

1/8 teaspoon freshly grated nutmeg

1/4 teaspoon sea salt

1/8 teaspoon freshly grated white pepper

1. **In a large saucepan,** combine the cream and butter. Over high heat, bring the mixture to a boil and cook, stirring occasionally, for 5 to 8 minutes, until thickened to a coating consistency (coats the back of a spoon and leaves a trail when your finger is drawn through it).

2. **While the sauce is simmering,** bring 3 quarts of water to a boil in a large pan and add 1 1/2 teaspoons fine sea salt or 1 tablespoon coarse sea salt. Add the fettucine and stir once or twice to distribute. Cook until al dente (see Pasta Cooking Notes on page 130). Homemade fresh pasta will take 3 to 4 minutes to reach the al dente stage.

3. **Drain the pasta well,** without rinsing. Immediately transfer to the pan with the cream-butter mixture and place over low heat. Toss to thoroughly combine, letting the cream coat all the strands of pasta evenly. Add the Parmigiano, nutmeg, salt, and pepper. Toss again, until all the ingredients are evenly blended and the pasta has absorbed most of the cream mixture. Taste and adjust seasoning with salt and pepper, if necessary.

4. **Divide the pasta** among 4 warmed plates or bowls. Serve immediately, passing a little extra Parmigiano on the side.

Fresh Pasta with Fried Sage Butter

Fresh sage makes an interesting infused butter that is absorbed into the pasta, while the crisp fried sage leaves add an interesting texture. This pasta is especially nice with Sautéed Veal Chops with a Parmesan Crust (page 175). It is imperative that the sage be completely dry, which means it must be slowly air-dried or freshly picked, not spun dry in a salad spinner or patted with paper towels. Any water left on the sage will splatter in the hot butter.

🌿 SERVES 4 AS A FIRST COURSE OR SIDE DISH

1/2 cup clarified butter (page 31)

20 to 25 fresh sage leaves, completely dry

1/2 pound Homemade Fresh Egg, Spinach, or Orange Pasta (pages 131, 133, and 134), or 7 ounces dried thin fettuccine

1. **In a small saucepan**, melt the butter over medium-high heat. Add the sage leaves in batches and sauté, without stirring, until they are crisp but not browned. As soon as the leaves become crisp, transfer with a slotted spoon to a double layer of paper towels. Be careful not to let the leaves burn, or they will turn bitter. Remove the butter from the heat and set aside.

2. **Bring 3 quarts of water** to a boil in a large pot and add 1 1/2 teaspoons fine sea salt or 1 tablespoon coarse sea salt. Add the fettucine and stir once or twice to distribute. Cook until al dente (see Pasta Cooking Notes on page 130). Homemade fresh pasta will take from 3 to 4 minutes to reach the al dente stage.

3. **Drain the pasta well**, without rinsing. Immediately transfer to a warmed serving bowl and add 1/4 cup of the sage cooking butter, tossing well to coat all the strands of pasta evenly. Taste, and if more butter is needed, add it a few tablespoons at a time. Reserving a few whole crispy sage leaves for garnish, crush the remaining ones and toss with the pasta. Divide among individual warmed plates and serve at once, garnished with the whole sage leaves. (Any remaining butter may be chilled or frozen and used to sauté chicken or fish.)

Pasta with Kale and Spicy Italian Sausage (SEE PHOTO INSERT)

This delightful mix of spicy sausage, deep green kale, and bright red Roma tomatoes has all the colors of the Italian flag and enough substance to satisfy the most hearty appetites. My favorite pasta shape, orrechiette ("little ears" in Italian), holds all the tiny bits of sauce and meat nicely. ✒ SERVES 4 AS A MAIN COURSE

3 cups kale, stemmed and cut into 2-inch-long strips

2 tablespoons olive oil

3 tablespoons unsalted butter

1 pound hot Italian sausage, casings removed

2 cloves garlic, minced

1 to 2 teaspoons crushed red pepper flakes

2 tablespoons unbleached all-purpose flour

2 cups Chicken Stock (page 40)

1/2 pound dried orrechiette or penne pasta

10 plum tomatoes, peeled, seeded, and chopped

10 fresh basil leaves, cut into chiffonade (page 5)

1 1/2 cups freshly grated Pecorino or Parmesan cheese

1. **Bring a large pot of salted water** to a boil. Add the kale and cook for 5 to 10 minutes, depending on the age and toughness of the leaves, until tender. Drain in a colander and immediately run cold water over the leaves to stop the cooking process and retain the bright green color. Set aside.

2. **In a large sauté pan,** heat the olive oil and 2 tablespoons of the butter over medium heat. Sauté the sausage for 5 minutes, until it is slightly browned, breaking it up with a wooden spoon. Add the garlic and pepper flakes and stir together for 1 minute, until the aroma is released. Add the flour and cook, stirring constantly, for 1 minute more, until the flour is well absorbed.

3. **Add the stock** and increase the heat to high. Bring the mixture to a boil, then decrease the heat and adjust to a brisk simmer. Simmer until the mixture has reduced to 1/2 to 3/4 cup. The sauce should be quite thick. Remove from the heat, cover, and keep warm while you cook the pasta.

4. **Bring 3 quarts of water** to a boil in a large pot and add 1 1/2 teaspoons fine sea salt or 1 tablespoon coarse sea salt. Add the orrechiette and stir once or twice to distribute. Cook until al dente (see Pasta Cooking Notes on page 130). Drain the pasta well, without rinsing.

5. **Return the reserved sauce** to low heat until warm. Whisk the remaining 1 tablespoon of butter into the warm sauce. Immediately add the tomatoes, kale, basil, and drained pasta. Toss together with tongs and warm for 1 or 2 minutes more to allow the pasta to absorb the sauce. Add 1 cup of the Pecorino and toss to distribute the cheese evenly. Divide the pasta among individual warmed plates or bowls, and sprinkle each portion with some of the remaining cheese. Serve immediately.

Seafood

WHEN I BEGAN COOKING IN THE EARLY SEVENTIES, the only fish to be found was frozen, and generally had a thick layer of bread crumbs pressed on top—the dreaded fish stick. Now, fortunately, fresh seafood has become readily available all across the country. Following my professional culinary training in the eighties, I began working with local markets and purveyors to provide the home cook with high-quality seafood. Fortunately, near my home and the school, we have a true artisan fishmonger. In the early years, I worked directly with Neil Schwarz, the owner of the shop. He would accommodate my requests for items not usually featured in his retail case. I generally ordered small amounts that were probably bothersome for Schwarz to procure, but I assured him that I would send customers to his store. As predicted, my students have become some of his best customers. No matter where you live, the key is to work directly with the local market managers to guarantee great quality and variety.

For this chapter, I have selected a variety of cooking methods—sautéing, poaching, grilling, cooking in paper, baking, and steaming—that will open the door to many other similar dishes. You will notice that I have left out broiling. Unless you have a well-made broiler, such as we have at the school, broiling most often produces "fish jerky"—too dry and with a too-strong flavor. Seafood must be cooked quickly, efficiently, and must never be overcooked. Sauces are included with many of the recipes that will enhance, but never mask, the flavor of perfectly prepared seafood. These are some of my favorite seafood recipes.

Poached Salmon with Pesto

(SEE PHOTO INSERT)

This is one of my favorite fast meals. Pesto is easily made in large batches and can be used for many quick meals. Here, versatile pesto accompanies a gently poached piece of salmon. To create a main course, this pairing can be joined with some freshly cooked pasta tossed with a little more pesto.

I use fillets here because salmon steaks are crosscut from a whole fish and thus contain both bones and skin. I find this cut bothersome to deal with. In many instances, "bone-in" means improved flavor. With salmon steaks, however, it means increased work. ✀ SERVES 6

POACHING LIQUID

16 cups water

1 cup dry white wine or dry vermouth

1/2 fennel bulb, coarsely chopped (optional)

1 thick slice onion

10 black peppercorns

3 sprigs thyme

3 sprigs parsley

1 Turkish bay leaf

2 (3-inch) lengths leek or celery

6 (6- to 8-ounce) salmon fillets, skin on

6 tablespoons pesto (page 33)

1. **To prepare the poaching liquid,** in a large casserole, combine the water, wine, fennel, onion, and peppercorns. Make a bouquet garni by tying the thyme, parsley, and bay leaf between the leek pieces with kitchen twine. Add the bouquet garni to the pan and place it over high heat. Bring the liquid to a boil and simmer for 3 minutes to allow the ingredients to infuse their flavor into the water.

2. **Add the salmon fillets** to the poaching liquid and adjust the heat to achieve a shimmer (page 20). Poach the fish for 10 to 12 minutes, until the salmon feels firm but still yields to the touch. The fish should be rare to medium rare in the center. Remove the fish from the liquid and carefully remove the skin from the fillets with a sharp knife.

3. **To serve, transfer each fillet** to individual warmed plates with a large slotted spoon or a fine-mesh, flat strainer, letting as much liquid as possible drain away. Top with 1 tablespoon of the pesto and serve immediately.

Steamed Monkfish with Vegetable Cream Sauce

Monkfish has the reputation of being the ugliest fish in the ocean, with its enormous, wide head and mouth. Only the tail meat is used. The meat is firm, somewhat mild, and holds up well in steaming. Monkfish matches perfectly with this simple vegetable cream sauce. If for some reason you're trying to cut cream out of your diet, it can be omitted and the fish served simply with steamed vegetables.

Steaming is a very simple cooking technique. If you do not have a steamer, you can rig one up by making a long "rope" using aluminum foil: tear off a length of foil about 18 inches long and then roll it up, lengthwise, into a rope. Curl the rope into a coil, leaving about one inch of space in between the ends of the rope. Place the coil on the bottom of a 3-quart sauté pan. Add steaming liquid to come just below the top of the coil and place a bowl about 2 inches smaller in diameter than the rim of the saucepan on top of the coil.
SERVES 4

STEAMING LIQUID

2 cups water

1 cup dry white wine or dry vermouth

2 leeks, white part only, thinly sliced

1¹/₂ pounds monkfish, cut into 4 fillets
Sea salt and freshly ground white pepper

SAUCE

1 large or 2 small carrots, peeled and julienned

1 leek, light green part only, julienned

¹/₂ cup heavy cream

2 tablespoons finely chopped fresh tarragon or basil

2 tablespoons cold unsalted butter, cut into 4 pieces

2 plum tomatoes, concassé (peeled, seeded, and diced)

Salt and freshly ground white pepper

Finely chopped fresh parsley, for garnish

1. **Place the water, wine,** and leeks in the bottom of a steamer pan. Bring the liquid to a boil, lower the temperature to achieve a simmer, and cook for 5 minutes to infuse the flavor of the leeks into the liquid. Season the fish with salt and pepper. Insert the steamer rack and arrange the monkfish inside. Cover the pan and steam for 7 to 8 minutes, until the fish is firm and opaque. Check the liquid level occasionally to be sure the pan does not boil dry; add more water if necessary to maintain a scant 1-inch level. Transfer the cooked fish to a warm platter, cover with foil, and keep warm in a low 200° oven while you finish the sauce.

2. **Pass the leftover steaming liquid** through a fine-mesh strainer into a small saucepan, discarding

continued

the solids, and place over medium heat. Add the carrot and leek and simmer for 5 minutes. Strain the broth again, reserving the liquid and vegetables separately. Return the liquid to the saucepan and reduce over high heat until only about 2 tablespoons remain. Stir in the cream and any juices that have collected on the fish platter. Simmer, stirring occasionally, for about 8 minutes, until reduced by half, to about 2/3 cup. The sauce should have thickened to a coating consistency (coats the back of a spoon and leaves a trail when your finger is drawn through it). Stir in the tarragon and simmer for 1 minute.

3. **Remove the pan from the heat** and add the cold butter all at once. Immediately begin whisking and whisk until the butter is completely incorporated. Add the carrot, leek, and tomatoes to the sauce and warm very gently, but do not allow the sauce to boil. Season with salt and pepper, taste and adjust the seasoning.

4. **Divide the monkfish** among individual warmed plates and spoon some of the sauce over the top. Scatter with a little parsley and serve immediately.

Sautéed Sea Bass with Lemon-Herb Butter

This is a good example of a dish that is quite excellent without a sauce and really superb with one. The recipe highlights several important cooking techniques: deglazing, reducing, and mounting the reduced liquid with butter. If you are looking for a quicker, easier meal, however, you can skip the reduction sauce and just place a tablespoon or so of the Lemon-Herb Butter on each fillet. A thick, firm-fleshed fish, such as salmon, will work well in place of the sea bass. I especially like the flavor of the fresh fennel tops, but any combination of tender fresh herbs will do. The French anise-flavored liqueur Pernod gives an enticing flavor to the sauce, but it is fine without it.

The caramelized juices of the fish provide a deep dimension of flavor that is crucial to the success of this dish. However, three important steps must be taken to ensure that the fish caramelizes rather than steams: First, the fish must be dried with paper towels to remove excess moisture. Second, once the fish is coated with flour it must immediately be placed into the hot sauté pan. (Floured meat and seafood become gooey in a short time and will not yield a crisp crust after cooking.) Third, be sure to leave at least one inch of space in between the pieces of fish in the sauté pan so that the steam can escape from the cooking surface. (Overcrowding creates a steam bath and prevents efficient caramelization.) 🌿 SERVES 6

LEMON-HERB BUTTER

1/2 cup unsalted butter, at room temperature

1/2 cup chopped feathery green fennel tops, or 3 tablespoons finely chopped fresh tarragon

10 fresh basil leaves, finely chopped

Finely chopped zest of 1 lemon

1 teaspoon freshly squeezed lemon juice

6 (3-inch-thick) pieces of skinless sea bass, 6 to 8 ounces each

3/4 cup finely chopped mixed fresh herbs, including feathery green fennel tops, tarragon, flat-leaf parsley, and basil

1/2 cup unbleached all-purpose flour

1 teaspoon sea salt

1/4 teaspoon freshly ground white pepper

Extra virgin olive oil, for sautéing

1/2 cup dry white wine or dry vermouth

1/4 cup Pernod (optional)

1. **To prepare the herb butter,** combine the butter, fennel, basil, and lemon zest and juice in a small bowl. Mix together well. Cover and refrigerate for at least 4 hours and up to 1 day. Or, freeze for 1 month.

continued

2. **Thoroughly dry the sea bass** with paper towels. With a small sharp knife, cut a 2-inch-long pocket in the middle of the side of each fillet, cutting halfway through the fillet. Fill each pocket with an equal amount of the mixed herbs.

3. **Preheat the oven to 375°.** In a large shallow bowl, whisk together the flour, salt, and pepper.

4. **Heat a large heavy sauté pan** over high heat and add enough olive oil to coat the bottom of the pan by 1/8 inch. When the oil is very hot and shimmering (page 20), dredge the fish in the flour mixture, coating all sides, and tap off the excess. Place the fish in the sauté pan and cook for 2 to 3 minutes, until browned and crisp. With a flexible metal turner, carefully turn the fish to the other side, keeping the crust intact, and cook for the same amount of time.

5. **Transfer the fish** to a wire rack placed inside of a baking dish and bake for 7 to 8 minutes, until the fish is firm but slightly yielding to the touch. If unsure, cut gently into the center of 1 fillet to make sure it is barely opaque. Be very careful not to overcook.

6. **While the fish is baking,** finish the sauce. Remove the prepared butter from the refrigerator and cut into 1/2-inch chunks. Remove any excess oil from the sauté pan by dabbing the pan with paper towels, leaving the flavorful brown drippings behind, but removing any that are blackened. Place the pan over high heat for about 30 seconds, until hot. Add the wine and stir to deglaze the pan, scraping up all the drippings. Cook for about 4 minutes, until reduced to about 1 teaspoon. Add the Pernod and cook over high for about 3 minutes more, until reduced to 1 or 2 teaspoons. Decrease the heat to very low and add the butter all at once. Immediately begin to incorporate the butter, either by shaking the pan back and forth over the burner, or by tipping the pan and whisking the butter into the pooled liquid. Do not allow the sauce to boil or it will separate. The idea is to emulsify the butter into the liquid with the use of gentle heat, thus forming a creamlike consistency. Remove the sauce from the heat and pass through a fine-mesh strainer. Season to taste with salt and pepper.

7. **Transfer the cooked fish** to individual warmed plates and drizzle the sauce over the fish. Serve immediately.

Shrimp with Shiitake Mushrooms over Pasta

This simple but luscious dish can be served as a rich appetizer or as a main course. Note that the chopped garlic is added with other ingredients, in this case the shrimp and mushrooms, to protect it from burning. To make your cooking process go smoothly, place the water on to boil for the pasta just before adding the wine to the sauté pan in step 2. ❦ SERVES 4

1 pound large shrimp, peeled and deveined

1/4 cup clarified butter (page 31)

1 tablespoon minced shallot

1 pound shiitake mushrooms, stemmed and quartered

1 clove garlic, minced

Salt and freshly ground white pepper

1/2 cup dry white wine

1 1/4 cups heavy cream

2 tablespoons chopped fresh herbs (chives, tarragon, parsley, or a combination)

3/4 pound angel hair pasta or thin fettuccine

1. **Thoroughly dry the shrimp** with paper towels. In a large frying pan, heat the butter over medium-high heat, until it starts to ripple. Add the shallot and cook, stirring, for about 30 seconds, until slightly softened. Add the shrimp, mushrooms, and garlic, and season with salt and pepper. Sauté, tossing frequently, for 3 to 5 minutes, until the shrimp are pink. With a slotted spoon, transfer the shrimp and mushrooms to a platter, leaving as much cooking liquid and juices in the pan as possible. Cover the platter with aluminum foil while you finish the sauce.

2. **Return the pan to** medium-high heat and add the wine. Adjust the heat so the wine simmers briskly, and cook for 2 to 4 minutes, until reduced to just a few tablespoons of liquid. Stir in 1 cup of the cream and continue to reduce for 6 to 10 minutes, until the mixture has thickened to a coating consistency (coats the back of a spoon and leaves a trail when your finger is drawn through it). Add 1 1/2 tablespoons of the herbs and return the shrimp and mushroom mixture to the pan. Stir for about 2 minutes, until warmed through. Taste and adjust the seasoning with salt and pepper. Keep warm until serving.

3. **In a large pot** of salted boiling water, cook the pasta until al dente. Drain in a colander and return to the empty saucepan over low heat. Add the remaining 1/4 cup cream and stir for about 1 minute, until it has all been absorbed into the pasta. Add the shrimp mixture and sauce and toss to coat evenly. Divide the pasta among warmed plates and garnish with the remaining 1/2 tablespoon herbs. Serve immediately.

Sole Fillets with Citrus Zest in Parchment

This quick, low-calorie recipe develops a wonderful flavor through the addition of finely chopped orange and lemon zest and fresh chives. The fish is cooked in parchment paper packets, allowing it to steam in its own juices. If you prefer to serve this with a sauce, try an Ecole de Cuisine favorite, Citrus Butter Sauce (page 60). For a truly dazzling dish, use all three of the butter sauces, White Wine (page 59), Tomato (page 61), and Citrus. The colors are striking and the taste exceptional.

Since you cannot see or touch the fish to test for doneness, I have found that 10 minutes is sufficient time for 10 to 12 ounces of fish per packet. The parchment will become spotted and brown at around the same time the fish is done. ✍ SERVES 6

12 (4- to 5-ounce) or 6 (10-ounce) sole or other lean
    white fish fillets

Sea salt and freshly ground white pepper

Finely chopped zest of 2 oranges

Finely chopped zest of 2 lemons

1/2 cup chopped fresh chives

2/3 cup Citrus Butter Sauce (optional, page 60),
    kept warm in a bain-marie (page 28)

1. **Preheat the oven to 425°.** Cut 6 pieces of parchment paper into heart shapes measuring about 12 inches long and 10 inches at the widest point (folding the paper in half lengthwise makes it easier to cut an even heart shape). At their widest point, the hearts should be at least 3 inches wider than the fish. Butter the inside of each heart to within 2 inches of the edges of the paper.

2. **Place 2 small or 1 large** sole fillet, skin side down, on one half of each heart, tucking the slender ends underneath the meatier portion of the fish to make an even thickness. Season with salt and pepper. Divide the orange and lemon zests and chives evenly among the 6 portions. Fold the uncovered half of each heart over the fish and align the edges. Fold the edges over by about 1/2 inch. Then, make a series of crimps, about 1/2 inch apart, all around the packet to seal the heart tightly. Place the packets on 2 large baking sheets and bake for 10 minutes.

3. **Remove from the oven** and cut each packet open with scissors. The fish will be creamy white in color. Using a large slotted spoon, transfer each serving to an individual warmed plate. Drizzle the sauce over the fish and serve immediately.

Preparing the Parchment

Cut the parchment into a heart shape

Fold the edges over by 1/2 inch

Make a series of crimps about 1/2 inch apart

The sealed package

Coquilles St. Jacques

(SEE PHOTO INSERT)

After having fresh, sweet scallops in France, I found the scallops sold in most American markets to be a sad substitute for the real thing. Most grocery store scallops are treated with tri-poly phosphate, a preservative that has about as much flavor as fish-flavored aluminum foil. These pumped-up, preserved scallops not only taste bad, but also shrink, when cooked, into tough hockey pucks. When buying scallops, ask for "diver caught" or "dry-packed," neither of which contains the preservative. The larger scallops are sea scallops, and the tiny scallops are bay scallops. Either one may be used in this recipe.

Specialty cookware shops (including my own, see page 251) sell scallop shells that have been packaged specially for making Coquilles St. Jacques. You can also use 4- to 5-ounce shallow ceramic baking dishes. ✍ SERVES 6

2 cups water

1 cup dry white wine

3 shallots, minced

1 Turkish bay leaf

Pinch of sea salt

1 pound sea scallops, side muscle removed, or bay scallops

SAUCE

1 teaspoon freshly squeezed lemon juice

3 tablespoons unsalted butter

3 tablespoons unbleached all-purpose flour

3/4 cup heavy cream

1/2 teaspoon sea salt

1/8 teaspoon freshly ground white pepper

6 tablespoons freshly grated Parmesan or shredded Gruyère cheese

1. **In a saucepan,** bring the water, wine, shallots, bay leaf, and salt to a boil over medium-high heat. Add the scallops and decrease the heat until the liquid is just shimmering (page 20). Sea scallops should be cooked for about 3 minutes, until opaque and with a slight spring, but not firm. The smaller bay scallops will take only about 1 minute.

2. **Pass the contents** of the pan through a fine-mesh strainer into another large saucepan and place it over high heat. Discard the bay leaf and place the cooked scallops in a bowl. Cover with aluminum foil and set aside while you make the sauce.

3. **To prepare the sauce,** bring the strained poaching liquid to a boil and add the lemon juice. Boil until the liquid is reduced to 1 cup. This will take 10 to 15 minutes.

4. **In a small saucepan,** melt the butter over medium-low heat. Thoroughly stir in the flour and cook, stirring occasionally, for 1 to 2 minutes, until the mixture is foaming but not brown. Remove from the heat and allow the mixture to cool slightly. Whisk a few tablespoons of the hot poaching liquid into the butter-flour mixture (called a roux), then whisk the entire butter-flour mixture back into the reduced poaching liquid. Whisk in the cream and place the pan over medium-high heat. Boil, stirring occasionally, for 5 to 10 minutes, until the mixture reaches a coating consistency (coats the back of a spoon and leaves a trail when your finger is drawn through it). Season with salt and pepper, taste, and adjust the seasoning as necessary.

5. **Divide the scallops** among 6 individual scallop shells or baking dishes and top each with an equal quantity of the sauce. Scatter 1 tablespoon of the cheese over each portion and place the shells on a large baking sheet. Bake immediately, or cover and refrigerate for up to 4 hours.

6. **Shortly before serving,** preheat the broiler until very hot. Set the baking sheet 4 inches from the heat and cook for about 1 minute, until the cheese topping is melted and bubbling. Serve immediately.

Shrimp in a Shell-Infused Sauce

This secret ingredient in this sauce is the shells. No, the shells are not eaten, but their tremendous flavor is released into the stock and cream in a process called infusion. After simmering, the mixture is pressed through a fine-mesh strainer and served with the cooked shrimp. It is simple and elegant. This dish can also be served with rice, over poached or sautéed scallops, or with Quenelles (page 162).

I was enchanted with the spectacular flavor of shell infusions when I took my first courses in Paris. There, this sauce is traditionally made with live crayfish. Called Nantua, that classic recipe is superb with scallops or any delicate white fish. If you are fortunate enough to be able to find live crayfish, see the variation after the recipe.

My shrimp version evolved when I received a shipment of cooked Cajun-spiced crayfish rather than live crayfish, so I couldn't make the Nantua. I came up with this recipe instead—it is easy to make year-round, since shrimp are available everywhere. If you have a fish shop or a store that peels and/or cooks shrimp, ask them to reserve shells for you. If you have extra shells, make this sauce with double the amount.

Never be tempted to use clam juice in place of fish stock. It has the taste of fish-flavored aluminum foil. If using chicken stock in this recipe, dilute it with water by half. ✿ SERVES 4 AS A FIRST COURSE

1 sprig thyme

1 sprig parsley

1 Turkish bay leaf

1/4 cup unsalted butter

2 shallots, finely chopped

2 carrots, peeled and finely chopped

2 pounds large raw shrimp, in the shell

2 tablespoons Cognac or brandy

1/2 cup dry white wine

3 cups Fish, Vegetable, or Chicken Stock (pages 43, 44, and 40)

Sea salt and freshly ground white pepper

1 1/2 cups heavy cream or crème fraîche (page 32)

1 rounded teaspoon tomato paste

Large pinch of ground cayenne pepper

1 pound angel hair pasta, cooked al dente

1. **With kitchen twine,** tie the thyme, parsley, and bay leaf together to make a bouquet garni. Melt the butter in a large sauté pan over medium-high heat. Add the shallots and carrots and cook for about 3 minutes, until softened. Increase the heat to high, add the shrimp, and sauté for about 2 minutes, until they just turn pink. Add the Cognac, wine, stock, and bouquet garni. Season with salt and pepper and simmer for about 4 minutes. Remove the pan from the heat. Transfer the shrimp to a bowl.

2. **When cool enough to handle,** peel the shrimp, separating and reserving the shells. Finely chop the shells, or you can crush them in a food processor. Return the shells to the stock mixture and place over medium heat. Simmer for about 20 minutes, until the liquid has reduced by about half.

3. **While the stock is reducing,** devein the shrimp by cutting a slit about 1/4 inch deep along the outer curved edge of each shrimp and removing the dark intestinal tract. Refrigerate the shrimp until serving.

4. **When the stock mixture has reduced,** stir in the cream. Simmer for about 20 minutes, until the sauce has thickened to a coating consistency (coats the back of a spoon and leaves a trail when your finger is drawn through it). In small batches, pass the sauce through a fine-mesh strainer or chinois into a clean saucepan, pressing hard on the solids in the strainer to extract every drop of cream. Discard the shell residue and bouquet garni.

5. **Stir the tomato paste** and cayenne pepper into the strained cream. Return the shrimp to the sauce and heat for about 4 minutes, until warmed through. Taste and adjust the seasoning with salt and pepper. Toss with the pasta, divide among individual warmed plates, and serve.

Variation

SAUCE NANTUA: There is very little meat in crayfish, so the shells are the significant ingredient in this application. Remove the intestine from 16 (4-inch) live crayfish by snapping the midsection of the tail over the back and then twisting the intestine out. Then add the entire crayfish to the very hot pan in place of the shrimp, as in the method above. Sauté the crayfish for 5 minutes, until bright red, then cool slightly. Finish the sauce as above, skipping the step of removing the shrimp meat from the shells, and serve with cooked scallops or any delicate white fish.

Quenelles with Shrimp-Infused Sauce

Quenelles are delicate dumplings made with pike fish, veal, or chicken. Here, little pike quenelles are accompanied by shrimp in an outstanding shrimp shell–infused sauce, which can be made a day in advance. The quenelles may be prepared, poached, and chilled ahead, then baked just before serving.

A tamis is a fine-mesh screen, like a flat strainer, that is used for refining smooth pastes such as these quenelles. Forcing the batter through the screen with a flat plastic scraper removes all the fibrous tidbits from the dumpling mixture, yielding a melt-in-your-mouth, silken result. You can use a food mill instead, but the result will not be quite as smooth. 🌿 SERVES 4

1 1/4 pounds skinless pike fillets, or 10 ounces sea scallops, muscles removed, plus 4 ounces sole fillet, skinned and boned

3 large egg whites

1/4 recipe Cream Puff Pastry dough (page 216)

1 cup heavy cream

2 1/2 teaspoons sea salt

1/8 teaspoon freshly ground white pepper

1/8 teaspoon freshly grated nutmeg

1 recipe Shrimp in a Shell-Infused Sauce (page 160), warm, for serving

1. **Place the fish fillets** in the bowl of a food processor and pulse until the fish is broken up. Process on high just until a smooth paste forms. Do not over-process. Pass the purée through a tamis or the finest screen of a food mill, discarding the fibrous residue remaining on the screen. Transfer the purée to a large bowl, cover, and nestle the bowl into a larger bowl filled with ice. Refrigerate for at least 1 hour.

2. **To prepare the quenelles**, in a bowl, lightly break up the egg whites with a whisk. Remove the bowl of fish purée with the ice bowl from the refrigerator. It is important to keep the mixture ice cold at all times by keeping it over the ice. Add the egg whites to the fish purée in 3 batches, incorporating each addition completely with a wooden spatula before adding the next. If the ingredients don't blend easily into each other, switch to a whisk and mix until blended. Beat in the pastry dough in 2 or 3 batches, again incorporating each addition before adding more. The mixture will look as if it will not come together; you can again use a whisk to help it along. In 4 batches, mix in the cream, and add 1/2 teaspoon of the salt, the pepper, and nutmeg. Cover the dumpling mixture and refrigerate, still over the ice bowl (replenish, if necessary), for another 1 hour.

3. **Fill a large sauté pan** about three-quarters full with water and bring to a boil over high heat. Add the remaining 2 teaspoons salt to the water. Dip 2 tablespoons in a bowl of cold water. Scoop up a large tablespoonful of the dumpling mixture with 1 spoon and shape with the interior of the other spoon. Pass the mixture back and forth between the spoons until an elongated oval is formed. You may also use a 1- or 2-ounce ice-cream scoop for this step. Drop the first quenelle into the water and decrease the heat to achieve a simmer.

4. **Continue shaping quenelles,** always dipping the spoons into cold water before making each one, dropping them into the boiling water as soon as they are formed. Work quickly so that they will cook evenly. Once you have about 10 quenelles in the water, decrease the heat to achieve a shimmer (page 20). The dumplings will drop to the bottom and then rise to the surface of the water as they cook. Once they have risen, continue to poach for 5 to 6 minutes, until firm. You should cook the quenelles in 2 batches to avoid overcrowding them.

5. **Preheat the oven to 375°** and butter a baking sheet. As they are done, remove the quenelles from the pan with a fine-mesh strainer and transfer to paper towels to drain. Arrange the drained quenelles on the prepared baking sheet.

6. **When all the quenelles** have been poached, drained, and transferred to the baking sheet, bake them for 4 to 5 minutes, until they rise slightly but do not brown. Transfer to individual warmed dishes and serve immediately with the shrimp sauce.

Meat and Poultry

THIS CHAPTER CONTAINS SOME OF MY FAVORITE regional French and Italian recipes. By cooking these dishes, you will learn the simple rules for roasting, braising, stewing, and sautéing that can be applied to many other recipes.

There's nothing magical about preparing good meals. Know the techniques, and you can make just about anything. The entrée recipes that I teach at the school can be used for quick everyday meals or for elegant dinner parties. This versatility is central to the way I teach—the techniques must be followed, but the resulting meal is all your own. Even an inexperienced cook can master these recipes, demystifying cooking in the process.

Herb-Roasted Rack of Lamb with Béarnaise Sauce (SEE PHOTO INSERT)

This has been the first lesson of my basic cuisine course since I founded the school, and it is also one of my favorite meals. A lot of people have the notion that lamb often tastes too strong, but this cooking method produced a delicious, richly flavored meat. Ask your butcher to "french" the ribs for you, so that the racks can be tied together with the bones crisscrossing each other (Frenching means removing the connective tissue between each rib bone and scraping the bones clean). The crisscrossing racks symbolize the crossing of swords in an honor guard, which is why this luxurious presentation is usually referred to as a "Guard of Honor." The racks are tied together with kitchen twine, and herbs are rubbed over the entire rack and sandwiched between them for maximum flavor. We serve this with Duchesse Potatoes (page 198), a decorative piped potato dish, and Green Beans in Hazelnut Butter (page 190). Sixteen ribs may seem a large quantity for four people, but the ribs are quite small by the time they have been frenched. SERVES 4

2 (8-rib) racks of lamb, frenched, at room temperature

8 sprigs thyme

8 sprigs rosemary

1 1/2 teaspoons sea salt

1/2 teaspoon freshly ground black pepper

1 cup Béarnaise Sauce (page 56), warm

1. **Preheat the oven to 475°.** Thoroughly dry the lamb with paper towels. Rub the herb sprigs gently all over the racks, and rub the salt and pepper evenly into both sides. Place the 2 racks facing each other, with the rib bones arching inwards, and place the herbs in between. Tie the racks together with kitchen twine, winding it around every 3 ribs or so. Place in a roasting pan (a rack is not necessary). It may be peppered, tied together with the herbs, and refrigerated up to 8 hours in advance, but should only be salted just prior to roasting.

2. **Place the lamb in the hot oven.** After 2 minutes, decrease the oven temperature to 400°. Depending on their size, the racks will take 25 to 30 minutes to reach medium-rare, approximately 144°. The racks will feel slightly springy to the touch. (Use an instant-read thermometer; do not let it exceed 148° or the lamb will be tough.)

3. **Remove from the oven** and tent the lamb loosely with aluminum foil (do not seal the foil tightly or the crisp exterior crust will soften). Let stand for 10 minutes.

4. **Transfer the lamb** to a warm serving platter or carving board. Carve into individual chops by slicing down between the bones. Serve 4 chops per person, with a large dollop of Béarnaise sauce on the side.

Pork Chops with Herbs, Balsamic Vinegar, and Olive Oil

Thick pork chops sautéed directly over high heat often end up tough and chewy because of the long cooking time needed to cook the meat through to the center. This dish is therefore a good place to apply the sear/finish in the oven method (pages 26–27). This two-stage technique yields a tender, juicy piece of meat. ✣ SERVES 6

6 (1¼- to 1½-inch-thick) bone-in pork chops

18 (2-inch) sprigs rosemary

18 (2-inch) sprigs sage or thyme

3 cloves garlic, thinly sliced

⅓ cup plus 2 tablespoons extra virgin olive oil, plus extra for sautéing

3 tablespoons balsamic vinegar

Sea salt and freshly ground black pepper

1. **Place the chops on** a rimmed baking sheet and tuck 2 sprigs of each herb and a few slices of garlic underneath each one. In a small bowl, whisk together the ⅓ cup olive oil and 2 tablespoons of the vinegar. Drizzle the mixture over the chops. Place another sprig of each herb and a few more slices of garlic on the tops of each chop. Cover with plastic wrap and marinate in the refrigerator for about 8 hours. Turn once or twice during the marinating time so that both sides absorb some of the oil and vinegar mixture.

2. **Preheat the oven to 375°.** Remove the chops from the marinade. Brush off the herbs and garlic pieces and thoroughly dry the chops with paper towels. Season both sides with salt and pepper and let stand for 10 minutes to come to room temperature.

3. **Heat a large, ovenproof sauté pan** over high heat. (If your largest sauté pan is not ovenproof, you can transfer the chops to a wire rack inside a roasting pan or over a baking tray to finish cooking.) When the pan is very hot, add enough olive oil to cover the bottom of the pan by about ⅛ inch. Heat the oil for about 30 seconds. Add the chops to the pan, making sure to allow at least 1 inch in between each chop (if necessary, sauté the chops in 2 batches or use 2 pans). Sear for 2 to 3 minutes, until the exteriors of the chops are caramelized and brown. Turn to the other side and sear for 2 to 3 minutes, until golden brown. Pour off the excess fat from the pan and transfer the pan to the hot oven. Continue cooking for 10 to 12 minutes longer, until firm to the touch for medium (page 22). Transfer the chops to a warm platter, tenting loosely with aluminum foil, and let stand for 5 minutes before serving.

4. **In a small bowl,** whisk together the 2 tablespoons olive oil and the remaining 1 tablespoon vinegar. Divide the chops among 6 warmed dinner plates, drizzle a little of the vinaigrette over each, and serve at once.

Pork Chops with Caramelized Apples, Calvados, Cider, and Cream (SEE PHOTO INSERT)

Calvados, the classic French apple brandy, will make this a true dish of Normandy—use it if you possibly can. Normandy is also known for its phenomenal variety of apples, rich butter, and cream. In the autumn, we in the U.S. have a wide choice of "antique apples." These classic varieties lack the storage power of more commercial apples and are only available for a few weeks. Take advantage of them, or just be sure to use hardy cooking apples that won't disintegrate under the heat. Look for unfiltered apple cider. Its flavor is far superior to the clear, pale juice. Pork, when overcooked, gets very tough and chewy. The sear/finish in the oven (pages 26–27) method works particularly well with pork chops. When using an aromatic spice like nutmeg, the taste should be barely detected, not jump out and overwhelm the other flavors. This recipe can be made without the alcohol, but it does add a nice dimension. I like to serve this dish with Spaetzle (page 138). ✍ SERVES 4

4 firm cooking apples, preferably an "antique variety," or Golden Delicious

4 (3/4-inch-thick) pork loin or veal chops

Sea salt and freshly ground black pepper

Freshly grated nutmeg

Clarified butter (page 31), or unsalted butter mixed with sunflower or safflower oil, for searing

1/4 cup Calvados, apple brandy, or brandy

1 cup unfiltered apple cider or apple juice

1/3 cup heavy cream

1. **Preheat the oven to 375°.** Peel, core, and quarter the apples. Cut each quarter lengthwise into 3 slices and set aside.

2. **Thoroughly dry the chops** with paper towels. Season both sides with salt, pepper, and a pinch of nutmeg. Heat a large sauté pan over high heat until very hot. Add enough clarified butter to cover the bottom of the pan by 1/8 inch and let heat for 30 seconds. Add the chops, without crowding (or sear in 2 batches or in 2 pans). Sear for 2 to 3 minutes, until nicely caramelized. Turn to the other side and sear for 2 to 3 minutes, until browned.

3. **Transfer the chops** an ovenproof platter or baking dish, and place in the oven to finish cooking for 10 minutes, until firm to the touch for medium (page 22).

4. **Add the sliced apples** to the sauté pan and sauté over medium-high heat, tossing occasionally, until golden brown, adding a little more clarified butter if the mixture seems too dry. When the apples are browned and tender all the way through without being mushy, use a slotted spoon to transfer them around the chops on the platter. Turn off the oven, tent the platter loosely with aluminum foil, and leave the oven door slightly ajar.

5. **Remove any excess butter** from the pan by dabbing with paper towels. Add the Calvados to the sauté pan, still over medium-high heat, and deglaze the pan, scraping up any brown bits with a metal spatula. Add the cider and continue to cook for 2 to 3 minutes, until reduced slightly. Transfer the sauce mixture to a small saucepan, again over medium-high heat. Boil the mixture for about 5 minutes, until it has reduced by two-thirds to about 1/3 cup. Stir in the cream and a small pinch of nutmeg. Continue to boil over medium-high heat for 4 to 5 minutes, until the sauce has reduced and thickened to a coating consistency (coats the back of a spoon and leaves a trail when your finger is drawn through it). Taste for seasoning and adjust with salt, pepper, and nutmeg if necessary.

6. **Transfer the chops** and apples to warmed dinner plates. Pass the sauce through a fine-mesh strainer, drizzling it over the chops and apples, and serve at once.

Steak with Peppercorns and Cognac (STEAK AU POIVRE)

This is a quintessentially French recipe. Simple, intensely flavored and very easy. Pink peppercorns are cultivated in Madagascar and imported via France, so they're usually fairly pricey, but can be found via mail order from the Spice House (page 252) or in gourmet stores. ✒ SERVES 4

4 (1 1/2- to 2-inch-thick) filet mignons, 6 to 8 ounces each

Sea salt and freshly ground black pepper

2 tablespoons clarified butter (page 31)

2 tablespoons olive oil

2 tablespoons unsalted butter

1 shallot, diced

1 tablespoon green peppercorns, drained

1/2 cup Cognac

1 cup heavy cream

1 tablespoon Meat Glaze (*Glace de Viande*, page 45) or soy sauce

1 teaspoon pink peppercorns

1. **Preheat the oven to 375°.** Thoroughly dry the steaks with paper towels. Season both sides with salt and pepper.

2. **Heat a large ovenproof sauté pan** over high heat until very hot. Add the clarified butter and olive oil and let them heat for 30 seconds. Add the steaks to the pan, making sure there is at least 1 inch between each (or sear the steaks in 2 batches or in 2 pans). Sear the steaks on one side for about 2 minutes, until caramelized and brown. Turn to the other side and sear for about 2 minutes, until crisp and caramelized. Set a rack inside a roasting pan or on a rimmed baking sheet. Transfer the steaks to the rack, place in the oven, and finish cooking to the desired doneness (about 10 minutes more for medium rare). Use the doneness test on page 22.

3. **Transfer the steaks** to a warm platter and tent loosely with aluminum foil. Let them rest for 5 to 6 minutes. Add 1 tablespoon of the unsalted butter and the shallot to the sauté pan and place over medium heat. Cook for 30 seconds, then add the green peppercorns and cook for 30 seconds more.

4. **Put the Cognac** into a measuring cup and pour it into the sauté pan (if you want to flambé, see page 21). Deglaze the pan, scraping up any brown bits with a metal spatula, watching out for flames as Cognac is highly flammable. Allow to reduce for 1 to 2 minutes, then add the cream and *glace de viande* and adjust the heat to achieve a boil. Boil for 4 to 5 minutes, until the sauce is thickened to a coating consistency (coats the back of a spoon and leaves a trail when your finger is drawn through it). About 1/2 cup of the sauce will be left. Taste for seasoning and adjust with salt and pepper if necessary.

5. **Decrease the heat** to medium-low and add any drippings that have drained from the steaks and the remaining 1 tablespoon butter. Whisk together thoroughly until the butter is incorporated. Add the pink peppercorns and warm gently, without boiling, for 1 minute. Transfer the steaks to heated plates and drizzle each one generously with the sauce.

Red Wine Beef Stew

(BOEUF BOURGUIGNONNE)

This rustic, intensely flavored beef stew with red wine, boiling onions, potatoes, bacon, and vegetables is a specialty of the Burgundy region of France. Any dry red wine will do, but it is best not to use an overly tannic wine. If in doubt, buy your wine from a knowledgeable wine shop. If you are in a hurry, you can eliminate the marinating process and add the bottle of wine in step 3 instead. Croûtons add an interesting texture counterpoint to this dish, and are a classic accompaniment.

Note: See Sauce Fixes on page 25 for tips on how to achieve a rich and flavorful result with braised and stewed dishes. 🌿 SERVES 6 TO 8

3 pounds boneless beef chuck, cut into 2-inch chunks

1 bottle dry red wine, such as burgundy or cabernet

2 cloves garlic, crushed

6 sprigs thyme

10 black peppercorns

1 tablespoon olive oil

1/3 cup clarified butter (page 31) or olive oil

1 yellow onion, coarsely chopped

2 carrots, peeled and coarsely chopped

1/4 cup brandy or Cognac

1/3 cup unbleached all-purpose flour

2 cups Brown Beef Stock (page 41)

2 shallots, coarsely chopped

4 garlic cloves, coarsely chopped

1 1/2 cups Fresh Tomato Sauce (page 139), or 2 tablespoons tomato paste

Sea salt

1/4 teaspoon freshly ground pepper

4 sprigs parsley

1 Turkish bay leaf

2 (4-inch) lengths celery

16 small red potatoes, peeled in a thin strip around the middle

18 white boiling onions (not pearl onions), about 1 inch in diameter

1 pound smoked slab bacon, cut into 1 1/2 by 1/2-inch strips (lardons)

1 1/2 pounds small white button or wild mushrooms, quartered

1/2 cup finely chopped fresh parsley, for garnish

6 to 8 croûtons (page 32)

1. **At least 4 or up to 8 hours** before you plan to cook the stew, combine the beef and wine in a large bowl and add the crushed garlic, 2 sprigs of the thyme, peppercorns, and olive oil. Toss the mixture just to combine. Cover and refrigerate, turning the meat 2 or 3 times during the marinating process.

2. **Preheat the oven to 350°.** Drain the marinating beef, reserving the wine. Pass the wine through a fine-mesh strainer into a bowl and set aside. Discard the garlic, peppercorns, and thyme. Dry the beef cubes thoroughly with paper towels. Heat a large Dutch oven or other deep heavy ovenproof pot or casserole over high heat until very hot. Add the clarified butter and heat for about 30 seconds. Add half the beef cubes and sear, turning occasionally with tongs, for about 7 minutes, until nicely browned on all sides. Transfer the beef to a platter and repeat the searing process with the remaining beef (if all the beef were added together, the meat would steam rather than sear). Transfer the second batch of beef to the platter.

3. **Add the yellow onion and carrots** to the pan and decrease the heat to medium. Cook, stirring occasionally, for about 3 minutes, until the vegetables are softened. Return all the browned meat to the pan. Add the brandy and deglaze over high heat for about 2 minutes, scraping up all the brown dripping from the base of the pan. The pan should be almost dry.

4. **Sprinkle the flour over the meat** and vegetables and cook over high heat, stirring occasionally, for 1 to 2 minutes to brown the flour slightly. Add the reserved wine, beef stock, shallots, chopped garlic, tomato sauce, 1 teaspoon of salt, and the pepper to the pot. Tie the parsley, remaining 4 sprigs thyme, and bay leaf in between the 2 pieces of celery with kitchen twine to make a bouquet garni; add to the pot. Uncovered, bring the liquid just to a boil, then cover and place in the hot oven. Cook for 2 hours, until the meat is very tender (see step 8 for doneness cue).

5. **While the stew is cooking,** place the potatoes in a large saucepan with enough water to cover by at least 1 inch. Bring to a boil and add 2 teaspoons of salt. Adjust the heat to maintain a brisk simmer. Cook for 10 to 15 minutes, until tender but not falling apart. Drain and reserve in a bowl at room temperature. Bring another saucepan of water to a boil and drop in the boiling onions. Adjust the heat so that the water simmers. Cook the onions for about 5 minutes, until tender. Drain well and rinse under cold running water. When cool enough to handle, peel and trim away the root ends carefully, without allowing the onions to fall apart. Drain the onions on paper towels.

continued

6. **In another saucepan,** combine the bacon and enough cold water to cover. Over high heat, bring to a boil and cook for 2 minutes to remove excessive salt and smokiness. Drain the bacon in a fine-mesh strainer and rinse under cold water. Shake the excess water from the bacon and pat dry with paper towels. In a sauté pan, cook the bacon over medium heat for about 5 minutes, until browned and crisp on the outside, yet still soft on the inside. Transfer the cooked bacon to a plate lined with paper towels. Reserve the bacon fat in the sauté pan.

7. **Add the peeled onions** to the sauté pan containing the bacon fat and place over medium-high heat. Sauté the onions for about 5 minutes, tossing occasionally, until nicely browned. With a slotted spoon, transfer the onions to a small bowl. Add the mushrooms to the sauté pan with the remaining bacon fat and sauté, tossing occasionally, for 10 minute, until deep, golden brown. Remove and set aside with the onions.

8. **After about 2 hours,** test the beef for doneness: stick one prong of a roasting fork into one of the cubes of beef and lift it from the pan. If the meat clings to the fork, it needs more cooking. If it drops off fairly easily, it is tender and ready to serve. Using a fine-mesh skimmer or a tablespoon, skim off any fat from the surface of the sauce.

9. **Add the potatoes, onions,** mushrooms, and bacon to the stew and mix together gently. Taste for seasoning and adjust with salt and pepper if necessary. Place the pot over medium heat and bring up to a simmer. Simmer for about 5 minutes, to warm the vegetables and allow the flavors to marry. Serve in warm bowls, garnished with a little of the chopped parsley and a croûton.

Sautéed Veal Chops with a Parmesan Crust

Veal has a rich yet mild taste that is enhanced by the intense flavors of fresh rosemary and thyme. Lamb, either loin or rib chops, may be substituted for the veal, in which case you will want to serve two chops per person. The key to a crisp crust is to cook the chops immediately after they are breaded, otherwise the crust will become gummy. I like to serve this dish with Spaetzle (page 138) Potato Gnocchi (page 135), or Duchesse Potatoes (page 198). ✒ SERVES 6

6 (1-inch-thick) veal chops, at room temperature

3/4 cup freshly grated Parmesan cheese

3 large eggs, well beaten

1 1/2 cups unseasoned fine dry bread crumbs

1 tablespoon finely chopped fresh rosemary

1 teaspoon finely chopped fresh thyme

1 1/2 teaspoons sea salt

1/2 teaspoon freshly ground black pepper

Olive oil or clarified butter (page 31), for sautéing

1. **Thoroughly dry the chops** with paper towels. Assemble 3 plates: place the Parmesan in one, the beaten eggs in the second, and the bread crumbs in the third. Add and thoroughly mix the rosemary and thyme into the Parmesan. Add and thoroughly mix the salt and pepper into the bread crumbs.

2. **Preheat the oven to 375°.** Place 1 chop onto the plate of Parmesan and firmly press some of the cheese into both sides with the heel of your hand or a meat pounder. Next, dip each side of the chop into the egg mixture. Finally, coat lightly with the bread crumbs. Repeat with the remaining chops, setting them aside on a baking sheet as they are prepared.

3. **Heat 2 large sauté pans,** or cook in 2 batches, over medium-high heat. When the pans are very hot, add enough olive oil to coat the bottom of each by about 1/8 inch and let heat for 30 seconds. Add the chops, leaving at least 1 inch between them to allow the steam to escape. Sear the chops for about 2 minutes, until a brown crust forms on one side, then turn and brown the other side for about 2 minutes. Place a large rack inside a roasting pan or on a rimmed baking sheet. With tongs, transfer the chops carefully (try not to break the crust) to the rack and finish cooking in the oven for about 8 minutes, until medium rare. Use the doneness test on page 22.

4. **Divide the chops** among 6 warmed plates and serve at once.

Osso Buco

Several years ago I spent a week in Milan, Italy, where Osso Buco is a specialty. While there, I tried several variations on this classic dish. It is traditionally served with saffron risotto, but I prefer it with Potato Gnocchi (page 135). In most recipes, the sauce is a rich, puréed tomato sauce. I like to use diced carrots, celery, and onions, which give the sauce texture and a lovely jewel-like appearance. It is also a good opportunity for my students to learn knife skills, since the vegetables should be cut into small, uniform dice. When this dish is plated, the heat from the shanks will release the garlic, lemon, and herb flavors from the gremolata, creating an enticing scented bouquet.

Note: See Sauce Fixes on page 25 for tips on how to achieve a rich and flavorful result with braised and stewed dishes. ❧ SERVES 8

10 ripe plum tomatoes, or 2 cups Fresh Tomato Sauce (page 139)

Olive oil, for cooking

1/2 cup unsalted butter

11/2 cups diced yellow onion (1/4-inch)

11/2 cups diced carrot (1/4-inch)

11/2 cups diced celery (1/4-inch)

2 cups unbleached all-purpose flour

Sea salt and freshly ground black pepper

8 (11/2- to 2-inch-thick) veal shanks

1 cup dry white wine

4 sprigs thyme

6 sprigs parsley

2 Turkish bay leaves

2 (4-inch) lengths celery

1/4 cup tomato paste

4 to 6 cups Brown Beef Stock (page 41)

GREMOLATA

2 tablespoons minced garlic

Finely chopped zest of 3 lemons

1/2 cup finely chopped fresh flat-leaf parsley

1. **If using fresh tomatoes,** cut out the stems and halve the tomatoes crosswise. Squeeze out most of the seeds and chop the tomatoes coarsely. Heat a sauté pan over medium-high heat and add the tomatoes and 2 tablespoons olive oil. Cook, stirring occasionally, for 5 to 6 minutes, until softened and most of the liquid has evaporated. Pass the tomatoes through a food mill, discarding the seeds and skins.

2. **Place a large Dutch oven,** casserole, or braising pan over medium heat and add the butter. Add the onion, carrot, and celery and sauté, stirring occasionally, for about 5 minutes, until softened. Set the pan aside.

3. **Preheat the oven to 350°.** On a large plate, mix the flour with 2 teaspoons salt and 1/2 teaspoon pepper. Pat the veal shanks dry with paper

towels and tie kitchen twine firmly but not tightly around the circumference of each, to hold them together during the braising process. Thoroughly coat each piece of veal in the seasoned flour, and shake off any excess. Heat a large sauté over medium-high heat until very hot. Add enough olive oil to cover the bottom of the pan by 1/8 inch and allow to heat for 30 seconds. Add the shanks and sear for about 3 minutes, until brown, then turn and sear the other sides for about 3 minutes. (Do not overcrowd the pan, there should be 1 inch between each piece; sear in batches if necessary.) As each shank is browned, transfer to the Dutch oven with tongs or a slotted spoon and place on top of the softened vegetables. Lean the pieces on each other so that they are stacked like fallen dominoes.

4. **Use a paper towel** to dab away the excess oil from the sauté pan. Place the pan over high heat for 30 seconds, then add the wine. Deglaze the pan, scraping up all the brown drippings with a metal spatula and mixing them into the wine. Simmer for 1 to 2 minutes to dissolve the smaller caramelized pieces into the wine. Strain the wine mixture with a fine-mesh strainer over the veal shanks.

5. **Tie the thyme, parsley,** and bay leaves in between the 2 pieces of celery with kitchen twine to make a bouquet garni and add to the pan. Add the puréed tomatoes, tomato paste, 1 teaspoon salt,

and 1/2 teaspoon pepper. Add enough beef stock to cover the shanks by two-thirds.

6. **Place the uncovered pan** on the stovetop and bring just to a boil over high heat. Immediately cover and transfer to the lower third of the hot oven. Cook for 2 hours. To test the meat for doneness, pick up 1 of the veal shanks with 1 tine of a roasting fork, if the meat slides easily off the fork, it is done. If not done, continue to cook for a few minutes and test again. Using a large slotted spoon or fine-mesh skimmer, carefully transfer all the meat to a warm platter. Do not let the shanks fall apart, if possible. Tent the platter with aluminum foil.

7. **To prepare the gremolata,** combine the garlic, lemon zest, and parsley in a small bowl and mix together well.

8. **Taste the sauce** and adjust the seasoning with salt and pepper if necessary. If the sauce is thin, place the pan over medium-high heat and reduce it for a few minutes, until thickened. Stir well occasionally to prevent the sauce from scorching on the bottom of the pan. (See page 25 for other sauce-fixing tips.)

9. **To serve,** spoon some sauce onto each plate and place 1 veal shank on top. Spoon a little more sauce over each, sprinkle with the gremolata, and serve at once.

Chicken in White Wine Cream Sauce with Mushrooms

I first had this dish in a tiny restaurant in Normandy on a cold winter night. It was served with gnocchi, crusty bread, vegetable soup, and apple tart. Simple perfection. When cooking chicken, it is important to remove white meat (the breasts) as soon at it is cooked. It will become stringy and tough if it stays in the pan as long as the legs and thighs. ✒ SERVES 4

1 (3 1/2-pound) chicken, cut into 8 serving pieces

1 1/2 cups unbleached all-purpose flour

1 teaspoon sea salt

1/2 teaspoon freshly ground white pepper

1/8 teaspoon ground cayenne pepper or paprika (optional)

Vegetable oil or clarified butter (page 31), for sautéing

4 tablespoons unsalted butter

2 shallots, finely chopped

2 cloves garlic, finely chopped

2 tablespoons Cognac or brandy

1/2 cup dry white wine

4 cups Chicken Stock (page 40)

5 sprigs parsley

3 sprigs thyme

1 Turkish bay leaf

2 green outer leaves of a leek, or 4-inch lengths of celery

3/4 pound mixed mushrooms, stemmed and quartered

1 cup crème fraîche (page 32) or heavy cream

1/4 cup chopped fresh flat-leaf parsley or chives, for garnish

1. **Rinse the chicken pieces** under cold running water and thoroughly dry with paper towels. In a bowl, combine the flour, salt, white pepper, and cayenne and blend together. Coat each chicken piece thoroughly with the seasoned flour and shake off the excess.

2. **Heat a large sauté pan** over medium-high heat until very hot. Add enough oil to cover the bottom of the pan by 1/8 inch. Add the chicken pieces, without overcrowding, and sauté, turning once, for about 5 minutes on each side, until golden brown. (Brown in 2 batches if the pan is not large enough to hold all the chicken with 1 inch between the pieces. Otherwise, the chicken will steam rather than brown.) As it is done, transfer the chicken to a platter. Pour off and discard all the fat, and remove any blackened drippings from the pan by dabbing with paper towels.

3. **Place the pan over medium** heat and add 2 tablespoons of the butter. Add the shallots and garlic and cook, stirring occasionally, for 1 to 2

minutes, until softened. Add the Cognac and cook for 1 minute. Add the wine and adjust the heat to achieve a boil. Cook for 2 to 3 minutes, until about 1/4 cup liquid remains in the pan. Add 2 cups of the stock to the pan.

4. **Tie the parsley, thyme,** and bay leaves in between the leek leaves with kitchen twine to make a bouquet garni. Return the chicken to the pan and add the bouquet garni and the remaining 2 cups stock. Cover the pan and, over very low heat, simmer for 30 to 45 minutes, until the chicken is tender, with no trace of pink remaining near the bone. Breast meat will always be done first, so test it after 30 minutes. To test, stick a skewer into the fattest part of the breast. The juices should run clear. Transfer the breasts to a warm platter and keep warm, loosely tented with aluminum foil. Continue cooking the dark meat until it is done, testing in the same manner in the thickest part of the thigh. Transfer the dark meat to the platter.

5. **While the chicken is cooking,** place another sauté pan over medium heat and add the remaining 2 tablespoons butter. When it is melted, add the mushrooms, and sauté, stirring occasionally, for 6 to 8 minutes, until pale golden and fairly dry. Set aside.

6. **When all the chicken** has been cooked, place the pan used to sauté the chicken over high heat and bring the liquid to a boil. Cook for 5 to 10 minutes, until reduced by about half. Whisk in the crème fraîche and continue to boil for 5 to 8 minutes, until thickened to a coating consistency (coats the back of a spoon and leaves a trail when your finger is drawn through it). Return the chicken pieces to the sauce and add the mushrooms. Simmer for 1 or 2 minutes more, to heat all the ingredients through. Turn the chicken pieces a few times so that they absorb the sauce. Transfer the chicken to heated plates, pour the sauce over, and garnish with the parsley. Serve immediately.

Chicken Breasts Stuffed with Pine Nuts and Spinach

(SEE PHOTO INSERT)

This tasty, make-ahead dish combines toasted pine nuts, spinach, crispy bacon, Parmesan, and Dijon for a really flavorful stuffing inside a boneless, skinless chicken breast. I like to pair this dish with a pasta like Penne alla Puttanesca (page 143) or the simpler Fresh Pasta with Fried Sage Butter (page 146).

⚜ SERVES 4

STUFFING

3 tablespoons unsalted butter, extra virgin olive oil, or a combination

2 cups finely chopped fresh spinach, well dried

2 tablespoons minced shallot

1 large clove garlic, minced

3 tablespoons pine nuts, toasted (page 30)

2 slices bacon, cooked until crisp and crumbled

1/4 cup freshly grated Parmesan cheese

1 tablespoon plus 1 1/2 teaspoons unseasoned fine dry bread crumbs

1 tablespoon finely chopped fresh basil, flat-leaf parsley, or tarragon

1 large egg yolk

Sea salt and freshly ground white pepper

4 boneless, skinless chicken breast halves

1 tablespoon extra virgin olive oil or unsalted butter, melted

1 tablespoon Dijon mustard

1/2 cup freshly shredded Gruyère cheese

1. **If you plan to serve the chicken** right away, pre-heat the oven to 400°.

2. **To prepare the stuffing**, in a sauté pan, melt the butter over medium-high heat. Add the spinach and cook for 1 minute, stirring. Add the shallot and garlic and cook for 1 to 2 minutes, until softened. Add the pine nuts, bacon, Parmesan, bread crumbs, basil, and egg yolk and season with salt and pepper. Remove from the heat. Mix together until evenly blended.

3. **Lightly butter a medium baking dish**, large enough to hold all the breasts with at least 2 inches between each. Thoroughly pat the chicken breasts dry with paper towels and lay them on a flat surface. Holding a small sharp knife parallel to the surface, cut a deep pocket into the longer side of one chicken breast. Season with salt and pepper on the inside of the pocket. Place one-fourth of the stuffing inside the pocket, packing it

*Pork Chops with Caramelized Apples, Calvados,
Cider, and Cream* (PAGE 168)

Chicken Breasts Stuffed with Pine Nuts and Spinach (PAGE 180)

Caramelized Apple Tart (Tarte Tatin)

(PAGE 236)

Grand Marnier Chocolate Cake with Shiny Chocolate Icing (PAGE 247)

in well so it stays inside during cooking. Repeat with the remaining breasts. In a small bowl, combine the olive oil and mustard, and rub the mixture into the outside of each breast. Season the outside of each breast with salt and pepper. Place the breasts in the prepared baking dish. Scatter the cheese evenly over the breasts. At this point, the chicken may be refrigerated, covered, for up to 8 hours. Return the chicken to room temperature for 10 minutes, and preheat the oven to 400° before continuing with the recipe.

4. **Bake the chicken breasts** for 20 to 30 minutes, until the meat is tender and the juices run clear when the thickest part of the meat is pierced with a skewer. Remove the chicken from the oven, place on a warm serving platter, and let stand for 5 minutes, loosely tented with aluminum foil. Serve on warmed plates.

Sautéed Duck Breasts with Cherry-Butter Sauce

While traveling in Burgundy, I encountered this bright, fruity butter sauce served with duck breast. The cherries perfectly complement the rich earthy flavor of duck. Sour red cherries are grown in Door County, a favorite Wisconsin vacation spot. Although sour cherries are available fresh for only a few weeks, they are readily available frozen. For those who are unable to find sour cherries, I have included an apple variation, below.

Duck breasts vary enormously in size, from 6 ounces to almost 12 ounces. The larger, thicker breasts can be used for this recipe, in which case you will need only 2 breasts. 🌿 SERVES 4

16 ounces frozen sweetened sour red cherries

1 cup cherry cider

4 duck breast halves, about 8 ounces each

Sea salt and freshly ground black pepper

3 to 4 tablespoons very cold unsalted butter, cut into tablespoon-sized pieces

1. **Thaw the cherries** in a fine-mesh strainer placed over a saucepan. When the cherries have thawed completely, press down gently to extract a little more juice. Reserve the drained cherries. Add the cherry cider to the saucepan with the juices from the frozen fruit and place the pan over high heat. Bring to a boil and reduce for 8 to 10 minutes, until only about 1/3 cup remains and the juice is syrupy. Watch carefully to avoid burning. Remove from the heat and set aside.

2. **Preheat the oven to 375°.** Score the skin of the duck breasts in a crisscross pattern, using a very sharp knife. Be careful not to cut into the flesh. Season both sides with salt and pepper

3. **Heat a large sauté pan** over high heat until very hot. Place the duck breasts in the pan, skin side down, and cook for about 3 minutes, until some of the fat has melted and the skin is brown and crisp. When the skin side has browned to a deep cinnamon color, turn the breasts over and cook for 3 minutes more. Pour off and discard the fat, place the pan in the oven, and cook for about 10 minutes, until medium rare. (Use the doneness test on page 22; exact cooking times will depend on the thickness of the breasts and the heat of the fire.) Transfer the breasts to a warm platter, skin side up, and tent loosely with aluminum foil. Let stand for 5 minutes.

4. **To finish the sauce,** return the reduced cider mixture to medium heat. When it is hot, whisk in the cold butter, to taste. Remove the pan from the heat while you continue to whisk until the butter has been incorporated and the sauce thickens. Return the pan to the burner, add the drained cherries, and decrease the heat to very low. Warm the cherries through for about 2 minutes, but do not allow the sauce to get too hot or boil, otherwise the butter may separate. Season with salt and pepper, taste and adjust if necessary.

5. **Slice the breasts about** 1/3 **inch** thick on the diagonal and divide among 4 warmed plates. Drizzle with the warm sauce and cherries and serve at once.

Variation

SAUTÉED DUCK WITH APPLES AND CIDER-BUTTER SAUCE: Peel and core 3 Golden Delicious apples and cut each one into 8 sections. Prepare and cook the duck breasts as in steps 2 and 3 above, then pour off all the remaining fat from the pan, leaving the brown drippings behind. Add 2 tablespoons of unsalted butter and melt over medium-high heat. Add the apples and sauté, stirring occasionally, until browned and tender but not mushy. If dark brown spots begin to appear on the bottom of the pan, add 2 tablespoons of the apple cider (used below) to deglaze the pan while the apples are cooking. With a slotted spoon, transfer the apple sections to a warm plate. Add 1 1/2 cups of fresh, unfiltered apple cider to the pan and increase the heat to high. Boil the cider for 8 to 10 minutes, until it has reduced and thickened to the consistency of thin syrup. Whisk in 4 to 6 tablespoons cold unsalted butter in tablespoon-sized pieces; remove the pan from the heat while you continue to whisk until all the butter has been incorporated and the sauce thickens. Serve the sauce over the duck, sliced as above, and the warm apples.

Vegetables and Potatoes

FRESH BROCCOLI, CAULIFLOWER, GREEN BEANS, asparagus, and carrots will handsomely complement any meal. In this chapter, I have included some very basic recipes for cooking vegetables. They can then be served with nothing more than butter, an infused butter or olive oil, or with the sauce of your choice.

When it comes to the boiling versus steaming question, there is no doubt in my mind. I much prefer cooking vegetables in salted boiling water—steaming leaves them rather bland. Vegetables need salt to enhance their flavor, but if it is added after cooking, you'll encounter crunchy salt particles when eating. The exception to this post-cooking rule is fleur de sel (page 7), a complex French salt that is used on cooked vegetables like fresh green beans or asparagus.

Vegetables cooked in water can be exceedingly tasty *and* healthful. Some say that boiling vegetables causes more of the nutrients to be lost, but actually the loss of nutrients occurs when vegetables are cooked beyond the al dente—firm but not crunchy—state, and that can occur with any less-than-careful cooking method. Having said that, there are some simple but very important rules that must be followed to obtain the optimal results when cooking vegetables. The most significant rule is that root vegetables are always started in cold water, which is then brought to a boil. Vegetables that grow above the earth are placed into already boiling water. See boiling, page 19, for more information.

For years, I have taught a (very popular) class on the versatile potato, including all the myriad dishes that can be created with it. Thus, you'll see quite a few potato dishes here (and don't miss my Potato Gnocchi in the pasta chapter on page 135). I've even included one of my childhood favorites, German Potato Dumplings (page 200)—a classic dish that has been made by generations of my family.

For many years, the only varieties of potatoes commonly available were the russet (sometimes known as a "baking" potato) and the smaller new potatoes. Russets grown in a rainy climate may be heavier and wetter than those grown in Idaho, where the dry climate produces a drier potato. In some recipes, the drier Idaho-grown potato produces a fluffier result—ingredients like butter, eggs, cream, or milk are more easily absorbed. We are beginning to see many more potato varieties, such as the superb Yukon Gold, but it will be some time before we can rival the seemingly endless range of potatoes I saw while travelling through Europe.

A fantastic potato grower in the Colorado Rocky Mountains called Rockey Farm is producing many interesting European varieties that are still relatively new in the United States. We had a great time in the school kitchen experimenting with these new treasures. Be proactive! Have your local market call their wholesaler to see if they can obtain some of these varieties from a local grower or from Rockey Farm (page 252).

While most of the dishes in this chapter work best as sides, others, such as Provençal Chard Tart (page 193) or Ratatouille (page 192), are slightly more complex and might stand alone as a vegetarian main course.

Broccoli and Cauliflower with Béchamel Sauce

Before cooking, soak both vegetables in a sink filled with cold water for a few minutes. If using your own, home-grown vegetables, dissolve a few tablespoons of salt in the water and let them soak for about 10 minutes to remove any garden pests, which will float to the top of the water.

There can be a lot of waste with broccoli. Peeling the tough stalks will yield more edible broccoli. If you prefer the look of the florets alone, as I do, remove the stalks, blanch them in salted boiling water for 3 minutes, then cool under cold running water and use as the base for a cream of broccoli soup. ✿ SERVES 6

1 head cauliflower, core and greens trimmed

2 heads broccoli, trimmed and stalks peeled

1 tablespoon coarse sea salt

1 cup medium Béchamel Sauce (page 49), warm

1/2 cup shredded Gruyère or Cheddar cheese

1. **Remove and discard the** cauliflower core. Break into bite-sized florets (the natural bouquets of the vegetable that break apart easily). Cut any larger florets lengthwise into bite-sized pieces.

2. **Remove the florets** from the broccoli in the same manner. If desired, use a sharp vegetable peeler to remove the peel from the broccoli stalks; cut the stalks into 1-inch pieces.

3. **Fill a large saucepan** with a generous amount of water and place over high heat. Cover and bring the water to a boil. Add the salt, broccoli, and cauliflower. Regulate the heat to maintain a brisk simmer and cook, uncovered, for 4 to 5 minutes, until they can just be pierced with the tip of a sharp knife.

4. **Drain the vegetables** in a colander. Immediately transfer to a warm serving dish and mix in the Béchamel sauce. Sprinkle the Gruyère over the top and serve at once.

Asparagus with Hollandaise Sauce

When buying asparagus, choose the thicker stalks because thin stalks are often stringy. To prevent the tips of thick asparagus from being overcooked before the stalks are cooked through, you'll need to peel the stalks. First cut off about 1 inch from the base, since it is usually dry and tough. (Don't snap off the ends—you'll end up discarding more of the stalk than you need to.) Using a Swiss peeler (page 18), begin peeling downward an inch or two beneath the flower end. This may seem like a laborious extra step, but when you taste the tender stalks and see the glorious green color, you'll be converted. This way, both tip and stalk are cooked to perfection at the same moment. I prefer to poach asparagus rather than steam them, since the salt water enhances their flavor. Rather than allowing the asparagus to float around the cooking pan bumping into each another, risking destruction of the delicate tops, I tie bundles of up to 6 asparagus together with kitchen twine.

Green asparagus with lemon-laced Hollandaise sauce is an exceptional treat. If you are fortunate enough to find fresh white asparagus, try the orange-flavored Maltese Sauce (page 54). White asparagus is actually the same plant as green asparagus. The grower painstakingly covers the asparagus stalks with straw every day as it grows, so that the spears never see the light of day. Thus, the usual reaction between sunlight and plant fibers to form the green chlorophyll never takes place (a similar process is used to keep Belgian endive white). ✒ SERVES 4

16 fresh thick stalks asparagus, stalks peeled

2 teaspoons coarse sea salt

1 cup Hollandaise Sauce (page 54), warm

1. **Fill a large sauté pan** or skillet three-quarters full of water and bring to a boil over high heat. Add the salt.

2. **With kitchen twine,** tie the asparagus together in bundles of 4 or 5 (tie them about two-thirds down from the top to avoid damaging the flower tips).

3. **Lower the bundles into** the boiling water and regulate the heat to maintain a simmer. Cook for 4 to 6 minutes, until the bases of the stems are tender and can be pierced with a knife. Using tongs, transfer the bundles to a double layer of paper towels. Immediately snip and discard the ties and transfer the asparagus to a warm platter or individual warm plates. Serve with a generous spoonful of the warm Hollandaise poured across the lower third of the stalks, extending onto the plates.

Sautéed Carrots with Shallots and Herbs

When cooking root vegetables, always start them off in cold water. Green beans, and any other vegetable that grows above the earth, are placed directly into boiling water. Here, the carrots are fully cooked in boiling water first, then slightly caramelized in a hot pan with some flavorful shallots. Sautéed carrots are also great served with Béchamel Sauce (page 49).

❦ SERVES 4 TO 6

8 carrots, peeled

2 teaspoons coarse sea salt

3 tablespoons unsalted butter

2 shallots, minced

2 tablespoons finely chopped fresh flat-leaf parsley or tarragon, or a combination

1/4 teaspoon freshly ground black pepper

1. **Slice the carrots** into 1-inch lengths on the diagonal. Put them into a saucepan and add enough cold water to cover by 1 inch. Over high heat, bring the water to a boil and add the salt. Regulate the heat to maintain a brisk simmer, and cook, uncovered, for about 10 minutes, until the carrots can be pierced all the way through with the tip of a knife. Do not overcook the carrots or they will be mushy. Drain and set aside.

2. **In a sauté pan**, melt the butter over medium heat. Add the shallots and cook, stirring, for about 3 minutes, until softened. Add the drained carrots to the pan and sauté for about 5 minutes, stirring with a metal spatula every minute or so, scraping the bottom of the pan to prevent the vegetables from scorching, until the carrots are slightly golden. Remove from the heat and scatter with the parsley and pepper. Serve at once.

Green Beans in Hazelnut Butter

Whenever possible, I prefer to use the tiny slim green beans known as haricots verts. Their flavor is bright and fresh, and you will never find large knobby seeds bursting from the bean. These beans make a beautiful accompaniment to Herb-Roasted Rack of Lamb (page 166) or Steak with Peppercorns and Cognac (page 170).

This is a good time to sprinkle a little fleur de sel (page 7) over the top of the finished dish, but you must still cook the beans in salted water or their flavor will be one-dimensional. You can substitute almonds, walnuts, or hickory nuts for the hazelnuts (none of them require skinning). 🌿 SERVES 4 TO 6

1/2 cup hazelnuts

1 teaspoon coarse sea salt

1 pound fresh haricots verts or standard green beans, trimmed

1/3 cup unsalted butter

1/4 teaspoon freshly ground black pepper

1. **Preheat the oven to 350°.** Spread the hazelnuts on a rimmed baking sheet and bake for 5 to 8 minutes, until golden. Allow to cool. Place a few nuts in the center of a paper towel or kitchen towel and rub off their skins. Repeat with the remaining nuts. With a large knife, chop the nuts coarsely.

2. **Bring a large saucepan** of water to a boil over high heat and add the salt. Add the beans and regulate the heat to maintain a brisk simmer. Cook until the beans are just tender, still slightly firm but not crunchy, about 4 minutes for haricots verts, 6 minutes for standard green beans. Drain the beans in a colander and immediately run under lots of cold water to stop the cooking and preserve the color.

3. **In a sauté pan,** melt the butter over medium-high heat and add the hazelnuts. Stir for a minute to warm, then add the beans and stir occasionally for about 2 minutes, until the beans are hot. Season with salt and pepper, toss to combine, and serve.

Mushrooms in a Dijon Cream Sauce

Almost any mushroom would taste good in this luscious cream and Dijon reduction, but my particular favorites are shiitakes. If unavailable, try the brown cremini, or even plain white button mushrooms.

❧ SERVES 4 TO 6

2 tablespoons unsalted butter

1 pound mixed mushrooms, stemmed and quartered

2 tablespoons plus 1 1/2 teaspoons minced shallot

1 teaspoon finely chopped fresh thyme

1/3 cup dry white wine

1 teaspoon freshly squeezed lemon juice

1 cup heavy cream

1 large egg yolk

1 to 2 tablespoons Dijon mustard

1/2 teaspoon sea salt

1/4 teaspoon freshly ground black pepper

2 tablespoons finely chopped fresh flat-leaf parsley

1. **In a large sauté pan**, melt the butter over medium-high heat. Add the mushrooms and cook, stirring occasionally, for 3 to 5 minutes, until the liquid has been released from the mushrooms. Add the shallot and thyme and continue cooking and stirring for about 3 minutes, until the shallots are translucent and the liquid has evaporated. Stir in the wine and lemon juice and regulate the heat so the mixture boils. Cook for about 3 minutes, until the wine had reduced to just a few tablespoons.

2. **Add all but 2 tablespoons** of the cream to the pan. Cook the mixture over high heat, stirring frequently, for about 10 minutes, until the sauce has thickened to a coating consistency (coats the back of a spoon and leaves a trail when your finger is drawn through it). Decrease the heat to low.

3. **In a small bowl**, whisk together the remaining 2 tablespoons cream, the egg yolk, and mustard to taste. Add to the mushrooms and stir together until the mixture has warmed through. Be careful not to let the sauce come to a boil or the egg yolk will scramble. Stir in the salt and pepper, adjust for seasoning, and serve at once, sprinkled with the parsley.

Ratatouille

This classic Provençal fare of tender vegetables simmered in olive oil makes a spectacular vegetarian main course, or it can accompany a light main course of fish or poultry. Use a sharp vegetable peeler to quickly and easily peel the eggplant. ✣ SERVES 4 TO 6

3/4 cup extra virgin olive oil

2 onions, sliced 1/4 inch thick

2 green bell peppers, cored, seeded, and thinly sliced lengthwise

1 teaspoon sea salt

12 plum tomatoes, peeled, seeded, and chopped

3 cloves garlic, finely chopped

1 teaspoon finely chopped fresh thyme

1 large eggplant, peeled and cut into 1 by 2-inch pieces

3 zucchini, ends trimmed, cut into 1 by 2-inch pieces

1/4 teaspoon freshly ground black pepper

10 large fresh basil leaves, finely chopped

1 tablespoon finely chopped fresh flat-leaf parsley

1 cup freshly grated Parmigiano-Reggiano cheese (optional)

1. **In a heavy pan** or enamel-coated cast-iron casserole, heat 1/4 cup of the olive oil over high heat for 1 minute. Add the onions and bell peppers and 1/2 teaspoon of the salt. Decrease the heat to medium-high and cook, stirring frequently, for about 5 minutes, until softened but not brown. Add the tomatoes, garlic, and thyme. Cook over medium-high heat for another 4 to 5 minutes, until the tomato juice has evaporated. Remove from the heat and set aside.

2. **In a large sauté pan**, heat another 1/4 cup of the olive oil over high heat for 1 minute. Add the eggplant and the remaining 1/2 teaspoon salt, and decrease the heat to medium-high. Cook for 8 to 10 minutes, stirring occasionally, until browned, adding a little more olive oil if the pan gets too dry. With a slotted spoon, transfer the eggplant to a colander in the sink and allow the excess oil to drain off. Return the sauté pan to medium-high heat and add the remaining 1/4 cup olive oil. After the oil has heated for 1 minute, add the zucchini and cook, stirring, for 6 to 7 minutes, until golden.

3. **Add the zucchini** and eggplant to the casserole with the onions, peppers, and tomatoes and place over medium-low heat for 2 to 3 minutes to warm and allow the flavors to marry. Add the black pepper, taste for seasoning, and adjust with salt and pepper if necessary. Add the basil and parsley and simmer for 1 minute more. Scatter the cheese over the vegetables just before serving.

Provençal Chard Tart

(TORTA DE BLEA OR TARTE BLETTE)

I have tried this Provençal specialty in many restaurants along the Riviera, but the tiny Le Merenda in Nice has by far the best Torta de Blea in all of southern France. For a long time, the establishment was owned by a couple, who have since retired. Happily, a renowned chef, attempting to escape the stress of his high-profile career, took the reins. As a result, the restaurant not only kept up the wonderful old specialties but also added some heavenly new dishes. The daily menu is quite short—it changes often and concentrates on seasonal foods. The restaurant seats only twenty-odd diners.

This dish features an unusual blend of ingredients, which result in a wonderful taste. I would consider this a vegetable side dish, a first course, or a main course, but in Provence it is served as a dessert.

☙ SERVES 6 TO 8

PASTRY

1 3/4 cups unbleached all-purpose flour

1 large egg

1/4 cup extra virgin olive oil

1 to 3 tablespoons water

1/2 teaspoon fine sea salt

FILLING

1 pound zucchini, grated

2 teaspoons coarse sea salt

2 1/4 pounds Swiss chard, washed, dried, and central stems removed

20 fresh basil leaves, cut into chiffonade (page 5)

1 small red onion, finely chopped

1/4 teaspoon freshly ground black pepper

1 cup golden raisins

1/2 cup pine nuts, toasted (page 30)

1/4 cup freshly grated Parmesan cheese

Finely chopped zest of 1 lemon

1 tablespoon sugar

1/4 cup extra virgin olive oil

3 large eggs, well beaten

1 tablespoon plus 1 1/2 teaspoons unbleached all-purpose flour

1 large egg beaten with 1/4 teaspoon salt, for the glaze

1. **To make the pastry**, place the flour in a mound on a large flat work surface. Make a well in the center of the flour with the base of a measuring cup. In a small bowl, whisk together the egg, olive oil, water, and fine salt. Place the egg mixture in the well. Roughly chop the flour and liquid together with a pastry scraper, scraping towards the center as the mixture begins to spread out. Then, using the heel of your hand, push the dough across the counter until the

continued

dough only just comes together. Do not overwork the dough or it will be tough. Divide the dough into 2 pieces, one roughly 20 percent larger than the other. Flatten them into disks and place in a plastic bag or wrap with plastic wrap. Refrigerate for at least 1 hour and up to 1 day.

2. **Preheat the oven to 375°.** Place the zucchini in a colander and sprinkle with the coarse salt. Toss together so the salt is evenly distributed. Let stand for 20 minutes, then toss again. Repeat once more, then let the zucchini stand for 10 more minutes. Place the colander under cold running water and rinse very thoroughly to get rid of as much salt as possible. Press down on the zucchini to squeeze out the excess liquid, then transfer to a triple layer of paper towels and fold them over the zucchini. Squeeze again to remove as much water from the zucchini as you possibly can.

3. **Finely chop the chard leaves.** In a large bowl, combine the zucchini, chard, basil, red onion, and pepper. Add the raisins, pine nuts, Parmesan, lemon zest, sugar, and olive oil. Toss together and taste for seasoning. Depending on how much salt was absorbed into the zucchini, a little additional salt might be needed. Stir in the beaten eggs. Sprinkle the flour over the top and toss the mixture together, gently but thoroughly.

4. **Roll out the larger piece of dough** into a 13-inch circle about 1/4 inch thick. Transfer it to a 10 by 2-inch-deep round tart pan with a removable bottom or a deep 10-inch pie pan. Gently ease the dough into the corners to line the pan. There should be an even 2 inches of excess dough all around the top edge.

5. **Scoop the filling into** the tart shell, spread it out evenly, and bring the overhanging crust up and over the filling. Brush the top rim of the crust lightly with the egg glaze; the glaze will seal the top to the bottom crust. Roll out the smaller piece of dough to a 10-inch circle about 1/4 inch thick and place over the tart, lining up the edges. Cut off any excess crust by pressing a rolling pin along the edge of the pan. Press the outer rim down gently to seal the 2 crusts together. With your fingers, tuck and lightly push the outer edge of the top crust down between the bottom crust and the edge of the pan. Brush the top of the pastry lightly with the egg glaze and prick in several places with a sharp knife to create a few small steam holes.

6. **Put the tart** on a rimmed baking sheet (to catch any spillovers) and bake for 45 to 55 minutes, until well browned. Cool on a wire rack for at least 30 to 45 minutes before slicing. Serve warm or at room temperature.

Garlic Mashed Potatoes

Each autumn, I escort small groups on a food tour of Paris. We go to my favorite markets, cookware shops and, of course, some restaurants. For many years we went to my favorite three-star restaurant in Paris, Jamin. Joël Robuchon made the most incredible garlic mashed potatoes. My groups were so impressed with the taste that the wait staff would bring us a bowl of the potatoes to pass with our main course (something rarely done in such formal establishments). This brilliant chef has since retired. The restaurant remains (though now with only two stars), still making very good food.

My Garlic Mashed Potatoes run a great second to those at Jamin. Of course this is a popular dish with many variations, but most have an overwhelming taste of raw or roasted garlic. In my preparation, the garlic is cooked with the potato and then puréed together. The potatoes are dried over heat after cooking to remove excess water—thus, they are able to absorb the cream and butter and make a luxurious purée. The cream is added before the butter, so it will be absorbed into the starch of the potato (if the butter is added first it greases the starch and prevents the cream from being absorbed). The mixture should resemble a soft mound, with a consistency similar to soft whipped cream; quite unlike our standard mashed potatoes. The mixture of Yukon Gold and russet potatoes is excellent, but you can use all russets if you are in a potato-deprived community.

🌿 SERVES 6 TO 8

1 pound Idaho-grown or other russet potatoes, peeled and cut into 1-inch chunks

1 pound Yukon Gold or Yellow Finn potatoes, peeled and cut into 1-inch chunks

10 large cloves garlic

1 tablespoon coarse sea salt

1 1/2 cups heavy cream

1/2 cup unsalted butter, at room temperature

1 to 2 teaspoons fine sea salt

1/2 teaspoon freshly ground white pepper

1/2 teaspoon freshly grated nutmeg

1. **Put all the potatoes** and the garlic into a large heavy pan or Dutch oven and add enough cold water to cover by 2 inches. Place over high heat and bring just to a boil. Add the coarse salt and regulate the heat to maintain a brisk simmer. Cook for about 15 minutes, until the potatoes are easily pierced with the tip of a knife.

2. **Warm the bowl of a stand mixer** by filling it with very hot water and letting it stand for about 10 minutes. Pour out the water and dry the bowl thoroughly before adding the potatoes. Drain the potatoes and garlic and return them to the original pan. Place over medium heat and shake back and forth for a minute to dry the vegetables thoroughly. Immediately pass the mixture through the fine disk of a

continued

food mill or press through a potato ricer into the completely dried warm mixer bowl.

3. **In a small saucepan,** heat the cream over high heat just until hot. Do not allow it to boil. Fit the paddle attachment to the mixer and turn to low speed. Add the cream slowly, allowing the potatoes to absorb it gradually. Add just enough cream to give the mixture a soft, mounding consistency, like cream whipped to soft peaks (you may not use all the cream). Add the butter, fine salt, pepper, and nutmeg and continue mixing for 1 to 2 minutes, until fluffy. Taste for seasoning and adjust with salt and pepper if necessary. Serve at once.

Dauphinoise Potatoes

Garlic and cream potatoes are simply scrumptious with many meat entrées. This French specialty is found throughout the country in neighborhood bistros. SERVES 6

2 cups heavy cream, or more

6 large cloves garlic, minced

2 teaspoons sea salt

1/2 teaspoon freshly ground white pepper

1/2 teaspoon freshly grated nutmeg

2 pounds Yellow Finn, Yukon Gold, or russet
  potatoes, peeled and sliced 1/8 inch thick

1 tablespoon unsalted butter, cut into 4 pieces

1. **Preheat the oven to 375°.** In a small saucepan, combine the cream, garlic, salt, pepper, and nutmeg. Bring the mixture just to a boil over high heat. Taste and adjust the salt, if necessary.

2. **Butter a large** deep glass or ceramic baking dish. Layer the potatoes evenly in the dish, overlapping them slightly, leaving 1 1/2 inches between the top of the potatoes and the rim of the dish. Pour the warm cream mixture over the potatoes. They should be barely covered with cream—add a little more cream if necessary. Dot the tops of the potatoes with the butter. Place the baking dish on a rimmed baking sheet (to catch any spillovers).

3. **Bake for 45 minutes to 1 hour,** until the potatoes are tender, well browned with a crust, and yield to the tip of a knife. Let stand for 10 minutes before serving.

Duchesse Potatoes

In this presentation, it is crucial that the potatoes be as dry as possible, so these decorative piped potatoes are dried twice: once after boiling, and then again after they have been pressed through the ricer. Adding the raw yolks to the hot riced potatoes "tightens" or strengthens them, so that the dough will hold its shape after piping. Then, the mixture is cooked over high heat for a minute, which further tightens and begins cooking the yolks. For an elegant dinner, pair these potatoes with Herb-Roasted Rack of Lamb (page 166) and Green Beans in Hazelnut Butter (page 190).

❧ SERVES 6 TO 8

2 1/4 pounds Idaho-grown, other russet, Yellow Finn, or Yukon Gold potatoes, peeled and cut into 1-inch chunks

1 tablespoon coarse sea salt

1/2 cup unsalted butter

6 large egg yolks

1 teaspoon fine sea salt

1/2 teaspoon freshly ground white pepper

1/8 to 1/4 teaspoon freshly grated nutmeg

1 large egg beaten with 1/4 teaspoon salt, for the glaze

1. **Put the potatoes into a large** heavy pan and add enough cold water to cover by 2 inches. Bring to a boil over high heat and add the coarse salt. Regulate the heat to maintain a brisk simmer and cook for about 15 minutes, until the potatoes are tender and can be easily pierced with the tip of a 1knife. Drain the potatoes and return them to the original pan. Place over medium heat and shake back and forth for a minute to dry thoroughly.

2. **If you plan to serve** the potatoes as soon as they are done, preheat the oven to 400°. In a small saucepan, melt the butter over low heat, stirring, until it has a creamy consistency. Remove from the heat just before all the butter has melted and stir until smooth.

3. **Pass the hot potatoes** through the fine disk of a food mill or press through a potato ricer. Return the potatoes to the original pan and place over medium heat for about 1 minute to remove any excess water. Remove the pan from the heat and immediately mix in the butter with a wooden spatula. Add and mix in the yolks, fine salt, pepper, and nutmeg. Taste and adjust the seasoning if necessary; you should just be able to distinguish the flavor of salt and nutmeg, otherwise the dish will be bland. Return the pan to medium heat for about 30 seconds to thicken (tighten) the yolks slightly. (This is a very important step, because the thickened yolks will allow the potatoes to hold their shapes better after being piped.)

4. **Grease 2 baking sheets** with butter. Spoon the potatoes into a pastry bag fitted with a 1/2-inch French star tip. Pipe onto the prepared baking sheets (I like to make shapes that resemble fir trees or chrysanthemums). Use approximately 2 tablespoons of the potato mixture for each

shape to make 24 to 36 portions. (The potatoes may be prepared up to 8 hours ahead of time to this point; simply cover the baking sheet with plastic wrap and refrigerate until ready to bake.)

5. **If the potatoes have been refrigerated**, return them to room temperature for about 15 minutes before baking, and preheat the oven to 400°. Brush each shape lightly with the egg glaze. Place in the oven and bake for about 15 minutes, until heated through and slightly browned.

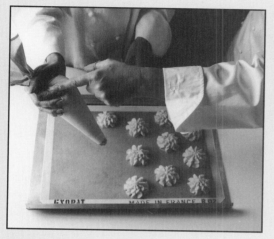

APPLY PRESSURE ON THE PIPING BAG WITH YOUR FINGERS AND . . .

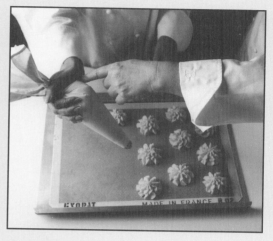

YOUR PALM.

HOLD THE BAG STEADY AND VERTICAL AS YOU SQUEEZE.

German Potato Dumplings

This is an old, cherished family recipe. It is usually served alongside pork roast with gravy or beef "birds" (pieces of thin round steak, rolled and stuffed with chopped parsley, chopped onion, and bacon braised in stock). My grandmother, mother, aunts, and I have all made this many times, and it will always be a favorite with my children. There are some recipes that evoke powerful memories of home. For me, one of the best is German Potato Dumplings.

Finely grated onion can only be made using the very finest holes of a grater. The onion is almost puréed. It is amazing to see how much onion it takes to make a teaspoon of grated onion. I usually make a double batch of this recipe since leftovers are fantastic. To reheat, slice the cooked dumplings into 1/2-inch slices and fry them in about 1/8 inch of butter or olive oil until golden.

Don't equate this dish with the Potato Gnocchi on page 135. In this recipe, the potatoes are boiled 8 to 12 hours before the dumplings are mixed, and only one egg binds them together. This is a much heavier dumpling than the gnocchi, which should be lighter-than-air. ✤ SERVES 6 TO 8

6 large Idaho-grown or other russet potatoes, unpeeled

1 tablespoon coarse sea salt

1 large egg, lightly beaten

1 teaspoon fine sea salt

1 teaspoon finely grated onion

1/4 cup finely chopped fresh flat-leaf parsley (optional)

1 to 1 1/2 cups unbleached all-purpose flour, plus extra for sprinkling

1. **Put the potatoes** into a large pot and add enough cold water to cover by 2 inches. Bring to a boil over high heat. Once the water boils, regulate the heat to maintain a brisk simmer and cook for 30 to 40 minutes, until the potatoes are tender all the way through when pierced with a sharp knife. Drain the potatoes, slit the skins open a bit, and set aside at room temperature for 8 to 12 hours to dry.

2. **Bring a stockpot** three-quarters full of water to a boil over high heat; add the coarse salt. Regulate the heat so that the water boils rapidly. Generously flour a baking sheet.

3. **Scoop the pulp out** of the potato skins and pass it through the fine disk of a food mill or through a potato ricer into a large bowl. Add the egg, fine salt, onion, parsley, and 1 cup of the flour. Mix together with a heavy wooden spoon or with

your hands. If the mixture is still sticky add a little more flour. The dough should hold together and not feel wet. You may not use all the flour. With clean, dry, lightly floured hands, scoop up about 1/3 cup of the mixture and shape into round dumplings. You'll end up with 14 to 16 dumplings. Repeat until all the mixture is used, placing the formed dumplings on the prepared baking sheet.

4. **In several batches,** drop the dumplings into the boiling water without crowding them. Regulate the heat so that the water maintains a brisk simmer at all times. The dumplings will sink to the bottom and rise after 2 to 3 minutes. Once they have risen, allow them to simmer for an additional 3 minutes. Remove the dumplings with a slotted spoon and drain on doubled paper towels. Serve immediately.

LESSON TWELVE

Desserts

THE GRAND FINALE OF THE MEAL SHOULD BE MEMORABLE—and if your dessert is well made, everyone is sure to remember it. The French have a reputation for using excessive amounts of butter and cream in desserts. While these rich ingredients are certainly used in the most exquisite desserts, it is the size of the dessert that is important. The goal is to create small, perfectly flavored desserts that look as though you may want to eat ten, but are so rich that you are completely content with one. A two-inch piece of my one layer Grand Marnier Chocolate Cake with Shiny Chocolate Icing (page 247) is so flavorful and satisfying that you will have trouble eating a second piece—even if you have a serious sweet tooth. In contrast, a piece of cake made from a box full of preservatives and accompanied by canned greasy frosting does not a dessert make.

Making desserts correctly requires patience, attention to rules, and perfect measuring. Dry ingredients should be spooned into measuring cups, then leveled off with a flat-edged knife. Teaspoons and tablespoons should also be leveled off with a knife. Never tap measuring cups on the counter or with a knife, otherwise the ingredients will compact, and you'll end up with more than the recipe calls for. Liquid ingredients should be measured in glass measuring cups on a flat surface so that you can accurately align the top of the liquid to the marked measure. I can't overstate this—improper measuring will cause failure in desserts. Think of dessert making as a science rather than an art—though it is that, too—and you'll understand the need for precision.

Use top-quality ingredients—including flour, sugar, vanilla beans and extract, and chocolate. These are everyday items, but your desserts will be much more tasty if you buy the best available products. If you don't use flour very often, buy small amounts at a time. (Never freeze flour because it will pick up the flavors in your freezer.) C&H is a good brand of sugar, and Nielsen-Massey makes a high-quality vanilla extract. Avoid the fraudulent vanilla sold as "vanillin," which is a foul chemical substitute for the real thing.

I use five excellent crusts at the school, all containing unsalted butter. The Butter and Lard Crust (page 207) is a sturdy yet very light and flaky crust, and it is used for the American-style pies. Lard is a natural product and therefore creates a more flavorful and flaky crust than shortening. Ultra-processed shortening can never come close to the flakiness produced by lard, even with numerous tricks like adding lemon juice, vinegar, or ice water. Another flavorful crust, Cream Cheese Crust (page 215) goes well with fruit or heavier fillings like pecans. Look for a high-quality cream cheese made without the use of thickeners.

I love going to the elegant restaurants in France when, after many courses of savory foods, the server brings a beautifully decorated plate of petit fours. Each looks like a jewel, almost too pretty to eat, and each has very different and intense flavors. After this array of petit fours, a remarkable dessert is served to finish the meal. My last bit of advice about desserts would be to set this goal for yourself—always serve delicious, hand-crafted desserts that perfectly complement the meal.

Crepes, both savory and sweet, are sold on street corners at small stands throughout Paris. The choices for fillings are endless. Sweet options include everything from chocolate, to butter and sugar, to butter and sugar with Grand Marnier. Crepes Suzette (page 240) is a classic dessert crepe presentation. The best crepes I've ever tasted were in a tiny restaurant called La Crêperie des Chevaliers de Malte, in Villedieu les Poêles, in Normandy. The tiny family-owned shop has the most magnificent selection of perfectly made crepes and galettes. My friend and I so enjoyed the meal that we returned three days in a row to sample the specialties and enjoy the company of the owners.

Crepe batter must rest for at least 30 minutes, preferably 1 hour, at room temperature before cooking, so the flour can absorb the liquid. If you're planning ahead, you can make the batter without the butter and refrigerate it, covered, for up to 8 hours. The batter should be brought back to room temperature and then the melted butter should be added just before cooking—otherwise it would solidify when chilled.

🍴 MAKES ABOUT 18 CREPES

1 cup unbleached all-purpose flour

3/4 cup whole milk

2 large eggs

1/4 teaspoon sugar

1/4 teaspoon salt

3 tablespoons clarified butter (page 31), melted, plus extra for cooking

1. **In a food processor or blender,** combine the flour, milk, eggs, sugar, salt, and melted butter. Process for approximately 10 seconds, until smooth. (To mix by hand, place the flour in a bowl and add the milk in a thin stream, whisking constantly, to make a perfectly smooth batter the consistency of thin cream. If necessary, add half a tablespoon or so of milk to thin the batter. Whisk in the eggs, salt, and clarified butter.)

2. **Cover and let the mixture stand** at room temperature for at least 30 minutes or up to 1 hour.

3. **Heat a 5-inch crepe pan** (page 14) over medium to medium-high heat until very hot. Drops of water scattered on the surface should dance and quickly evaporate. Brush the pan lightly with clarified butter (instead of scorching a good pastry brush, you can make your own by tying a folded paper towel around the tins of a fork with kitchen twine). Pour 1/4 cup of the batter into the center of the hot pan and quickly tilt it in all

continued

directions to lightly coat the entire base of the pan; immediately pour out any excess. (The exact amount of batter used depends upon the size of the crepe pan, and it's better to have more than not enough.) After 30 seconds or so, the bottom of the crepe should be golden brown, with a lacy pattern.

4. **Loosen the edges** of the crepe with an offset spatula. Flip over and heat for just a few seconds to cook any remaining raw spots. This side will be the inside of the crepe; the lacy side that was cooked first is called the "presentation side," and is always on the outside.

5. **Continue making crepes** in the same way, transferring them to a baking sheet or a large platter lined with plastic wrap. The crepes can be stacked, slightly overlapping each other, while hot. Use immediately, or cool and store covered in the refrigerator for up to 2 days, or freeze for several weeks.

Butter and Lard Crust

This is the ultimate crust for American-style pies. The lard makes it sturdy and flaky, and the butter lends a rich flavor—the best of both worlds. It can be baked with the Apple Pie filling on page 229 or baked blind (pre-baked, cooled, and then filled) with the Lemon Filling on page 218. This is also a good crust choice for dense fillings like pumpkin. If you are making a lemon pie, add finely grated or chopped lemon zest to the dough. ✍ MAKES 2 (9-INCH) CRUSTS

1 3/4 cups unbleached all-purpose flour, chilled in the freezer for at least 30 minutes

3/4 teaspoon sea salt

1/2 cup lard, chilled and cut into 1/4-inch dice

1/2 cup unsalted butter, chilled and cut into 1/4-inch dice

6 tablespoons ice water

1. **On a clean surface** or a large cutting board, combine the chilled flour, salt, lard, and butter. Quickly chop the fat into the flour with a plastic pastry scraper until the mixture looks like plump peas. Do not blend the mixture; there must be small but visible chunks in order for the pastry to be flaky. Use the pastry scraper to cut the water into the flour mixture, using a scraping and chopping motion.

2. **Lightly flour your kneading** surface and, using the pastry scraper, quickly gather the dough in a mass. (Do not touch the dough with your fingers too much, or it will warm up and yield a tough crust.) With the heel of your hand, smear the dough across the counter, a section at a time, until the dough just comes together. Repeat the smearing procedure only 4 or 5 times. It is very important not to overwork the dough. Small chunks of visible butter ensure a flaky crust, so do not attempt to make a smooth, homogeneous dough.

3. **Form the dough into a ball** and flatten into a 5-inch disk. Place in a plastic bag or wrap with plastic wrap and refrigerate for at least 2 hours and up to 2 days before using. (The dough may also be wrapped in plastic wrap, placed in a freezer bag, and frozen for up to 2 months. Thaw in the refrigerator for several hours before using.)

4. **Remove the dough disk** from the refrigerator and let stand for 5 to 10 minutes at room temperature. Divide the dough into 2 pieces (you can make 2 single-crusted pies or 1 double-crusted). On a lightly floured surface, roll out 1 piece of the dough into a circle, 1/8 inch thick, sprinkling with flour when necessary to prevent sticking. It will be about 10 1/2 inches in diameter.

continued

Carefully fold the dough into quarters and transfer to a 9-inch heavy aluminum pie pan. Gently unfold the dough and press it into the pan, easing it into the corners with your knuckles. Trim the dough so the edge extends 1 inch from the outermost edge of the pan; fold the overlap back under itself to form a smooth edge. Crimp the edge with your fingers or a fork. (If making a double-crusted pie, roll out the other piece of dough as above and place between 2 pieces of plastic wrap before chilling.) Chill for 30 minutes before filling and baking as directed in the chosen recipe. (At this point, the lined pie pan can be refrigerated for 1 day or frozen for 2 months. Wrap in plastic wrap and then in foil, to avoid freezer burn.)

5. **If the crust will be baked blind** (without filling), preheat the oven to 400° and place a rack in the middle of the oven. (If using a pure convection oven (page 11), set it for 375° and bake on any shelf.) Prick the base of the shell 12 times with a fork and line it with aluminum foil or parchment paper. Fill the shell with aluminum or ceramic pie weights. Place the pan on a baking sheet and bake for 10 to 15 minutes, until the pastry begins to brown around the edge. Remove the pie weights and foil from the crust and return the pastry shell to the oven. Continue baking for 10 to 12 minutes, until the base of the crust is lightly browned. Cool on a wire rack for 10 minutes before filling.

Lining a Pie or Tart Pan

Fold the dough into quarters and transfer to the pan

Gently unfold the dough

Ease the dough into the corners with your knuckles

Flaky Butter Crust

This melt-in-your-mouth buttery crust can be used in many recipes. It is important for the butter to remain cool during the process, or the crust will be tough. A classic French method for keeping the butter cool involves using a rolling pin to beat cold-from-the-fridge butter on the counter until it becomes pliable. You should be able to flatten the butter and, then, with a pastry scraper, fold it in half, up over itself, without the butter showing any cracks. A smooth fold indicates that the butter is just the right temperature to begin incorporating into the flour. Convection ovens work particularly well for baking pastry, because the moving air dries the bottom of the crust quickly.

MAKES 2 (9-INCH) CRUSTS

1 3/4 cups unbleached all-purpose flour

1/2 teaspoon sea salt

1 1/2 cups cold unsalted butter

1 large egg, lightly beaten

1 tablespoon cold water

1. **On a clean surface** or large cutting board, combine the flour, salt, and butter. Chop the butter and flour together with a plastic pastry scraper until a rough, crumbly mixture forms, scraping up the flour into the butter as you chop. Make a well in the center of the flour-butter mixture. Place the egg and water in the well. Roughly chop the flour together with the egg and water using the pastry scraper. Then, using the heel of your hand, smear the dough across the counter, and repeat 4 to 5 times until the dough just comes together. Do not overwork the dough, or it will be tough. Small chunks of butter should still be visible in the dough when it comes together—this will ensure a flaky crust.

2. **Form the dough into a ball** and flatten into a 5-inch disk. Place in a plastic bag or wrap with plastic wrap and refrigerate for at least 1 hour and up to 24 hours before using. If you refrigerate the dough for more than 2 hours, it should be brought to room temperature before proceeding to step 3. (The dough may also be wrapped in plastic wrap, placed in a resealable freezer bag, and frozen for up to 1 month. Thaw in the refrigerator for several hours before using.)

3. **Divide the dough into** 2 pieces (you can make 2 single-crusted pies or 1 double-crusted). On a lightly floured surface, roll out 1 piece of the dough into a circle, 1/8 inch thick, sprinkling with flour when necessary to prevent sticking and keeping it as round as possible. It will be about 10 inches in diameter. Carefully fold the dough into quarters and transfer it to a 9-inch heavy aluminum pie pan. Gently unfold the dough and press it into the pan, easing it into the corners with your knuckles. Trim the dough so the edge extends 1 inch from the outermost edge of the pan; fold the overlap back under itself to form a smooth edge. Crimp the edge with your fingers or a fork. (If making a double-crusted pie, roll out the other piece of dough as above and place between 2 pieces of plastic wrap before chilling.) Chill the shell for at least 30 minutes, until firm. (At this point, the lined pie pan can be refrigerated for 1 day or frozen for 2 months. Wrap in plastic wrap and then in foil, to avoid freezer burn.)

4. **If the crust will be baked** blind (without filling), preheat the oven to 400° and place a rack in the middle of the oven. (If using a pure convection oven (page 11), set it for 375° and bake on any shelf.) Prick the base of the shell 12 times with a fork and line it with aluminum foil or parchment paper. Fill the shell with aluminum or ceramic pie weights. Place the pan on a baking sheet and bake for 10 to 15 minutes, until the pastry begins to brown around the edge. Remove the pie weights and foil from the crust and return the pastry shell to the oven. Continue baking for 10 to 12 minutes, until the base of the crust is lightly browned. Cool on a wire rack for 10 minutes before filling.

Sweet Sugar Crust

This is a fragile melt-in-your-mouth, cookie dough–like crust. A high sugar content dough such as this one makes for difficult rolling out, so it's really only appropriate for small tarts, not for full-size pies. The sugar crystals act as tiny razor blades, cutting the dough as you work it. It is a good base for individual Fresh Fruit Tarts (page 228), Mocha Filling (page 219), or Chocolate Mousse Filling (page 220). The empty tart shells can be baked ahead and frozen, or simply kept in an airtight container for several weeks. This dough is always baked blind and cooled before adding the filling. ✍ MAKES 36 (1-INCH) CRUSTS

1 cup unsalted butter, at room temperature

1/3 cup sugar

Finely grated zest of 1 orange or lemon

1 large egg

1 teaspoon vanilla extract

2 1/2 cups unbleached all-purpose flour

1. **In the bowl of a stand mixer** fitted with the paddle attachment, beat the butter, sugar, and zest on medium speed for 2 minutes, until pale and fluffy. Add the egg and vanilla and continue to mix just until combined. With the mixer off, add the flour, then mix on low speed just until blended; continue to mix on low speed for 30 seconds.

2. **Divide the dough** in half and shape each portion into a flat disk about 8 inches in diameter. Place in a plastic bag or wrap with plastic wrap and refrigerate for at least 1 1/2 hours or overnight before using. (The dough may also be wrapped in plastic wrap, placed in a resealable freezer bag, and frozen for up to 1 month. Thaw in the refrigerator for several hours before using.)

3. **Preheat the oven to 350°** and place a rack in the lower third of the oven. (If using a pure convection oven (page 11), set it for 325° and bake on any shelf.)

4. **For individual tarts,** you do not roll out the dough. Pull off 36 small balls of dough and press into 1-inch tart tins. Prick the base of the each tart 1 time with a fork. (At this point, the lined pie pan(s) can be refrigerated for 1 day or frozen for up to 1 month. Wrap in plastic wrap and then in foil, to avoid freezer burn.)

5. **Place the tins** on a baking sheet in the refrigerator for 30 minutes.

6. **With the tins still on the baking sheet,** bake for 6 to 8 minutes, until the pastry is thoroughly dry and lightly browned. Some of the shells may bake faster than others, so remove them as they brown. Cool on a wire rack and fill as directed in the chosen recipe. (Once baked, the shells can be held for 1 week in a tightly covered container before filling.)

Nut Crust

This crust is perfect for fruit tarts or those with rich chocolate fillings that require a pre-baked crust. The finely ground nuts provide flavor and color. Almonds, pecans, or hazelnuts can be used. Hazelnuts and pecans have a very distinct flavor, so before you decide which nut to use, consider how it will complement the filling. Chocolate fillings are excellent with pecans or hazelnuts. Fruit tarts filled with pastry cream are enhanced by the somewhat bland almond—stronger-tasting nuts might overwhelm the delicate flavor of the filling. Like the Sweet Sugar Crust (page 212), this dough has a high sugar content, which makes rolling it out somewhat difficult.

🌿 MAKES 2 (9-INCH) OR 2 (2-INCH) CRUSTS

3 1/2 cups unbleached all-purpose flour

3/4 cup ground almonds, pecans, or hazelnuts

Finely chopped zest of 2 oranges or lemons, or a combination

2/3 cup superfine sugar (page 8)

Large pinch of sea salt

1 1/2 cups cold unsalted butter, cut into tablespoon-sized pieces

2 large egg yolks

1 large egg

1 tablespoon rum (optional)

1. **In the bowl of a stand mixer** fitted with the paddle attachment, combine the flour, nuts, citrus zest, sugar, salt, butter, egg yolks, egg, and rum. Mix on medium speed for 1 to 1 1/2 minutes, until the ingredients are just blended and the dough comes together.

2. **Turn the dough out onto** a lightly floured surface or large cutting board and divide into 2 balls. Flatten the balls into disks. Place into separate plastic bags or wrap each with plastic wrap; refrigerate for at least 45 minutes or up to 2 hours before using. (The disks can also be wrapped in plastic wrap, placed in a freezer bag, and frozen for up to 2 months. Thaw in the refrigerator for several hours before using.)

3. **Remove the dough disks** from the refrigerator and let rest at room temperature for 10 minutes before rolling. Preheat the oven to 350° and place one rack in the lower third of the oven and another in the upper third. (If using a pure convection oven (page 11), set it for 325° and bake on any shelf.)

4. **For full-size pies**, you can make 2 single-crusted pies, or 1 double-crusted. Note that this is a fragile dough, so it will be a little difficult to roll out. Roll only until it begins to break apart. You can finish by pressing the dough into the tins. Roll out 1 of the disks of dough between 2 pieces

continued

of plastic wrap or on a generously floured surface, to 1/8 inch thick, sprinkling with flour when necessary to prevent sticking. It will be about 10 inches in diameter. Carefully fold the dough into quarters and transfer it to a 9-inch heavy aluminum pie pan. Gently unfold the dough and press it into the pan, easing it into the corners with your knuckles. Trim the dough so the edge extends 1 inch from the outermost edge of the pan; fold the overlap back under itself to form a smooth edge. Crimp the edge with your fingers or a fork. Prick the base of the shell 3 or 4 times with a fork. (If making a double-crusted pie, roll out the other piece of dough as above and place between 2 pieces of plastic wrap before chilling.)

5. **For individual tarts**, do not roll out the dough. Pull off 24 small balls of dough and press into 2-inch tart tins. Prick the base of each tart 1 time with a fork. (At this point, the lined pie tin(s) can be refrigerated for 1 day or frozen for up to 1 month. Wrap in plastic wrap and then in foil, to avoid freezer burn.)

6. **Place the tins** on a baking sheet in the refrigerator for 30 minutes.

7. **Bake the large tins** for 20 minutes and the individual tins for 10 minutes, until the crusts are browned. Some of the individual shells may bake faster than others, so remove them as they brown. Cool on a wire rack and fill as directed in the chosen recipe. (Once baked, the shells can be held for 1 week in a tightly covered container before filling.)

Cream Cheese Crust

A simple crust that complements Southern-Style Pecan Pie (page 233) or Apple Pie (page 229), this crust must be baked with a filling; it cannot be pre-baked. ✍ MAKES 1 (9-INCH) CRUST

**1 cup cold unsalted butter, cut into
    tablespoon-sized pieces**

**1 (8-ounce) package cold cream cheese, cut into
    tablespoon-sized pieces**

2 cups unbleached all-purpose flour

1/2 teaspoon sea salt

1. **In the bowl of a stand mixer** fitted with the paddle attachment, combine the butter and cream cheese and mix on low speed for 2 to 2 1/2 minutes. Scrape down the sides of the bowl with a spatula. Add the flour and salt. Continue to mix just long enough to incorporate all the ingredients. Small chunks of visible butter ensure a flaky crust, so do not attempt to make a smooth, homogeneous dough. It is very important to not overwork the dough or it will be tough.

2. **Form the dough into a ball** and flatten into a disk. Wrap with plastic wrap and refrigerate for about 1 1/2 hours or up to 1 day before using. (The dough may also be wrapped in plastic wrap, placed in a resealable freezer bag, and frozen for up to 2 months. Thaw in the refrigerator for several hours before using.)

3. **Remove the dough disk** from the refrigerator and let rest at room temperature for 10 minutes before rolling. On a lightly floured surface or large cutting board, roll out the dough to 1/8 inch thick, sprinkling with flour when necessary to prevent sticking. It will be about 10 inches in diameter. Carefully fold the dough into quarters and transfer it to a 9-inch heavy aluminum pie pan. Gently unfold the dough and press it into the pan, easing it into the corners with your knuckles. Trim the dough so the edge extends 1 inch from the outermost edge of the pan; fold the overlap back under itself to form a smooth edge. Crimp the edge with your fingers or a fork. Lightly prick the bottom with a fork. Chill the shell for at least 30 minutes before filling and baking in the chosen recipe. (At this point, the lined pie pan can be refrigerated for 1 day or frozen for 2 months. Wrap in plastic wrap and then in foil, to avoid freezer burn.)

Cream Puff Pastry

(CHOUX PASTRY OR PATE À CHOUX)

This versatile dough is used for many recipes, ranging from appetizers to desserts. It can be filled, have additional ingredients added, or simply topped with sugar. Everyone should have this useful recipe in his or her repertoire.

I never know what to call this because the French name choux sounds like "shoe," but "cream puff pastry" implies American puffs filled with whipped cream. Whenever I say a French word on my TV show, translations are placed on the screen so that my viewers understand what I am talking about. So for now, I usually refer to this recipe as "choux pastry."

The classic French use for choux pastry is to make profiteroles—small puffs filled with French Custard Ice Cream (page 224) and coated with a chocolate glaze such as Shiny Chocolate Icing (page 248). (If you don't have ice cream, Pastry Cream (page 225) is an acceptable substitute.) The first time I had these in Paris, I was fascinated by the wonderful taste of the puff itself. The cream puff dough I knew was always heavy and wet. The trick, my pastry chef told us, was to bake the puffs until the cracks of the pastries were tanned. He teased us, saying that blonde American girls were good but that blonde pastries were bad. In order for any pastry container to taste good, whether it be a pastry or a pre-baked tart crust, it must be well-baked. Baking brings out the flavor of the ingredients. Under-baked pastry is doughy, flat, and tasteless.

Another specialty is the Champagne Sugar Puff found most often in the Champagne region of France. Gruyère Cheese Puffs are from the Burgundy region and are excellent served with red wine or even ice-cold beer.

Making pastries is a science. It requires exact measurements and has rules that must be followed to ensure success. Read all the instructions carefully and make sure that you are gauging the completion of each step by what the dough looks like, not how much time has passed. ✒ MAKES 18 TO 24 PUFFS

1/2 cup unsalted butter, cut into 1/4-inch dice

1 cup water

1/2 teaspoon sugar (optional, used only for dessert recipes)

1/4 teaspoon sea salt

1 cup unbleached all-purpose flour

4 large eggs

1 large egg or more, well beaten

1. **In a heavy saucepan** (do not use nonstick or it will be difficult to see the "haze" in step 2), combine the butter, water, sugar, and salt. Place over high heat and swirl the pan occasionally to make sure the butter melts evenly. Watch carefully as you only want the butter to melt. You do not want the water to boil.

2. **The moment the water reaches** the boiling point and the butter has all melted, remove the pan from the heat and add the flour all at once. Using a wooden spoon, stir to blend in the flour until the mixture is smooth. Once the mixture forms a ball and pulls away from the sides of the pan, return the pan to high heat and dry it out by moving and beating the dough constantly back and forth until a haze forms on the bottom of the pan (a dry dough will absorb more egg in the next step). This will take from 1 to 2 minutes, depending on the strength of the heat. Remove from the heat.

3. **Adding only one at a time**, add the 4 whole eggs, stirring briskly with the wooden spoon to thoroughly incorporate each egg before adding the next. Add just enough of the 1 beaten egg to make a glossy mixture that falls slowly from the spoon in a thick shiny sheet. It should not hold in a clump on the spoon or slide off quickly. You may not need all of the beaten egg. For recipes that call for cream puff pastry dough, stop here.

4. **Preheat the oven to 400°** and place a rack in the lower third of the oven. (If using a pure convection oven (page 11), set it for 375°.) Allow the dough to cool for 5 to 6 minutes to make it easier to handle. Line a baking sheet with parchment paper. Spoon the dough into a pastry bag fitted with a 1/2-inch plain tip. Pipe out rounds onto the prepared baking sheet that are 1 inch high and 1 to 1 1/4 inches in diameter. Using a pastry brush, glaze the tops of the rounds with a little of the beaten egg, using another egg if necessary. Be careful not to let the egg to drip off of the rounds onto the baking sheet, as this will prevent the puffs from rising.

5. **Bake for about 15 minutes**, until the dough has risen and puffed. Open the oven door a few inches to allow the excess steam to escape, then close the door and continue to bake for 5 to 10 minutes, until the cracks covering the puffs are golden brown, not white. Cool the puffs on wire racks, leaving space between each one to allow the steam to escape. If placed too close together, the puffs will get soggy. Allow to cool for 30 minutes before filling. Filled puffs can be refrigerated for up to 6 hours, but any chocolate coating should be applied just before serving.

Variations

CHAMPAGNE SUGAR PUFF: After brushing with the egg wash, sprinkle each puff generously with pearl sugar and bake as directed.

GRUYÈRE CHEESE PUFF: Add 1/3 cup finely shredded Gruyère cheese to the batter after all the egg has been added in step 3. Pipe the dough as directed, brush with egg glaze, and sprinkle a little more finely shredded cheese on the top of each puff. Bake as directed.

Lemon Filling

Use a pre-baked Sweet Sugar Crust (page 212), Butter and Lard Crust (page 207), or Nut Crust (page 213) with this filling.

🌿 MAKES ABOUT 2 CUPS

2 large eggs

2 large egg yolks

1 cup sugar

1/3 cup freshly squeezed lemon juice, strained

Finely grated zest of 1 lemon

6 tablespoons unsalted butter, cut into tablespoon-sized pieces

Tart Fillings

At elegant French restaurants, tiny tarts, which the French consider petit fours, are often precursors to the main dessert: an appetizer to tempt your sweet tooth before the main attraction. Any of the following three fillings make a fine main dessert or can be served as petit fours. I especially like to serve a variety of petit fours, made with different fillings, at luncheons.

1. **In the bowl of a stand mixer** fitted with the paddle attachment, combine the whole eggs, egg yolks, and sugar. Beat on medium-low speed for about 2 minutes, until thick, fluffy, and light yellow. Add the lemon juice and zest and mix to combine. Pour the mixture into a small saucepan and place over medium heat. Cook, stirring constantly, for 3 to 5 minutes, until it reaches a creamy consistency. Remove from the heat and stir in the butter until melted and smooth.

2. **Preheat the oven to 375°** and place a rack in the lower third of the oven. (If using a pure convection oven (page 11), set it for 350°.) Pour the hot lemon filling into baked and cooled crusts. (It will be easier to pour if you transfer the hot mixture to a heatproof glass measuring cup with a pouring spout). Place the filled tart(s) in the oven for 2 to 3 minutes for individual tarts and about 5 minutes for a full-size tart, just to set the filling. Let cool and serve at room temperature.

Mocha Filling

This is one of the most luxurious tart fillings of all. I love coffee, but for those who don't, the coffee can be omitted. Use espresso powder from Italy, if possible—it has a lovely, rich flavor. Choose either a pre-baked Sweet Sugar Crust (page 212) or Nut Crust (page 213) for this filling. ✒ MAKES ABOUT 2 CUPS

2 cups heavy cream

6 tablespoons sugar

1 teaspoon instant espresso powder

2 ounces finely chopped bittersweet chocolate

1/4 cup grated bittersweet chocolate, for garnish (optional)

1. **In a heavy tall-sided** saucepan (which will prevent the cream from boiling over), combine the cream, sugar, and espresso powder. Place the pan over medium-low heat and stir until the sugar has dissolved. Increase the heat to medium-high and bring to a boil, stirring occasionally and watching carefully so the cream doesn't boil over. Cook for 8 to 10 minutes, until thickened and reduced to about 1 1/3 cups. Remove from the heat, add the chopped chocolate, and stir until the chocolate is completely melted.

2. **Let the mixture cool** for 10 minutes before spooning or pouring into a pre-baked and cooled crust(s). Refrigerate for 20 to 30 minutes. When the tart(s) have set, bring back to room temperature, decorate the top(s) with the grated chocolate, and serve.

Chocolate Mousse Filling

Use with a pre-baked Sweet Sugar Crust (page 212) or Nut Crust (page 213). This filling is also good spooned into ramekins, chilled, and served as a mousse. ✒ MAKES ABOUT 2 CUPS

4 ounces chopped bittersweet chocolate

2 tablespoons Chambord, Grand Marnier, or rum

4 large eggs, separated, at room temperature

1 teaspoon vanilla extract

1/2 teaspoon cream of tartar (optional)

1/4 cup sugar

Grated bittersweet chocolate and/or fresh raspberries, for garnish

1. **In a heavy saucepan**, combine the chocolate and the Chambord. Place the pan over very low heat and stir constantly until the mixture has almost melted. Remove from the heat. The heat of the pan will continue to melt any remaining small pieces. Do not allow the chocolate to get too hot or it may curdle. When the chocolate has melted, add the egg yolks, one at a time, whisking slightly after adding each yolk. Whisk in the vanilla. Transfer the chocolate to a large bowl and set aside.

2. **In the bowl of a stand mixer** fitted with the whisk attachment, or a clean copper bowl using a balloon whisk, whisk the egg whites until they are slightly foamy. Add the cream of tartar (add only if not whisking in a copper bowl; see page 35) and continue beating until soft peaks form. Add the sugar and continue whisking for 30 to 45 seconds more, until stiff, glossy peaks form.

3. **Gently fold a spoonful** of the egg whites into the chocolate mixture to lighten it (so it will more easily blend into the remaining whites). Add the remaining whites in 3 batches, gently folding between each addition. Gently spoon or pipe the filling into the baked and cooled tart shell. Chill in the refrigerator for about 2 hours, until set. To serve, garnish with grated chocolate and/or fresh raspberries.

Buttercream Frosting

This recipe, which I learned from Richard Grausman in the mid-seventies at a cooking demonstration in Chicago, opened the door to French cooking for me. When I tasted this luxurious frosting, I realized that the only bad thing about my cooking skills were the bad cookbooks, calling for margarine and powdered sugar in their inferior recipes. The result should have been called chemical cream, not buttercream.

Amazingly, this classic recipe is made by pouring a 239° sugar syrup (a syrup that has reached the "soft-ball" stage, as defined in candy-making terminology) into raw egg yolks, and then beating the mixture until it forms a thick, voluptuous mass. When the mixture has cooled, seeming mounds of unsalted butter are added. It's all worth it. ❧ MAKES ABOUT 3 CUPS

1 cup sugar

1/2 cup water

6 large egg yolks, at room temperature

1 1/2 cups unsalted butter, at room temperature

2 teaspoons vanilla extract

1. **Combine the sugar** and water in a small saucepan. Place over low heat and stir until the sugar has dissolved. Dip a pastry brush in cold water and wash the sides of the pan down to remove all the sugar crystals. Increase the heat to medium-high and cook until the syrup reaches the softball stage (239°) on a candy thermometer. (If you don't have a thermometer, keep a glass of ice water on hand and drop a few drops of the sugar syrup into the water occasionally as it begins to thicken. The softball stage is reached when the syrup forms a soft, pliable ball as soon as it hits the water.)

2. **Place the egg yolks** in the bowl of a stand mixer fitted with the paddle attachment. Turn the mixer on slow speed just to break up the yolks. Add the hot sugar syrup in a thin stream, pouring slowly so that the syrup reaches the yolks between the side of the bowl and the paddle, until all of the syrup is added. Once the sugar syrup has been added, increase the speed to medium-high. Beat for 5 to 6 minutes, until the mixture has cooled and is thick and pale yellow. You should not be able to feel any heat on the underside of the bowl.

3. **Add the softened butter** 1/4 cup at a time, beating after each addition, just until incorporated. After all the butter has been added, add the vanilla extract and beat for 30 to 60 seconds on medium-high, until the mixture is shiny and has a creamy, spreadable frosting consistency.

Variation

LIQUEUR BUTTERCREAM: In place of the vanilla extract, use Grand Marnier or Chambord. Begin by adding 2 tablespoons of your liqueur of choice, and taste. Each liqueur has a different flavor strength. Try to achieve a pleasant hint of flavor, not an overwhelming punch.

Basic Vanilla Custard Sauce

(CRÈME ANGLAISE)

French cooking often builds on itself. Once you have mastered one technique, you'll often find that, with slight alterations or the addition of other ingredients, you have mastered several other important dishes too. And so it is for Crème Anglaise, a rich custard sauce. As is, the sauce can be served under dense chocolate cakes or to accompany poached fruit. Almost double the amount of sugar in the recipe and you have the base for French Custard Ice Cream (page 224; anything that is chilled or frozen must have the flavor enhanced, the extra sugar brings an otherwise bland dessert to life). Adding starch, like flour, rice flour, or cornstarch will make the thicker Pastry Cream (page 225), which can be used in éclairs or other desserts as a filling. Add unflavored gelatin and the sauce can be poured into a mold, thus becoming a Bavarian (page 226).

I have found that grocery store egg yolks have gotten smaller in the past several years and are rather pale in color. Then, I started having problems with custard not thickening. If your yolks are small, use 10 for this recipe. The best eggs have orange-tinted yolks, indicating a rich corn-fed diet. If you are fortunate enough to have farm eggs from corn-fed chickens, or if you buy your eggs from high-quality markets, you will have the best custard creams this side of the Atlantic.

Note that if you add fruit to this mixture, like apple peels for an apple-infused ice cream, you must bring the cream and milk to a boil before adding the fruit. The proteins of the milk are changed by boiling and will then be able to accept the acids in the fruit without curdling. ✒ MAKES 4 CUPS

2 1/2 cups whole milk

1 cup heavy cream

2 whole vanilla beans, or 2 teaspoons vanilla extract

8 to 10 large egg yolks

3/4 cup sugar

1. **(If you plan to use vanilla extract,** it will be added at the end, so step 1 can be skipped.) In a heavy saucepan, combine the milk and cream. On a cutting board, cut the vanilla beans in half lengthwise and scrape the seeds out with the tip of a sharp knife. Add the seeds and pods to the milk mixture and place over high heat. Bring this mixture just to a boil and whisk to aid in the extraction of the vanilla seeds from the pods. Remove the pan from the heat and let it stand for at least 30 minutes so the vanilla beans can infuse their flavor into the milk. (This may be done a day ahead, in which case the milk should be refrigerated.)

2. **In the bowl of a stand mixer** fitted with the paddle attachment, beat the yolks and sugar together on medium speed for about 2 minutes, until the mixture is thickened, fluffy, and pale yellow. You should be able to write your initial on the top of the batter and have it stay visible for half a second. Remove the bowl from the mixer.

3. **Remove the vanilla pods** from the milk mixture and using 2 fingers, press any remaining seeds from the pods into the pan. Discard the pods. Bring the milk-cream mixture just back to a boil over high heat heat. Add about 1/2 cup of the milk to the egg mixture and mix with a flat heat-resistant spatula to temper the yolks. Now, stirring all the time with the spatula, add all the egg mixture back into the pan and continue stirring until evenly blended.

4. **Place the pan over medium-low** heat and, using a wooden spoon, continually stir the mixture in a figure 8 pattern, making certain that you are stirring and involving all the mixture on the bottom of the pan and also getting into the corners.

5. **Cook, stirring constantly,** for 5 to 10 minutes, until the mixture has thickened to a coating consistency (coats the back of a spoon and leaves a trail when your finger is drawn through it). If the mixture stays separated and leaves a distinct path without the two sides running together, the cream is ready. If the mixture seeps back together after your finger passes, return it to the heat for a few more minutes, then retest. It should be about the consistency of heavy cream, or slightly thicker.

6. **Half fill a large bowl** with ice water. Immediately pass the finished cream through a fine-mesh strainer into a medium bowl and place it carefully in the large bowl of ice water, making sure it does not sink down so far that ice water runs over the edge into the cream. If using vanilla extract stir it in now. Stir the cream occasionally, until cooled. Store tightly covered for up to 2 days in the refrigerator.

Variations

LEMON AND ORANGE CRÈME: Add the finely chopped zest of 3 or 4 fresh lemons or oranges after the milk has boiled in step 1. Strain after the milk mixture has infused for at least 30 minutes. Serve orange crème over fresh sliced strawberries, raspberries, or orange segments. Serve lemon crème over fresh blueberries.

MINT CRÈME (REQUIRES TWO DAYS): Add 2 cups chopped and packed fresh peppermint to the milk-cream mixture after it has come to the boil in step 1. Store, covered, in the refrigerator overnight. The next day, pass the mixture through a fine-mesh strainer, pressing hard on the leaves to extract as much liquid as possible. Then continue with step 2 of the recipe. Be certain that you use peppermint, not spearmint. Occasionally, I see spearmint labeled simply as "mint." This herb will produce a flavor like toothpaste, so be sure to get peppermint, or grow your own!

CARDAMOM CRÈME: Add 2 teaspoons ground cardamom, 1/2 teaspoon ground ginger, and 1/2 teaspoon ground cinnamon in step 1, along with the vanilla. There is no need to strain the mixture. The cardamom flavor goes great with sautéed apple slices or an apple streusel.

French Custard Ice Cream

Unlike Philadelphia-style, French-style ice cream contains egg yolks. Of course I prefer the French variety. It's important to freeze the bowl that the ice cream will be stored in, as well as the utensil used to remove it from the ice cream machine. Otherwise, the warmth of the bowl or utensil can cause water to separate from the cream and create an ice layer.

A cup of shaved chocolate, chopped nuts, or fruits may be added to the ice cream during the last few minutes of churning. Or, make ice cream out of any of the Basic Vanilla Custard Sauce variations on page 223, such as Mint Crème or Lemon and Orange Crème. ✱ SERVES 6 TO 8

4 cups Basic Vanilla Custard Sauce (pages 222-223) made with 1 1/4 cups sugar, cooled

1. **Churn the custard sauce** in an ice-cream maker for 30 to 40 minutes, according to the manufacturer's instructions. Cover and freeze until ready to serve.

Variation

PUMPKIN ICE CREAM: This only works as an ice cream, not a sauce. Whisk together 1 cup canned puréed pumpkin, 3 tablespoons ground cinnamon, 1 teaspoon freshly grated nutmeg, 1/2 teaspoon ground cloves, and 1/2 teaspoon ground allspice until evenly blended. Add this mixture to the hot sweetened custard sauce, cool completely, and churn according to the manufacturer's instructions.

Pastry Cream

(Crème Patisserie)

Pastry cream is usually used as filling—especially as a base for fruit tarts or in Profiteroles. It's the thickened version of the Basic Vanilla Custard Sauce (page 222).

MAKES 3 CUPS

2 cups whole milk

1 whole vanilla bean, or 2 teaspoons vanilla extract

1/2 cup sugar

6 large egg yolks

3 tablespoons unbleached all-purpose flour

2 tablespoons cornstarch

1 tablespoon cold unsalted butter

1. **(If you plan to use** vanilla extract, it will be added at the end of the cooking time, so step 1 can be skipped.) Place the milk in a large heavy saucepan. On a cutting board, cut the vanilla bean in half lengthwise and scrape the seeds out with the tip of a sharp knife. Add the seeds and pod to the milk and place over medium-high heat. Bring this mixture just to a boil and whisk to aid in the extraction of the vanilla seeds from the pod. Remove the pan from the heat and let it stand for at least 30 minutes so the vanilla bean can infuse its flavor into the milk. (This may be done a day ahead, in which case the milk should be refrigerated.)

2. **Remove the vanilla pod** from the milk mixture and using 2 fingers, press any remaining seeds from the pod into the pan. Discard the pod. Place the pan over medium heat and warm the milk until hot, but not boiling.

3. **In the bowl of a stand mixer** fitted with the paddle attachment, combine the sugar and egg yolks and beat on medium speed until the mixture is pale yellow and thickened. Add the flour and cornstarch and beat until blended and thick pale yellow ribbons form. Remove the bowl from the mixer. Add one ladleful (about 1/4 cup) of the hot milk into the egg yolk mixture and mix with a flat heat resistant spatula to temper it. Then add the egg mixture to the pan of hot milk, stirring constantly. Place the pan over medium heat and whisk for 5 to 8 minutes, until quite thick and smooth. The mixture will get lumpy at first, as it begins to thicken; simply keep whisking and it will become smooth. There should be no floury taste remaining—cook for a couple minutes longer if you can still taste the flour. If using vanilla extract, stir it in now.

4. **Cool the pastry cream** quickly by spreading it out onto a platter. Place the cold butter on a fork and rub back and forth over the surface of the hot cream. As soon as the cream cools, transfer to a bowl and refrigerate until needed. Pastry cream may be stored, covered, for up to 2 days.

Bavarian

(BAVAROIS)

A Bavarian is simply Basic Vanilla Custard Sauce *(page 222) with the addition of unflavored gelatin. Try serving this wonderful dessert at your next buffet. Made with raspberry or strawberry purée and surrounded by piles of fresh berries, it makes a stunning presentation. To unmold large desserts, fill a sink or very large bowl with hot water and hold the mold in the hot water for 10 to 15 seconds, being careful to not get any water inside the mold. Or, for an easier presentation, pour the mixture into a pretty crystal dish and serve it with a spoon.*

MAKES 8 CUPS; SERVES 6 TO 8

1 1/2 cups heavy cream

2 cups whole milk

2 whole vanilla beans, or 1 tablespoon vanilla extract

3 envelopes unflavored gelatin

2/3 cup cold water

6 large egg yolks

2/3 cup sugar

1. **Place the cream in the bowl** of a stand mixer fitted with the whisk attachment. On high speed, whip the cream until it forms soft, mounded peaks. Do not allow it to form stiff peaks. Use immediately or refrigerate for up to 3 hours, until ready to use.

2. **(If you plan to use** vanilla extract, it will be added at the end of the cooking time, so step 2 can be skipped.) Pour the milk into a heavy saucepan. On a cutting board, cut the vanilla beans in half lengthwise and scrape the seeds out with the tip of a sharp knife. Add the seeds and pods to the milk and place over high heat. Bring this mixture just to a boil and whisk to aid in the extraction of the vanilla seeds from the pods. Remove the pan from the heat and let it stand for at least 30 minutes so the vanilla beans can infuse their flavor into the milk. (This may be done a day ahead, in which case the milk should be refrigerated.)

3. **In a small bowl,** soak the gelatin in the cold water for 10 minutes.

4. **Remove the vanilla pods** from the milk mixture and using 2 fingers, press any remaining seeds from the pods into the pan. Discard the pods. Reheat the milk mixture over high heat until hot but not boiling. Remove from the heat.

5. **In the bowl of a stand mixer** fitted with the paddle attachment, beat the egg yolks and sugar together on medium speed, until pale yellow and thickened. Remove the bowl from the machine. Stirring the mixture constantly, add a ladleful (about 1/4 cup) of the hot milk to the

egg mixture to temper the yolks. Add the egg mixture to the pan of hot milk and whisk to blend. Cook over medium-low heat, stirring constantly, for 4 to 6 minutes, until the mixture is thickened to the consistency of heavy cream.

6. **Pour the custard through** a fine-mesh strainer into a medium bowl. If using vanilla extract, stir it in now. Add the softened gelatin and whisk until the gelatin has dissolved. Fill a large bowl with ice cubes and enough cold water to come one-third up the side of the bowl.

7. **Place the bowl of custard** inside the ice-filled bowl, taking care that none of the water spills into the custard. Stir constantly until the mixture is very cool, but not so cold that the gelatin begins to set. Remove the mixture from the ice bowl and quickly fold in the whipped cream.

8. **Scoop the mixture into** an 8-cup mold, individual molds, or a pretty serving bowl. Chill large molds for 6 to 8 hours, small molds for about 3 hours. Unmold the bavarian by placing the base of the mold(s) into hot water for about 15 seconds, then inverting onto a platter. Or serve directly from the bowl.

Variations

RASPBERRY OR STRAWBERRY BAVARIAN: Purée 1 pound of fresh berries in a food processor. Stir in 1/4 cup sugar or to taste, stirring until the sugar has dissolved. If seeds remain in the purée, pass it through a fine-mesh strainer, using a rubber spatula to press the pulp through. At the end of step 5, stir the purée into the custard mixture.

CHOCOLATE BAVARIAN: At the end of step 5, stir in 12 ounces of grated bittersweet chocolate. Stir until melted and smooth.

COFFEE BAVARIAN: Add 2 tablespoons of Italian espresso powder to the milk before it comes to a boil in step 2.

Fresh Fruit Tart

This tart may be made with a thin layer of pastry cream underneath the fruit or simply with sliced fresh fruit. Melted red current or apricot jelly brushed onto the base of the crust will help prevent sogginess. It also makes a shiny glaze on top of the fruit and provides a lovely flavor. A pre-baked Nut Crust is the best bet for this filling—it is sturdier and will withstand the weight of the fruit better than the fragile Sweet Sugar Crust (page 212). People who cannot eat nuts will be quite happy with the Flaky Butter Crust (page 210). I also sometimes make this as individual tarts—this recipe will make six 5-inch tarts.

❧ MAKES 1 (9-INCH) TART

3/4 cup red currant or apricot jelly (do not use preserves or jam because of the chunks of fruit in the mixture)

2 tablespoons water, Grand Marnier, or Chambord

1 (9-inch) Nut Crust (page 213), baked and cooled

1 1/2 cups Pastry Cream (page 225; optional)

3 cups sliced strawberries, blueberries, raspberries, kiwi, and grapes

1. **In a small saucepan,** melt the jelly with the water over medium-low heat, whisking until the mixture flows freely. Using a pastry brush, coat the interior of the baked and cooled crust with the melted jelly.

2. **For a pure fruit filling** proceed to step 3. For the pastry cream filling: Spoon the pastry cream into a pastry bag fitted with a plain tip and pipe a 1/4-inch-thick layer of cream into the crust. Or, spoon the cream directly into the crust and spread into an even layer with a rubber spatula.

3. **Arrange the fruit** in a decorative pattern, extending the slices to overlap the edges of the crust slightly and cover the pastry cream completely. Use the remaining melted glaze to coat the fruit: So that the fruit will not be shifted out of place, drench the pastry brush with the warm glaze and allow it to drip generously over the fruit. The glaze should coat the fruit and also fill the gaps between the pieces, forming a smooth and glossy surface across the top of the tart. Rewarm the glaze slightly if it is not flowing freely. Cover the tart loosely with plastic wrap and refrigerate until serving. Cut into wedges and serve on individual plates.

Apple Pie

This all-American favorite is often made by tossing apples with flour and spices, placing the apples into the crust, and dotting them with pieces of butter. I find the resulting taste to be floury, and the butter does nothing more than melt onto to the bottom, making an oily tasting and soggy crust. When testing recipes for the Perfect Pie episode of my TV show, I wanted a pie that did not taste floury, rather more like the classic French Caramelized Apple Tart (Tarte Tatin, page 236). It is a good idea to use all the same variety of apple, to ensure even cooking times.

    Do not dump the apples into the crust. Take a minute to arrange the slices neatly next to each other so that when they cook and collapse, large gaping spaces are not created between the top crust and the cooked apples. The top of the pie is brushed with an egg glaze rather than the standard sprinkling of sugar, which often burns. ✹ MAKES 1 (9-INCH) PIE

6 large or 8 medium Golden Delicious, Granny Smith, or other baking apples

1/2 cup freshly squeezed orange juice

1 recipe Butter and Lard Crust dough (page 207)

1/2 cup firmly packed light brown sugar

1/4 cup granulated sugar

2 tablespoons cornstarch

1 teaspoon ground cinnamon

1/4 teaspoon freshly grated nutmeg

1/2 teaspoon fine sea salt

1 tablespoon rum or bourbon (optional)

1/4 cup cold unsalted butter, cut into 1/2-inch cubes

1 large egg, well beaten

1. **Peel and core the apples,** then slice them into 1/2-inch wedges. Place the apple wedges in a large bowl, pour the orange juice over them, and toss to coat. Set aside.

2. **Divide the dough** into 2 pieces. On a lightly floured surface, roll out 1 piece of dough into a circle about 1/8 inch thick and 10 inches in diameter, sprinkling with flour when necessary to prevent sticking. Carefully fold the dough into quarters and transfer it to a 9-inch heavy aluminum pie pan. Gently unfold the dough and press it into the pan, easing it into the corners with your knuckles. Trim the dough so the edge extends 1 inch from the outermost edge of the pan. Roll out the other piece of dough and place on a baking sheet. Cover the doughs with plastic wrap and refrigerate until ready to bake.

3. **In a small bowl,** blend together the brown sugar, granulated sugar, cornstarch, cinnamon, nutmeg, and salt. Add to the apples and toss thoroughly, so that all the apples are well coated. Let the mixture stand at room temperature for 1 hour, turning the ingredients over a

continued

few times. Drain the juices from the apple mixture into a small saucepan and stir in the rum. Heat the apple liquid over medium-high heat for 3 to 4 minutes, until reduced to a thickened, syrupy consistency. Remove from the heat and whisk in the butter until melted.

4. **Arrange one layer of apple** slices in concentric circles in the prepared crust. Arrange a second layer, reversing the direction. Continue alternating directions. Stack the apples neatly, overlapping without leaving unnecessary space between the slices or the layers. Keep layering until the apples are about 2 inches above the rim, with the center of the pie being a bit higher than the edges. Pour the reduced juice mixture over the apples to evenly coat.

5. **Preheat the oven to 425°** and place a rack in the lower third of the oven. Brush the rim of the bottom crust with water and cover the apples with the reserved circle of dough. Trim the top crust to extend 1 inch beyond the outer edge of the pie plate, matching the edge of the bottom dough. Save the scraps. Press the top to the bottom crust and fold the overlap back onto itself to form a smooth edge. With the thumb and forefinger of one hand, hold the dough edge steady and pull inward with the forefinger of your other hand to make a flute (it should look like the letter "U"). Continue making the flutes around the entire edge. Or, use the tines of a fork to press the top and bottom crusts together (but this is not as pretty as the fluted "U" edge).

6. **Brush the top crust** and edge of the pie with the beaten egg. Cut out several leaf or apple shapes from the reserved dough scraps and arrange them decoratively on top of the pie. Brush the decorations with the egg glaze. Pierce the top crust with the tip of a knife in about 10 different spots around the decorations, or cut a decorative pattern in the top crust with the tip of a knife (this will allow the steam to escape). Place the pie on a baking sheet to catch any spillovers. Bake for 15 minutes, then decrease the temperature to 350° and bake for 45 minutes more, until a wooden or metal skewer easily pierces the apples in the center of the pie. Cool on a wire rack, then cut into wedges and serve.

Lemon Meringue Pie with Italian Meringue

Combine a simple cooked meringue (called Italian meringue) with a flaky crust enhanced by lemon zest and you have the perfect lemon pie. Have the lemon filling and the meringue completely prepared and ready to go when you start assembly, because the filling must be hot when poured into the crust and the meringue must be used almost immediately. The whole process will go much faster and more efficiently if you are organized in your kitchen!

Cooking a meringue not only ensures that it will hold its shape, but also kills any bacteria that may be present. Using a hot sugar syrup, as opposed to just whipping while adding sugar, produces a perfect meringue. You'll need a candy thermometer for this recipe. ✒ MAKES 1 (9-INCH) PIE

ITALIAN MERINGUE

1 1/4 cups sugar

1/3 cup water

4 large egg whites, at room temperature

6 large egg yolks

2 large eggs

1 1/2 cups sugar

2/3 cup cornstarch

1/4 cup unbleached all-purpose flour

2 cups water

3/4 cup freshly squeezed lemon juice

3 tablespoons unsalted butter

1/4 teaspoon sea salt

1 teaspoon vanilla extract

1 (9-inch) Butter and Lard Crust (page 207), finely chopped zest of 2 lemons added to the dough with the flour, baked and cooled

1. **Preheat the oven to 350°** and place a rack in the lower third of the oven. (If using a pure convection oven (page 11), set it for 325° and still bake in the lower third of the oven.)

2. **To prepare the meringue,** put the sugar and water in a small saucepan over medium-high heat. Stir slightly just to moisten all the sugar. Dip a pastry brush in cold water and wash the sides of the pan down to remove all the sugar crystals. Bring the mixture to a boil. Wash down the sides again, if necessary, dipping the brush into water each time. Boil, without stirring, for 6 to 8 minutes, until the sugar reaches the hard-ball stage (244 to 246°) on a candy thermometer. (If you don't have a thermometer, keep a glass of ice water on hand and drop a few drops of the sugar syrup into the water occasionally, as it begins to thicken and form clear (not golden), slow-popping bubbles. The hard-ball stage is reached when the syrup forms a hard ball, i.e., not soft or sticky on the fingers, as soon as it hits the water.)

continued

If you're using a gas stove, the flame beneath the saucepan should be adjusted so that it is as high as possible but is only underneath the pan, not lapping up the sides.

3. **While the sugar is cooking,** beat the whites in the bowl of a stand mixer fitted with the whisk attachment until stiff but not dry (page 35). Try to make sure the whites and sugar are both ready at about the same time. Tilt and cool the bottom of the saucepan under cold running water to stop the syrup from continuing to cook. Pour the syrup into the beaten whites in a thin stream, whisking constantly and aiming the stream of syrup nearer to the side of the bowl, not directly over the whisk attachment. When all the syrup has been added, continue beating for 2 to 3 minutes, until the mixture is smooth, shiny, and begins to cool. Use immediately.

4. **In a bowl, combine the yolks** and whole eggs and whisk together until thoroughly blended.

5. **In a saucepan** (not over heat), combine the sugar, cornstarch, flour, and water. Whisk together until the mixture is smooth and thick. Place over medium heat and cook, stirring constantly, for about 3 minutes, until thickened. Remove from the heat and taste. If the mixture tastes starchy from the flour, return the pan to the heat and cook for another 1 to 2 minutes to cook out the starchy taste.

6. **Temper the beaten eggs** by whisking a large spoonful of the hot flour-sugar mixture into the bowl. Mix just until thoroughly blended and then pour the egg mixture into the saucepan. Mix well, using a whisk, and return the saucepan to the heat. Cook over medium-low heat for 3 minutes, whisking constantly until smooth and well-blended.

7. **Remove the pan from** the heat and whisk in the lemon juice, butter, salt, and vanilla. Pour the hot filling into the pre-baked crust. Spread the meringue over the top of the pie, making sure that it touches the crust all around, forming it into a mounded dome shape. To decorate, either make swirls with the back of a spoon, smooth the top, or dip a spoon into meringue and pull it up to make little tips all over the meringue. Or, spread about one-fourth of the meringue onto the pie, again making certain that the meringue touches the crust all around. Then spoon the remaining meringue into a pastry bag fitted with a large star tip and decorate the pie with rosettes or shells.

8. **Bake for 20 to 30 minutes,** until the meringue begins to brown lightly. Cool to room temperature on a wire rack. Refrigerate, uncovered, so the meringue topping will not be disturbed, for at least 2 or up to 8 hours, before cutting into 8 wedges and serving.

Southern-Style Pecan Pie

My favorite part of having a nationally televised public television show is hearing from viewers from all corners of the country. Mara Trotter, a viewer from Louisiana, sent me this classic recipe for pecan pie, along with fresh pecans that she had shelled from her own tree!

I have added a little bourbon to the recipe, and I like to serve it drizzled with *Shiny Chocolate Icing* (page 248) or even melted bittersweet chocolate. Whipped cream sparingly flavored with bourbon and vanilla makes another nice complement.

✿ MAKES 1 (8- OR 9-INCH) PIE

1 recipe Cream Cheese Crust dough (page 215)

1/2 cup sugar

1 cup light corn syrup

2 tablespoons bourbon (optional)

3 tablespoons unsalted butter, cut into 1/2-inch cubes

3 large eggs, well beaten

1 cup chopped pecans

1 teaspoon vanilla extract

1/8 teaspoon salt

2 ounces melted bittersweet chocolate (optional)

1 cup heavy cream whipped to soft peaks with 1 tablespoon bourbon, 1/2 teaspoon vanilla, and 2 tablespoons sugar (optional)

1. **On a lightly floured surface,** roll out the dough to 1/8 inch thick and 10 inches in diameter. Carefully fold the dough into quarters and transfer it to an 8- or 9-inch heavy aluminum pie pan. Gently unfold the dough and press it into the pan, easing it into the corners with your knuckles without stretching it. Trim the dough so the edge extends 1 inch from the outermost edge of the pan; fold the overlap back under itself to form a smooth edge. Crimp the edge with your fingers or a fork. Chill the crust for 1 hour.

2. **Preheat the oven to 350°** and place a rack in the lower third of the oven. In a saucepan, combine the sugar, corn syrup, and bourbon and place over high heat. Bring to a boil, stirring occasionally until the contents are blended. Add the butter, allow it to melt, and remove from the heat.

3. **Stir the eggs, pecans,** vanilla, and salt into the mixture and pour into the prepared crust. Bake for 50 to 60 minutes, until the filling is set. Cool on a wire rack.

4. **Slice the pie into** 8 wedges and serve on individual plates. Drizzle each serving with 2 tablespoons of the melted chocolate and/or top with a dollop of the flavored whipped cream.

Warm Bittersweet Chocolate Tarts

These delicious flourless chocolate tarts have a warm and liquidy chocolate center. You must use a high quality bittersweet chocolate for this recipe. It can easily be divided in half—use 3 whites for a half recipe. I use individual tart pans, but 4-ounce ramekins will also work well. For some added luxury, serve with a drizzle of Basic Vanilla Custard Sauce (Crème Anglaise) or any of the variations (page 222), or Raspberry Coulis (page 248). ✄ MAKES 8 (4-INCH) TARTS

1 pound finely chopped bittersweet chocolate

1/2 cup unsalted butter, cut into tablespoon-sized pieces

12 large egg yolks

2/3 cup plus 1 tablespoon sugar

5 large egg whites

1/2 teaspoon cream of tartar (optional)

Sifted cocoa powder, for dusting

Sifted confectioners' sugar, for dusting

1. **Spray eight 4-inch diameter,** 1 1/2-inch deep tart tins with removable bottoms with vegetable-oil cooking spray. (Or, spray eight to ten 4-ounce ramekins.)

2. **Preheat the oven to 450°** and place a rack in the lower third of the oven. (If using a pure convection oven (page 11), set it for 425° and bake in the lower third.)

3. **In a small heavy saucepan,** combine the chocolate and butter. Place over low heat and stir occasionally until the chocolate begins to melt and look glossy. Remove from the heat and continue to stir until the chocolate has melted. If there are large chunks remaining, return the pan to the heat for a few seconds to gently encourage the chunks to melt. Let cool slightly, until lukewarm.

4. **In the bowl of a stand mixer** fitted with the paddle attachment, combine the egg yolks and the 2/3 cup sugar. Beat on high speed for 3 to 4 minutes, until the yolks are thickened, fluffy, and pale yellow. The mixture should hold its shape for a moment if you write your initial on top of the batter with a fork. Fold the warm chocolate mixture into the yolk mixture.

5. **In the bowl of a stand mixer** fitted with the whisk attachment, or a clean copper bowl using a balloon whisk, whisk the whites for 1 minute, until frothy. Add the cream of tartar (add only if not whisking in a copper bowl; see page 35) and continue beating just until soft peaks form and the mixture begins to pull away from the sides of the bowl. Add the remaining 1 tablespoon sugar and whisk for 30 to 60 seconds more, until the whites are glossy and the peaks hold their shape with slight curl at the ends.

6. **Fold a large dollop** of the egg whites into the chocolate-yolk mixture to lighten it. Fold in the remaining whites in 3 batches, folding just enough to incorporate the whites. Pour into the prepared dishes.

7. **Bake for 5 to 6 minutes**, until the edges are firm but the centers are still slightly wobbly. The size of the container and the material it is made of are all variables in the baking time. Remove from the oven and cool on wire racks for 2 to 3 minutes.

8. **Dust individual plates** with cocoa powder. Turn a tart out onto each plate so that the bottom becomes the top, dust the tops with confectioners' sugar, and serve warm.

Caramelized Apple Tart

(TARTE TATIN) (SEE PHOTO INSERT)

There are many stories about how this famous tart originally came about, but the most often repeated tells of the Tatin sisters in a Loire Valley village in the mid-1800s. They were making an apple tart and simply forgot the bottom crust. After the apples were baked, they realized that there was no crust, so they topped the caramelized apples with a raw crust, put it in the oven, and then turned it upside down on a serving platter once the crust was well browned. The sisters used a metal oven placed over charcoal, which gave the apples that characteristic deep amber color.

We use the traditional copper, tin-lined Tarte Tatin mold with slanted sides. Copper conducts heat far better than anything else: the tin-lined copper creates the spectacular deep amber color. After my students try this dessert, they usually decide to invest in the pan. The tart can also be made in a 12-inch sauté pan, but the color is never the same.

Make sure you use a hardy baking apple such as Golden Delicious (my favorite) or Granny Smith, which can withstand the extended cooking time without falling apart. This tart is great served with French Custard Ice Cream (page 224), but it is traditionally served without any accompaniments because it is just so good all by itself. ✐ SERVES 8 TO 12

1 recipe Flaky Butter Crust dough (page 210), refrigerated for at least 1 hour

3/4 cup unsalted butter, cut into 1-inch cubes

2 cups sugar

1 tablespoon water

1 tablespoon freshly squeezed lemon juice

7 pounds large Golden Delicious, Granny Smith, or other hard cooking apple, peeled, halved lengthwise, and cored

1. **Remove the dough** from the refrigerator and let stand for 10 minutes. On a lightly floured surface, roll out the dough into a circle, 1/4 inch thick and 13 inches in diameter (it should be 2 to 3 inches larger than the diameter of the mold). Transfer the dough circle to a tray or baking sheet and refrigerate, covered with plastic wrap, for at least 15 minutes or up to 1 day, until ready to use.

2. **Put the butter into** the bottom of the tarte tatin mold and place the mold over medium heat. Melt the butter, then stir in the sugar, water, and lemon juice. Remove from the heat.

3. **Slice off a small piece** of one of the narrow ends of each apple half, to create a stable base. Arrange the apples upright in concentric circles in the mold, with their bases standing in the butter and sugar mixture. They should fill the

mold and be tightly packed together. One or 2 apple halves may be left over. Set them aside.

4. **Place the mold over medium** heat and cook for 35 to 55 minutes, until a medium-colored caramel is formed. In the first few minutes of cooking, the apples will shrink. When this happens, fit 1 or 2 more halves into the pan so that it remains tightly filled. During the cooking, regulate the heat so that the liquid simmers briskly and, as always where caramel is involved, do not leave the kitchen. At first, the liquid will be pale and thin from the juices of the apples. Keep cooking so that the water evaporates and the sugar and apple juices caramelize and are absorbed by the apples. Use potholders to move the pan around on the burner so that the heat is evenly distributed, otherwise any hot spots may turn into burned spots. And remember that caramel keeps cooking for 1 to 2 minutes after it is removed from the heat, so stop cooking just before your ideal cinnamon-amber color is achieved.

5. **Preheat the oven to 350°** and place a rack in the upper third of the oven. Place the chilled circle of dough on top of the hot apples. Turn the rim of overhanging pastry back on itself to form a rough crust, keeping the apples completely covered. Bake for 20 to 30 minutes, until the pastry is crisp and brown. Remove from the oven and let the tart cool for 5 minutes in the mold. Place a heat-resistant serving plate upside down over the mold, and invert the two together to unmold the tart onto the plate. Give it a good downward shake to help all the apples come away. If any apple sticks to the bottom of the pan, remove it with a metal spatula and replace on the tart. Serve warm or cold.

Tuiles à l'Orange

These thin wafers are said to resemble the shape of French roof tiles. You can serve them simply as a cookie, use them as a garnish, or make them into an edible bowl for ice cream or fresh fruit.

✔ MAKES 12 TO 18 COOKIES

2/3 cup sifted confectioners' sugar

2 large egg whites

1 teaspoon vanilla extract

6 tablespoons unsalted butter, cut into 6 pieces

1/2 cup cake flour, sifted

Finely grated zest of 1 orange or lemon

1. **Preheat the oven to 400°.** (If using a pure convection oven (page 11), set it for 375°.) Lightly butter several heavy aluminum or nonstick baking sheets.

2. **In a bowl, combine the sugar,** egg whites, and vanilla. Whisk together for about 30 seconds, until foamy. Over very low heat, melt the butter in a small saucepan, swirling until creamy (not hot or separated). Immediately remove from the heat and add to the egg whites. Add the flour and citrus zest and whisk until all the ingredients are blended.

3. **Using a tablespoon,** drop level spoonfuls of the batter onto the prepared baking sheets, leaving several inches between each to allow for spreading. Spread the batter with the back of the spoon so that it is very thin and round.

4. **Bake for 5 to 10 minutes,** depending on size, until the tuiles are browned around the edges and golden in the center. It is very important to bake the tuiles until they are crisp and light brown. An undercooked tuile will be chewy, rather than fragile and crisp.

5. **Working quickly** while they are still hot and pliable, use a metal spatula to remove the tuiles from the baking sheets and place them over a rolling pin. Mold each one around the pin, so it assumes the shape of a curved ceramic roof tile. Use a clean, dry towel to help mold the warm cookies around the pin if necessary. If the cookies get too cool they will not bend. Simply return them to the oven for about 30 seconds and then shape as above. Let the tuiles cool on the rolling pin for about 1 minute, then remove and use immediately or store for up to a week in a tightly sealed container.

Chocolate-Orange Biscotti

Biscotti are simple Italian cookies. These can be made with or without the chocolate and citrus zest. They are prefect for nibbling while sipping a cup of coffee. The key to perfect biscotti is to return them to the oven to dry out after the initial baking.

MAKES ABOUT 30 COOKIES

3/4 cup whole blanched almonds

3 large eggs

3/4 cup sugar

2 1/2 cups unbleached all-purpose flour

1 teaspoon baking soda

Pinch of salt

1/3 cup finely chopped bittersweet chocolate

Finely chopped zest of 2 large oranges

1 large egg white

1. **Preheat the oven to 375°.** (If using a pure convection oven (page 11), set it for 350°.) Lightly butter and flour 2 baking sheets.

2. **Spread the almonds** on a third, rimmed baking sheet and bake for 8 to 12 minutes, until golden. Allow to cool a little, then finely chop half of the nuts and coarsely chop the other half.

3. **In the bowl of a stand mixer** fitted with the paddle attachment, combine the eggs and sugar and mix on medium-low speed for 30 seconds. Add the nuts (both finely and coarsely chopped), flour, baking soda, salt, chocolate, and orange zest and mix on medium speed for 2 minutes, just until the mixture holds together. Divide the dough into 4 equal pieces and dust them with flour. Flour your hands and then shape each piece into long log about 1 inch in diameter, rolling back and forth with the palms of your hands to achieve an even thickness. Place the logs on 1 of the prepared baking sheets. In a bowl, beat the egg white until slightly frothy, and brush on the tops of the dough logs. Bake for 20 minutes, until lightly golden. Decrease the oven temperature to 225°. (Decrease a pure convection oven to 220°.)

4. **Remove the rolls from** the oven, and while still warm, cut each roll with a serrated knife diagonally on a 45-degree angle into 3/4-inch-thick slices. Lay the slices flat on both of the baking sheets. Bake for 20 minutes more, until firm. Remove from the oven and cool on wire racks. Serve immediately or store in an airtight container for up to 1 month.

Crepes Suzette

Traditionally, this dessert is made by rubbing orange rind onto sugar cubes, dissolving them in butter, and then flaming the dessert with Cognac just before serving. I have found that the dish tastes just as good if you do a syrup with the zest, sugar, and butter and skip the grand regalia of flambéing. At the school, we flame the dessert, just for the sake of showing the procedure, but we also have the proper equipment with a great deal of open space to eliminate the possibility of something catching on fire. The orange butter can be made up to 2 days in advance and kept, covered, in the refrigerator. ☙ SERVES 6

Finely grated zest of 2 oranges

2/3 cup sugar

1 cup unsalted butter, at room temperature,
    cut into pieces

1/4 cup freshly squeezed orange juice, strained

1/4 cup Grand Marnier

1/4 cup Cognac or brandy

1 recipe Dessert Crepes (page 205)

1. **In a food processor,** combine the orange zest and sugar. Pulse for 30 seconds to break up the zest. Add the butter and process, scraping down the bowl sides, until smooth. Add the orange juice and Grand Marnier process until mixed thoroughly. This mixture may be used immediately or left at room temperature for up to 8 hours. Don't worry if all the liquid is not absorbed into the butter—it will cook together into a syrupy mass.

2. **In a large wide sauté pan** or copper crepe pan, melt the orange-butter mixture over medium heat. Add the Cognac and simmer, stirring, for 6 to 8 minutes, until the mixture is a syrupy consistency.

3. **Working with one crepe** at a time, dredge both sides in the orange-butter mixture. With the pretty, lacy side out, fold the crepe in half and then in half again to form a triangle. Place the folded crepes to one side of the pan. As the crepes are soaked, place them neatly next to each other, slightly overlapping, filling the pan.

4. **Increase the heat** to high and let the mixture bubble for 1 minute to infuse the orange-butter and Cognac into the crepes. Serve on individual heated plates, drizzling a little of the extra syrup over each.

Crème Caramel

Crème Caramel and Crème Brûlée (page 243) are the quintessential French desserts. Crème Caramel is a milk-based custard made with a hard-crack caramel that liquefies to make a sauce for the unmolded custard. This (actually quite easy) dessert has lengthy directions that carefully describe the making of the caramel and the lining of the ramekins. Once you have done this for the first time, you'll be amazed at how quickly this dish can be made. Also, it is best made a day in advance to give the hard caramel more time to liquefy—if you keep it in the refrigerator for twenty-four hours before serving, you'll end up with more caramel sauce. I prefer to use the prettier individual ramekins for my guests. The custard will also set more quickly in the smaller dishes. If desired, you can eat this dessert within a few hours of baking.

❧ MAKES 1 (6-CUP) DESSERT OR 8 (4-OUNCE) INDIVIDUAL SERVINGS

CARAMEL

1 1/3 cups sugar

6 tablespoons water

CUSTARD

2 1/2 cups whole milk

1 whole vanilla bean, or 2 teaspoons vanilla extract

3 large eggs

4 large egg yolks

1/2 cup sugar

1. **In a small saucepan** over low heat, dissolve the sugar in the water, stirring once or twice just to moisten the sugar. Increase the heat to high and bring the mixture to a boil. If you're using a gas stove, keep the flame just under the pan, not coming up the sides. In the first 3 minutes of cooking, wash the sides of the pan 2 or 3 times with a pastry brush dipped in cold water. This prevents the sugar crystals that may be clinging to the sides of the pan from re-crystallizing the caramel, which would make it grainy rather than fluid. When the syrup cooks to a dark cinnamon color, remove from the heat.

2. **Working quickly** but very carefully (caramel is very hot) pour the caramel into a 6-cup soufflé dish or individual heatproof 4-ounce ramekins. Holding just the rim, tilt the dish and then swirl the caramel on the inside to coat the bottom and three-quarters up the sides, always leaving the base of the dish resting on the counter. The caramel will harden very fast. Try to coat the sides and bottom evenly. It is important to get all the ramekins swirled and coated quickly, as the caramel hardens fast. Use immediately or set the prepared dish(es) aside (they can sit for up to 2 hours).

3. **(If you plan to use** vanilla extract, it will be added just before adding the milk to the egg mixture, so step 3 can be skipped.) To prepare

continued

the custard, place the milk in a heavy saucepan. On a cutting board, cut the vanilla bean in half lengthwise and scrape the seeds out with the tip of a sharp knife. Add the seeds and the pod to the milk and place over high heat. Bring this mixture just to a boil and whisk to aid in the extraction of the vanilla seeds from the pod. Remove the pan from the heat and let it stand for at least 30 minutes so the vanilla bean can infuse its flavor into the milk. (This may be done a day ahead, in which case the milk should be refrigerated.)

4. **In the bowl of a stand mixer** fitted with the paddle attachment, combine the whole eggs, egg yolks, and sugar. Beat together on medium-low speed for 2 to 3 minutes, until thickened and pale yellow.

5. **Preheat the oven to 325°** and place a rack in the lower third of the oven. Return the pan of vanilla-infused milk to low heat and, if using vanilla extract, stir it in now. When the milk is hot but not boiling, pour a ladleful (about 1/4 cup) of the warm milk into the egg mixture, stirring all the time, to temper the eggs. Stir in the remaining hot milk and pass the mixture through a fine-mesh strainer into a large measuring cup; discard the vanilla pod. Let the mixture settle for 10 minutes, and then use a fine-mesh skimmer or a flat spoon to remove all of the foam from the top.

6. **While the custard is resting,** heat a kettle of water for the bain-marie. Ladle the custard into the prepared dish(es) and place them into a large roasting pan. Add enough of the very hot, but not boiling, water to the roasting pan, to come

about two-thirds of the way up the sides of the dish(es). Be careful not to spill any water into the custard mixture. Bake for about 30 minutes for individual dishes and about 1 hour for a large dish, until set. The custard should not come to a boil. When it is done, the custard will look set but will still be slightly wobbly in the middle. Touch the very center lightly with a fingertip. If some of the custard comes off on your finger, it needs more time. If the center is wobbly but your finger pulls away clean, the crème is done.

7. **On a wire rack, cool the custard(s)** to room temperature. Cover and refrigerate the large dessert for at least 4 hours. Individual custards should be refrigerated for at least 2 hours. To unmold, run a sharp knife around the edges, keeping the blade slanted toward the side of the bowl to avoid cutting the custard. Place a plate over the custard and invert, giving the dish and plate a few sharp downward jerks to dislodge the custard. As you remove the dish, allow as much caramel as possible to drizzle over the custard. Serve cold.

Variation

ORANGE OR LEMON CRÈME CARAMEL: After the milk and vanilla have come to a boil in step 3, add the finely grated zest of 3 oranges or lemons. Allow the flavors to infuse for at least 1 hour. Proceed with the cooking process and strain out the zests with the vanilla pods in step 5. Proceed as directed.

Crème Brûlée

Crème Brûlée is a thick cream- and milk-based custard. After baking and chilling, it is sprinkled with sugar, which is then caramelized with a household blowtorch to produce a thin, hard shell. Arguably the best Crème Brûlée in all of France is served at the Thoumieux Hotel and Restaurant in Paris, my home-away-from-home. It is made with an infusion of vanilla beans. The beans themselves are strained out, but the tiny seeds remain behind and sink to the bottom of the custard, flavoring the entire dessert.

Select a low, flat porcelain dish with straight or fluted sides for this recipe. We sell several versions of this classic shape that can be used for many other applications. I use dishes that hold 4 to 8 ounces of custard. The custard can be made several days in advance and kept, tightly covered, in the refrigerator until the sugar topping is added and caramelized.

🌿 SERVES 4 TO 6

3 cups heavy cream

1/3 cup whole milk

3/4 cup plus 2 tablespoons sugar

1 whole vanilla bean, or 2 teaspoons vanilla extract

6 large egg yolks

1 large egg

1 teaspoon vanilla extract

4 to 6 tablespoons sugar, for topping

1. **In a large heavy saucepan,** combine the cream, milk, and 1/2 cup of the sugar. Place the pan over high heat and bring to a boil, watching carefully to prevent a boil-over, then remove from the heat. On a cutting board, cut the vanilla bean in half lengthwise and scrape the seeds out with the tip of a sharp knife. Add the seeds and the pod to the pan. Let the mixture stand and infuse for about 30 minutes.

2. **In the bowl of a stand mixer** fitted with the paddle attachment, combine the yolks, whole egg, and vanilla extract with the remaining 1/4 cup plus 2 tablespoons sugar. Beat the mixture on medium speed for 2 minutes, until thick, creamy, and pale yellow,

3. **Remove the vanilla pod halves** from the cream mixture and using 2 fingers, press all the seeds from the pod into the pan. Discard the pod. Reheat the cream until hot, but not boiling. Add a ladleful (about 1/4 cup) of the hot cream into the egg mixture, stirring constantly, to temper the eggs. Stirring all the time, add the rest of the hot cream to the egg mixture.

4. **Let the mixture stand** for about 20 minutes, then use a flat spoon or skimmer to remove the foam from the top. Preheat the oven to 275° and place a rack in the lower third or half of the oven.

continued

5. **Ladle the custard mixture** into individual ramekins, filling them halfway. Place the dishes into a large roasting pan. Pour hot water into the pan, so that the water comes about halfway up the sides of the dishes; be careful not to spill any water into the custard mixture.

6. **Bake for 1 to 1 1/2 hours.** When it is done, the custard will look set but will still be slightly wobbly in the middle. Touch the very center lightly with a fingertip. If some of the custard comes off on your finger, it needs more time. If the center is wobbly but your finger pulls away clean, the crème is done.

7. **On a wire rack, cool the custards** to room temperature. Cover and refrigerate for at least 2 to 3 hours or up to overnight, until well chilled.

8. **Preheat the broiler** or use a blowtorch (the blowtorch will make the process much easier). Sprinkle the top of each dish with an even layer of sugar, about 1/16 of an inch deep, reaching all the way to the edges. Be careful not to make the layer too thick. If using a blowtorch, heat the sugar until it caramelizes and turns a cinnamon color. If using a broiler, pack the dishes in ice and place under the broiler, about 4 inches from the heat source, until the sugar melts and browns. This method works well in professional-quality ovens designed for home use that produce more even heat. Most home broilers don't get hot enough to correctly caramelize the sugar. Therefore I recommend the blowtorch method for best results. After caramelizing the sugar, allow the crème to cool for 3 minutes, and serve immediately.

Classic French Chocolate Mousse

(MOUSSE AU CHOCOLAT)

This, one of the simplest of desserts, has a few rules that must be followed carefully to ensure perfection. First, chop the chocolate before melting so it will melt more evenly in the pan. Then melt it over very low heat, in a heavy saucepan. The chocolate mixture must get quite warm, but not hot, which would cause it to curdle. When the chocolate feels comfortably hot to your touch (yes, you can then lick your fingers), the eggs can be added. The raw egg yolks are "set" by the warmth of the chocolate, but very hot chocolate would cook the yolks. On the other hand, if the chocolate has cooled too much and begins to solidify even a little, it will not blend easily into the whites. ✎ SERVES 6 TO 8

8 ounces chopped good-quality bittersweet chocolate

1/4 cup unsalted butter

3 tablespoons water

3 tablespoons Grand Marnier, Chambord, or rum

5 large eggs, separated, at room temperature

1/2 teaspoon cream of tartar (optional)

1. **In a small heavy saucepan,** combine the chocolate, butter, and water. Over low heat, stir occasionally until the chocolate is melted and the mixture is smooth. Stir in the Grand Marnier. Remove from the heat and let cool for 2 minutes.

2. **When the chocolate feels** comfortably hot to the touch, add the yolks all at once; quickly and thoroughly stir them in.

3. **Using a clean copper bowl,** whisk the egg whites with a balloon whisk until they are slightly foamy. Add the cream of tarter (add only if not whisking in a copper bowl; see page 35) and continue beating until soft peaks form. With a flat spatula, gently fold 1/2 cup of the whites into the chocolate mixture to lighten the chocolate (see next page). Fold the chocolate–egg white mixture into the remaining whites until no streaks are visible.

4. **Carefully, so that you** don't deflate the air in the mixture, spoon the mousse into individual ramekins or a 1 1/2-quart bowl. Cover and let the mousse set for at least 4 hours in the refrigerator. Bring to room temperature for about 5 minutes before serving.

Chocolate Mousse: How to Fold in Egg Whites

FOLD 1/2 CUP OF THE WHITES INTO THE CHOCOLATE . . .

TO LIGHTEN THE CHOCOLATE.

ADD THE CHOCOLATE–EGG WHITE MIXTURE TO THE REMAINING WHITES.

FOLD UNTIL NO STREAKS ARE VISIBLE.

Grand Marnier Chocolate Cake with Shiny Chocolate Icing

(SEE PHOTO INSERT)

For three consecutive years in the early years at the school, Julia Child taught a series of classes. One of her recipes, a classic French Reine de Saba (an almond-chocolate cake) is the predecessor to this cake. A student who was taking my classic cuisine courses told me that she was allergic to nuts. Not wanting any one of my students to go without dessert, I revised the recipe, used my shiny chocolate icing, and have since made this my signature cake. I teach the students how to decorate plates with Basic Vanilla Custard Sauce (Crème Anglaise, page 222) and the raspberry coulis, and then serve wedges of the cake on top of the sauces.

This dense and delicious chocolate cake may be varied to taste by substituting a wide range of liqueurs, nuts, and zests (see my variations below). It is very important to have all the ingredients at room temperature and the chocolate fluid but not too warm, before mixing them with the egg whites: barely warm ingredients blend together more easily, and less air will be lost from the mixture. Buy the best chocolate you can find for both the icing and the cake. The French Valrhona is my favorite, just make sure you use bittersweet, not unsweetened (see Sources on page 252). If Valrhona is unavailable, use any high-quality bittersweet chocolate.

For the icing, the cream should be just hand-hot, as chocolate will curdle or separate if it gets too hot. The chopped chocolate will melt very quickly once the warm cream is added to it. This icing can also be used as a glaze for desserts or chilled as a ganache for a truffle. This glaze can be made in advance and stored in the refrigerator for up to 1 month. Be sure, however, to reheat it carefully and gently over very low heat before icing the cake.

Just like any flavor, chocolate is more difficult to taste when served cold. Be sure to serve this cake at room temperature, rather than directly from the refrigerator. ✎ SERVES 8

4 ounces good-quality bittersweet chocolate, finely chopped

1/2 cup unsalted butter, at room temperature

1/2 cup plus 2 tablespoons sugar

Finely chopped zest of 2 oranges

3 large eggs, separated, at room temperature

2 tablespoons Grand Marnier

3/8 teaspoon cream of tartar (optional)

Pinch of salt

1/2 cup less 1 tablespoon cake flour

1/2 cup grated bittersweet chocolate, for decoration

continued

7 ounces good-quality bittersweet chocolate, finely chopped

2/3 cup heavy cream

7 tablespoons clarified butter (page 31)

RASPBERRY COULIS

1 quart ripe raspberries, or 1 (12- to 16-ounce) bag frozen unsweetened raspberries

2 to 4 tablespoons granulated sugar

2 2/3 cups Basic Vanilla Custard Sauce (Crème Anglaise, page 222)

1. **Preheat the oven to 325°** and place a rack in the lower third of the oven. Cut a circle of parchment paper to the exact size of an 8-inch round cake pan, using the pan's base as a template. Lightly butter the sides and bottom of the pan, place the parchment circle on the bottom, and butter the parchment. Lightly flour the sides and bottom of the pan, and tap out the excess.

2. **To make the cake batter,** place the chocolate in a small saucepan over very low heat. When the chocolate begins to look glossy and melted, remove from the heat and stir to be sure it is completely melted. Return to the heat for a moment, if needed, to finish melting. Let cool until barely warm before proceeding.

3. **In the bowl of a stand mixer** fitted with the paddle attachment, cream the butter, 1/2 cup sugar, and zest on medium-low speed for 2 to 3 minutes, until softened and very fluffy. Add and beat in the egg yolks and Grand Marnier for 30 seconds, until smooth. Scoop the warm chocolate into the egg mixture and beat on medium-low speed until blended and smooth.

4. **In a separate clean bowl** of a stand mixer fitted with the whisk attachment, or a clean copper bowl using a balloon whisk, whisk the whites until they are slightly foamy. Add the cream of tartar (add only if not whisking in a copper bowl; see page 35) and salt and continue beating until soft peaks form. Add the remaining 2 tablespoons sugar and continue to whisk for 20 to 30 seconds, until stiff, glossy peaks form.

5. **Using a wide rubber spatula,** fold a large spoonful of the egg whites into the chocolate mixture to lighten it. Put the flour into a fine-mesh strainer, sift a few tablespoons over the chocolate mixture, and fold in. Continue adding and folding the egg whites and the flour into the batter, alternating between them. Using a light hand, fold in each addition almost completely before adding the next. The mixture should be completely smooth, but take care not overmix the batter or it will lose precious air. The batter should be light and somewhat fluffy.

6. **Pour the batter into** the prepared pan and use an offset or flat spatula to gently spread the batter evenly. Bake for about 25 minutes, until the center of the cake is moist and leaves moist crumbs when pierced with a toothpick. The edges will be dry 2 to 3 inches in from the rim of the pan. Transfer to a wire rack and let cool for about 30 minutes before unmolding. Loosen the edges with a small knife and gently invert and unmold the cake onto the cooling rack. Carefully peel away and discard the parchment paper. When the cake is completely cool, brush any loose crumbs from the sides and top.

7. **To prepare the icing,** put the chocolate into a small saucepan. Put the cream in another saucepan and heat over low heat, just until hand-hot; do not let it reach the simmering point. Pour the cream over the chocolate (the pan of chocolate should not be over the heat). Whisk the mixture gently, just enough to finish melting the chocolate. (If there are stubborn chunks of chocolate that have not melted, place the pan over very low heat for a few moments to melt them.) Add the clarified butter and whisk together gently until blended.

8. **To glaze the cake with the icing,** begin by pouring the icing onto the center of the cake. Spread with an icing spatula so that the icing runs down the sides and covers the whole cake. Press the grated chocolate into the icing on the sides of the cake while the icing is still soft. In a cool room or in the refrigerator, let the cake stand until the icing is set, about 30 minutes. (If refrigerated for too long, the icing will lose its shine. To bring the shine back, place the cake in warm 350° oven for 5 seconds, no more.)

9. **To prepare the raspberry coulis,** pass the berries through the fine disk of a food mill. If seeds remain, press the mixture through a fine-mesh strainer using a flexible spatula. There will be a lot of juice and it will seem very thin. Be sure to scrape off the thick pulp that clings to the bottom of the food mill or strainer. Mix the juice and pulp together. Sweeten to taste with the sugar, stirring until the sugar has dissolved.

10. **Using a wide flat turner** or large spatula, carefully transfer the cake to a platter. The cake may be refrigerated in an airtight container for up to 3 days, but should be returned to room temperature before serving. Slice the cake into 8 wedges.

11. **To serve, place about** 1/3 cup of the custard sauce (crème anglaise) on each individual plate. Carefully spoon small circles of the raspberry coulis on the rim of each plate. Draw the tip of a knife around in a circle, through each dot of coulis, to create a swirl effect. Place a wedge of cake on each plate and serve immediately.

Variations

RASPBERRY: For the cake, replace the Grand Marnier with Chambord. Add a little Chambord to the icing. Omit the orange zest. Decorate the top edge of the cake with fresh raspberries and, using a pastry brush, glaze them carefully with a mixture of 2 tablespoons red currant jelly and 1 tablespoon water that have been melted together.

HAZELNUT OR ALMOND: For the cake, replace the Grand Marnier with Frangelico (hazelnut) or Amaretto (almond) liqueur. Add a little of either liqueur to the icing. The orange zest is optional. After mixing the batter, gently fold in 1/3 cup chopped toasted hazelnuts or almonds. Instead of the grated chocolate, garnish the sides of the cake with additional toasted and chopped nuts.

COFFEE: For the cake, replace the Grand Marnier with coffee liqueur (or 1 teaspoon Italian espresso powder dissolved in 2 tablespoons water). Add 1 tablespoon coffee liqueur to the icing. Omit the orange zest. In addition to garnishing the sides with grated chocolate, place a ring of pure chocolate coffee beans along the top edge of the cake.

Sources

Jill Prescott's Ecole de Cuisine
Cooking school and retail cookware and
  specialty food store
*French porcelain, skimmers, strainers, bakeware,
  sea salt, vanilla beans and extracts, Valrhona
  chocolate*
765 H Woodlake Road
Kohler, WI 53044
(920) 451-9151
www.jillprescott.com

Kitchen Equipment

August Lotz Co., Inc.
Quality wood products
146 N. Center Street
Boyd, WI 54726
(715) 667-5121
www.augustlotz.com

Dacor Distinctive Appliances
*Professional appliances designed for
  home use*
950 South Raymond Avenue
Pasadena, CA 91105
(800) 772-7778
www.dacor.com

General Espresso Equipment
*Top-quality home and commercial espresso
  machines*
7912 Industrial Village Road
Greensboro, NC 27409
(336) 393-0224
www.geec.com

George Watts & Son, Inc.
China, tabletop ware, flatware
761 N. Jefferson Street
Milwaukee, WI 53202
(414) 291-5120
www.TablewareAmerica.com

Illuminations
Candles and table accessories
1995 South McDowell Boulevard
Petaluma, CA 94954
(800) CANDLES
www.illuminations.com

John Boos & Company
Butcher block tables and wooden cutting blocks
315 South First Street
Effingham IL 62401
(217) 347-7701
www.johnboos.com

Pickard China
China dinnerware
782 Pickard Avenue
Antioch, IL 60002-1574
(847) 395-3800
www.PickardChina.com

Richardson Furniture Emporium
Artisan-made wood diningroom furniture
202 Pine Street
Sheboygan Falls, WI 53085
(920) 467-6659
www.richardsonbrothers.com

Romancing Provence
Hand-painted specialty pottery and painting
from Provence
225 5th Avenue, Suite 502
New York, NY 10010
(212) 481-9879
www.romancingprovence.com

Ingredient Sources

D'Artagnan
Duck, duck fat, foie gras, rabbit
280 Wilson Avenue
Newark, NJ 07105
(800) 327-8246
www.dartagnan.com

Egg Farm Dairy
Cultured butter, clabber cream, wild-ripened
cheeses
2 John Walsh Boulevard
Peekskill, New York 10566
(800) CREAMERY
www.creamery.com

Golden Guernsey Dairy
Top-quality milk and butter
2101 Delafield Street
Waukesha, WI
(800) 289-7787
www.foremostfarms.com

King Arthur Flour Company
Quality flours
P.O. Box 876
Norwich, VT 05055
(800) 827-6836
www.kingarthurflour.com

Rockey Farms
Specialty potato producer in Colorado
Contact: Culinary Specialty Produce
(908) 789-4700
potech@fone.net

Schwarz Fish Market
Smoked fish and specialty products
Neil Schwarz and Leslie Winter
828 Riverfront Drive
Sheboygan, WI 53081
(800) 966-3685

The Spice House
Freshly ground spices, dried herbs, sea salts
3 retail stores in the Midwest
(312) 274-0378
www.thespicehouse.com

Urbani Truffles USA
Truffles and truffle oils
29-24 40th Avenue
Long Island City, NY 11101
(800) 281-2330
www.urbani.com

Wild Flour Bakery
Artisan breads
15425 West Howard Avenue
New Berlin, WI 53151
(262) 860-1613
www.wildflour.net

Index